Time Out Of Mind

The Rising
of an
Old Master

To Marga

Even if the flesh
Falls off my face
It won't matter as long
As you're there

Contents

Encore

These songs of mine, I think of as mystery plays, the kind that Shakespeare saw when he was growing up. I think you could trace what I do back that far. They were on the fringes then, and I think they're on the fringes now. And they sound like they've been traveling on hard ground.

- Bob Dylan, MusiCares speech, 2015

You make everything yours

When Dylan butterflies around his gypsy gal in the early sixties, the toddler Suzanne Vega is playing on the streets in the same Spanish Harlem. She may have fleetingly noticed the shabby folk hero back then, but from puberty onwards, the maestro has played a growing role in her artistry. In interviews, the Grammy winner and "mother of mp3" (the inventor of mp3, Karlheinz Brandenburg, uses her song "Tom's Diner" for his first audio compression) keeps mentioning Dylan's name as her source of inspiration and personal hero. "From Bob Dylan," she says for example, "I learned to expand my mind and the power of the image and metaphor."

In 2013, when asked, she does not call her breakthrough hit "Luka" the highlight of her career, but: "My highlight was opening for Bob Dylan. Childhood hero, way more friendly and kinder than I could have imagined."

The accompanying selfie is posted on her twitter account in January 2016 with the title The ghost of electricity howls in the bones of her face, the well-known song line from "Visions Of Johanna". Undoubtedly out of fear for plagiarism accusations, Vega adds loud and clear the name of the author; "Bob Dylan #selfie".

That caution is a legacy of the hot late summer of 2006, when a rampant Plagiarism Or Inspiration discussion in the various online Dylan groups skips to the grown-up world and even sets the opinion pages of The New York Times on fire, briefly. One of the most striking names among the letters submitted in the Times is Suzanne Vega's, who in her movingly naive letter stands up for her hero. Dylan did not deliberately copy some lines of poetry by 19th-century poet Henry Timrod, she argues:

> "Maybe he has a photographic memory, and bits of text stick to it. Maybe it shows how deeply he had immersed himself in the texts and times of the Civil War, and he was completely unconscious of it."
>
> (The Ballad Of Henry Timrod, *New York Times*, September 17, 2006)

Babe in the woods. Her closing words are a lot less wide-eyed, though. Quite captivating even, as a matter of fact: "He's never pretended to be an academic, or even a nice guy. He is more likely to present himself as, well, a thief. Renegade, outlaw, artist. That's why we are passionate about him."

The fat hit the fire thanks to the digging of Scott Warmuth, a New Mexico musician, passionate Dylan fan and excellent, very worth reading Dylan blogger, who finds on *Modern Times* a dozen rather literal Timrod quotes, especially in "Spirit On The Water", "When The Deal Goes Down" and "Workingman's Blues #2". Coincidence is indeed out of the question, so soon the discussion divides the fans, critics and know-it-alls into Shruggers, Defenders, Attackers and Disappointed. The Disappointed stumble over the pattern that is now beginning to emerge; on *"Love And Theft"* (2001) the poet did copy exuberantly too, without mentioning the source (from Ovid, for example, and from *Confessions Of A Yakuza*, the fascinating memoirs of a Japanese gangster, written down by his doctor).

Now the floodgates are open. In the decades that follow, right up to today, fascinated Dylanologists set to work, searching and finding sources for Dylan's songs in the man's oeuvre from 1961 to the present day. *À La Recherche Du Temps Perdu* in Dylan's autobiography *Chronicles*, Harry Belafonte in "She Belongs To Me", Bertolt Brecht in "The Times They Are A-Changin'", Dante and Jerry Lee Lewis in "Mississippi"... the list of quotations, paraphrases and borrowings is colourful, eclectic and endless.

It all goes to show: Dylan is not a revolutionary. Not an avant-garde artist who creates a new art on the ruins of his destroyed predecessors. Dylan is like Mozart and like Rembrandt and like Shakespeare: he builds bridges, he is a crossroads, he stands on the shoulders of giants, as Sir Isaac Newton would say, he takes the best of ten worlds and creates one work of art from the best of ten worlds. From folk songs by Woody Guthrie, blues monuments by Robert Johnson, bluegrass classics by The Stanley Brothers, poems by Baudelaire and Rimbaud and T.S. Eliot, novels by Proust and Melville, plays by Shakespeare and Homer, songs by Elvis, Hank Williams and Johnny Cash, film noirs from the 1950s and F. Scott Fitzgerald and old magazines.

And for *Time Out Of Mind* Warmuth finds yet another unlikely source as the purveyor: poetry by Henry Rollins, the ferocious all-round artist from Washington DC.

The same applies to the musical support for his Nobel Prize-worthy lyrics. "Like A Rolling Stone" is the chord progression of "La Bamba". "Blowin' In The Wind" is the old slave song "No More Auction Block". Dylan simply copies the music for his Oscar-winning "Things Have Changed" from a Marty Stuart song. The most enchanting song on his most recent album, 2020's *Rough And*

Rowdy Ways, "I've Made Up My Mind to Give Myself to You" is Offenbach's "Barcarolle" from *Les Contes d'Hoffmann*, after which comes the irresistible "Crossing The Rubicon": a nicked lick from Little Walter's "I Can't Hold Out Much Longer".

Dylan, in short, is a prospector, a miner who knows how to forge the most fantastic jewels out of lumps of ore and raw precious metal. *"Love And Theft"*, indeed.

But: it works both ways. Dylan takes and Dylan gives. Dylan's output influences generations of artists. There are hundreds of top artists who say it all started with Dylan. Roger Waters, David Gilmour, George Harrison, Brian Wilson, John Lennon, Eddie Vedder, Joni Mitchell and Bono... in every decade artists in the Premier League can explain what Dylan meant to them, and that is usually: the spark to write songs.

The admiration and influence is even more tangible in the tens of thousands of Dylan covers; Dylan is the most covered musician in the world ("Yesterday" is the most covered song, Dylan the most covered artist). The Byrds owe their world fame to Dylan's "Mr. Tambourine Man", Adele's breakthrough is "Make You Feel My Love", Guns and Roses score a world hit with "Knockin' On Heaven's Door", Johnny Cash with "It Ain't Me, Babe", UB40 und Robert Palmer with "I'll Be Your Baby Tonight", Jimi Hendrix enters the stratosphere with Dylan's "All Along The Watchtower"... the list is long. Rolling Stones' Ronnie Wood, a seasoned Dylan fan, does have an explanation. "I could have filled my album with only my own songs, but I think that a Dylan song is not out of place on any album, from anyone," says Ronno when asked why the Dylan cover "Seven Days" was included on the Stone's solo album *Gimme Some Neck*.

It is a cover that illustrates a third, tangible pillar of Dylan's significance for the Arts. Dylan has written about 700 songs. He rejects about 30% of that body of work - songs he never records himself, or discards after a studio recording. "I Shall Be Released", "Rock Me Mama Like A Wagon Wheel", "Love Is Just A Four Letter Word", "This Wheel's On Fire", "Farewell Angelina", "Quinn The Eskimo", "You Ain't Going Nowhere"... it's a long list of brilliant songs that Dylan indifferently rejects, only for The Byrds, Joe Cocker, Joan Baez, Manfred Mann, Old Crow Medicine Show and all the others to gratefully pick them up and score hits.

"Part of the folk tradition," say the fans who, despite the positive give-and-take balance, feel some discomfort with all that borrowing by Dylan. And so does Dylan, one of the very rare times he speaks out about all that borrowing. Henry Timrod is the first source to which a defensive Dylan, years later, acknowledges some indebtedness. The acknowledgement takes place in the Rolling Stone interview with Mikal Gilmore, 27 September 2012:

> "And as far as Henry Timrod is concerned, have you even heard of him? Who's been reading him lately? And who's pushed him to the forefront? Who's been making you read him? And ask his descendants what they think of the hoopla. And if you think it's so easy to quote him and it can help your work, do it yourself and see how far you can get. Wussies and pussies complain about that stuff. It's an old thing – it's part of the tradition. It goes way back. [...] It's called song writing. It has to do with melody and rhythm, and then after that, anything goes. You make everything yours. We all do it."

A bit too assertive perhaps, but paradoxically too modest as well. After all, Dylan gives much more than he takes.

1   Love Sick

They may be a bit awkward and bewildering sometimes, but more often they are touching still, the advertising miniatures Dylan occasionally lends himself to in the twenty-first century. The Pepsi commercial is slick, sweet and not very subtle, but actually gives a giant respectful and fun upgrade to "Forever Young", thanks also to Will.i.am. The sober Apple advertising for the iPod and iTunes from 2006 (with "Someday Baby") is contagious and stylish, and the film in which Dylan drives through an empty landscape in a Cadillac Escalade confirms the words of Liz Vanzura, Cadillac's marketing director of: "We tried to be very respectful of the fact that he's a legend."

That succeeds partly because the bard, as in those other commercials, says nothing qualitative about the product to be praised. And because Pepsi, Cadillac and Apple are *true Americans*, just like Dylan, with some tolerance and repression of overly critical thoughts one could suspect Dylan's recommendation is heartfelt.

Perhaps because the master talks more, this is a bit more difficult with the IBM advertising. But then again the words of the talking computer Watson fascinate, claiming to have analysed all of Dylan's songs.

"Your main themes are," Watson concludes, "Time Passes and Love Fades."

"That sounds about right," Dylan replies amused.

Watson's claim actually *is* about right. IBM spokeswoman Laurie Freedman officially reports that the researchers really have fed 320 Dylan songs to Watson and his analysis truly has distilled the aforementioned themes. Wilson's capabilities of "personality analysis, tone analyzer and keyword extraction" has helped to better understand the data.

Granted, 320 is not all songs, but still: more than half.

The appreciation for Dylan's commercial trips is anything but widely shared. The fact he allowed the Bank Of Montreal in 1996 to use "The Times They Are A-Changin'", already did taste a bit tricky, but could at least still be classified under the safe heading *Irony*. That escape is less credible with the first time that Dylan also physically features in a product promotion, for *Victoria's Secret* in 2004. Only the seasoned connoisseurs smile, because they immediately remember the giggly 1965 press conference:

> Q: Mr. Dylan, Josh Dunson in his new book Freedom In The Air implies that you have sold out to commercial interests and the topical song movement. Do you have any comments, sir?
> BD: Well, no comments, no arguments. No, I sincerely don't feel guilty.
> Q: If you were going to sell out to a commercial interest, which one would you choose?
> BD: Ladies' garments.

Lo and behold! A Biblical forty years prior to the fact the Prophet is already announcing his appearance in a lingerie advertisement.

The song chosen for the soundtrack is "Love Sick" and thereby Dylan casts a second shadow over the beauty of the song.

Dylan cannot be blamed for the first Great Distractor. At the presentation of the Grammy Awards in 1998, where he picks up his three Grammys for *Time Out Of Mind*, Dylan plays "Love Sick". During the performance one of the background dancers breaks loose, uncovers the upper body, on which with large letters *Soy Bomb* is written, and performs a somewhat spastic-looking dance right next to Dylan, until he is removed.

The man is a self-proclaimed performance artist, one Michael Portnoy. The purpose of his disturbance was, as he explains later, to "send positive vibrations to viewers at home." The words *soy bomb* are a poem that he, on request, also is willing to explain: "*Soy*... represents dense nutritional life. *Bomb* is, obviously, an explosive destructive force. So, soy bomb is what I think art should be: dense, transformational, explosive life."

That crystal clear message did not completely come across. Portnoy blames this, somewhat regretfully, on a miscalculation: "*Soy bomb* was intended to be a simple poem, but my arms stole all the attention."

It does, however, draw continuing attention to Portnoy, unfortunately. He is allowed to make his fuzzy say in all major newspapers, gets a stage for his, presumably meant ironically, but still utterly infantile croaking ("Bob Dylan is a thing of the past, I am the future of music" - *Daily News*) and even true artists like pop artist Eels sustain the stolen fame ("Whatever Happened To Soy Bomb" on *Blinking Lights And Other Revelations*, 2006).

All in all, the squabbles overshadow the beauty of Dylan's performance and the extraordinary power of "Love Sick". On the bonus DVD with the Limited Edition of *Modern Times* (2006), Portnoy is flawlessly cut away and the glory is artificially restored.

The second Great Distractor is the use of the song in that *Victoria's Secret* commercial. Featuring top model Adriana Lima, dressed as sparse as Portnoy at the time, but much more attractive, obviously. The clip offers hardly a story. Lima squirms and seduces, an unaffected Dylan throws, a little surly, his hat on the floor and leaves, Adriana puts on the hat. There is the connection to the soundtrack: apparently the man does not desire love - perhaps he is sick of love.

The stylized aesthetic of the images certainly detracts from the raw splendour of the song itself. As the opening track for the album, it may be an equally remarkable choice (as the finale of an album full of decline and deterioration, it seems more appropriate), but it is actually a great introduction as well.

Producer Daniel Lanois deserves praise. The first six seconds of the album is rudderless sounds, studio buzz, musicians sitting down with their instruments, or something, then the staccato organ hits from Augie Meyers ("that little back beat skank organ," as Lanois calls it pleasantly disrespectful) and then that wonderful sound of Dylan's singing. As if he is calling from an old telephone booth somewhere along a deserted Arizona road to the studio in Miami.

It certainly is a wonderful find from Lanois and/or Dylan; by disconnecting the singer from the song, from the recording, as it were, he prevents the song from becoming whining, he avoids it becoming an embarrassing exposé of self-pity and exaggeration. Recorded this way, the despondent words of the washed out narrator get the stately opulence of a nineteenth-century symbolist. "I'm walking through streets that are dead", "weeping clouds", "you destroyed me with a smile", "silence like thunder" ... old-fashioned imagery that could have been produced by a fellow Nobel Prize winner like pessimist Maurice Maeterlinck (1862-1949) or Baudelaire ("The sound of music, tormenting and caressing / Resembling the distant cry of a man in pain"). But the direct inspiration comes from the Bible again, this time from the Song of Songs: "I am sick of love" is literally there (5:8).

The simple but compelling pulse of the song is just as tempting - the song is popular with colleagues. The well-known contribution of Mariachi El Bronx to the Amnesty project *Chimes Of Freedom* (2012) eases the angularity of the original and also has a distinctive arrangement (Mexican trumpets, abundant percussion and kitschy gypsy violins). Really appropriated, though, the song is by The White Stripes; "Love Sick" is about a hundred times on the set list and Jack White brings it so intense, loving and driven, that a whole generation of fans thinks it is actually a Jack White song.

In terms of intensity, however, that version is (more than) surpassed by our Flemish friends from Triggerfinger. Ruben Block opts for a similar voice distortion and a similar arrangement as the original, but the performance of the three-man band is - of course - even more meagre. And therefore perhaps even more desperate and ominous than Dylan's. It is definitely the most beautiful cover, and one that may stand next to the master himself.

Worth mentioning, hors concours, is the rendition by one of the maternity assistants, an assistant who contributed to the original version: Duke Robillard, one of the guitarists on *Time Out Of Mind*. Robillard is a veteran (born 1948) and a versatile blues guitarist who seems to mature with the years; especially since the 90s, his popularity among colleagues has been flourishing and he is increasingly being asked for session work. In between, he makes meritorious solo albums, dozens by now, on which the same respect for tradition can be heard as on Dylan's later albums. *New Blues For Modern Man* (1999), the album he records shortly after his work with Dylan, presents in addition to his interpretation of "Love Sick" also an admirable cover of Charley Patton's "Pony Blues" - probably not by chance one of Dylan's great loves. Robillard's "Love Sick" is a very pleasant, soulful and sultry homage. His singing skills are not too heavenly, unfortunately, but the rest is masterful. Particularly his B.B. King- and Snowy White-like guitar work.

2   Dirt Road Blues

I   They going down 61 Highway

Mozart, Van Gogh, Garrincha, Charley Patton, Nick Drake, Baudelaire... our history is rich with exceptionally gifted artists who, for various reasons, do not manage to cash in on their otherworldly talent and die penniless and forgotten. Especially painful in that shameful list are the artists who live long enough to see others make use of their work and become rich and famous with it. Arthur Crudup, of course, is a prime example. The man who wrote "That's All Right Mama" and "My Baby Left me", the songs that catapulted Elvis into the stratosphere. Crudup was eventually fobbed off with $10,000, three years before his death in 1974, after years of lawyer's sabre-rattling and embarrassing legal wrangling.

His genius seems to have touched Dylan, too. Apart from "That's All Right Mama", which Dylan will continue to play over the years (including with Johnny Cash in the studio, 1969), a dusty Crudup single also seems to have been among the "reference records", the records Dylan gives as homework to producer Daniel Lanois and studio staff before recording *Time Out Of Mind* and "Dirt Road Blues". Like engineer Mark Howard, who tells *Uncut*:

"All these old blues recordings, Little Walter, guys like that. And he'd ask us, 'Why do those records sound so great? Why can't anybody have a record sound like that anymore? Can I have that?' And so, I say, "Yeah, you can get those sound still."

Similar to how engineer Chris Shaw describes his experiences of searching for the right sound: "He might say, 'Well, I'm kinda hearing this like this old Billie Holiday song.' And so we'll start with that, the band will actually start playing that song, try to get that sound, and then he'll go, 'Okay, and this is how my song goes.' It's a weird process." And fitting with what Lanois reveals about his preparations for *Time Out Of Mind*:

> "I did a lot of preparation with Pretty Tony in New York City. I listened to a lot of old records that Bob recommended I fish out. Some of them I knew already – some Charley Patton records, dusty old rock'n'roll records really, blues records. And Tony and I played along to those records."

Charley Patton is, of course, a spirit that hovers over *Time Out Of Mind* anyway, and especially over its successor *«Love And Theft»* (2001). In lovingly stolen riffs ("Highlands"), complete songs ("High Water"), fragments of lyrics and, indeed, *sound*. Patton's stamp on "Dirt Road Blues" seems rather obvious. After all, one of Patton's best-known songs is the smashing "Down The Dirt Road Blues" from 1929, with the opening lines expressing the same, world-weary state of mind as Dylan's protagonist:

> *I'm goin' away to a world unknown*
> *I'm goin' away to world unknown*
> *I'm worried now, but I won't be worried long*

... and, obviously, the same classic blues text structure - each verse a repeated opening line, followed by a rhyming closing line. And coincidentally, almost as many words even (170 vs. 179). Yet this doesn't seem to be the "reference record" around which Dylan constructs his song - the sound doesn't match. In this respect, Crudup's adaptation, "Dirt Road Blues", which he recorded in Chicago in October 1945, is closer. From which, by the way, Arthur will lift the second verse, turning it into the Big Bang of rock'n'roll:

> *Well now, that's all right now, mama, that's all right for you*
> *That's all right, baby, any way you do*
> *Now, I ain't goin' down, baby, by myself*
> *You know, the one that I love, moving down with someone else*

... the verse with the lyrics, the drive and the melody that will become "That's All Right Mama", rock'n'roll's ground zero, which Crudup will record eleven months later as "That's All Right", a B-side to "Crudup's After Hours". That music-historical fact of Crudup's "Dirt Road Blues" eclipses everything else, but in 1997 Dylan seems to be particularly touched by the sound - at least, he takes the stomp, the rhythm, the guitar pattern and the rattling, shrill guitar sound with him. The atmosphere is different, though – Dylan's song is *spooky*. Thanks to a fairly simple artifice: reverb on Dylan's vocals and the ethereal, wispy, unearthly organ sound of Augie Meyers' keys.

Dylan is asked about it, in interviews after the release of *Time Out Of Mind*. By *Newsweek*'s David Gates, for example. In the week of 21 September 1997, a week before the release of *Time Out Of Mind*, three journalists are invited, one after the other, to a Santa Monica hotel suite. They have already heard the recordings, and Gates did notice both the overall desolate theme and the extraordinary sound. "It is a spooky record," Dylan agrees, "because I feel spooky. I don't feel in tune with anything."

Bleak, lugubrious words. Spoken by a man who is still recovering from an encounter with Death four months earlier - that viral infection in the sac around the heart. Who, the doctors explain, presumably contracted his infection by inhaling fungal spores down some dirt road in Indiana, Tennessee or Illinois. Who declares after his discharge from hospital: "I really thought I'd be seeing Elvis soon." And Patton, Robert Johnson and Arthur Crudup, we might add. That heavenly choir would probably have had strike up "Dirt Road Blues" as welcome song. Although Crudup most likely would have called for his own "Death Valley Blues":

> Tell all the women
> Please come dressed in red
> They going down 61 Highway
> That's where the poor boy he fell dead

"Man, you must be puttin' me on," Dylan probably would have said, before joining in.

II   The troublingest woman I ever seen

> Gon' walk down that dirt road, 'til someone lets me ride
> Gon' walk down that dirt road, 'til someone lets me ride
> If I can't find my baby, I'm gonna run away and hide

They do walkabout, the poor protagonists of Dylan's *Time Out Of Mind*. "I'm walking through streets that are dead" is the opening line of the album ("Love Sick"), "Standing In The Doorway", the song after "Dirt Road Blues" starts with *I'm walking through the summer nights*, then comes "Million Miles" and "Tryin' To Get To Heaven", in which the I-person has to walk *through the middle of nowhere,* to *wade through high muddy water* and is *just going down the road feeling bad,* and like this, it goes on. In "Not Dark Yet" he follows the river, he is twenty miles out of town in Cold Irons Bound, he goes to the end of the earth To Make You Feel My Love and the album's closing track is a restless wanderer again, with his heart in the Highlands.

Already after one verse, "Dirt Road Blues" seems to be a similar lament as the lamentations of the other lamenters on this album; scourged by heartbreak, abandoned by the woman he can't live without. Not that those first few words are that explicit - but after about seventy years of blues tradition, it certainly is an educated guess; most of us have been conditioned to the point that *walking down the dirt road* can only mean: that poor sucker just lost the love of his life. A Pavlovian association that can be traced all the way back to Tommy Johnson, presumably.

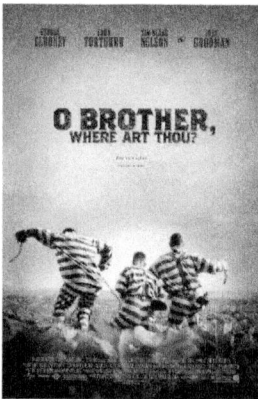

"Sing in me, O Muse, and through me tell the story," the Odyssey quote with which Dylan concludes his Nobel Prize lecture, is also the opening of the brilliant 2000 Coen Brothers film *O Brother, Where Art Thou.* Dylan publicly expresses his great admiration for the film, which has a lot to do with George Clooney, but even more with the soundtrack. And with the wildly colourful script of course, which playfully, unobtrusively and extremely imaginatively incorporates hints and nods to classic films, Homer, American history and music. Like the role for Tommy Johnson:

HITCHHIKER: Thank you fuh the lif', suh. M'names Tommy. Tommy Johnson.
Delmar is genuinely friendly:
DELMAR: How ya doin', Tommy. I haven't seen a house in miles. What're you doin' out in the middle of nowhere?
Tommy is matter-of-fact:
TOMMY: I had to be at that crossroads las' midnight to sell mah soul to the devil.

Indeed, of the legendary blues Founding Father Tommy Johnson the story was spread that he owed his exceptional guitar skills to a deal with the devil on the crossroads, a story that somehow got transferred to Robert Johnson. In the film, the Soggy Bottom Boys take him to the studio, where, with Tommy as guitarist, they record an irresistible version of "Man Of Constant Sorrow", the song that is somewhere in Dylan's personal Top 40.

Dylan got to know Tommy Johnson's work as early as 1960 in Minnesota, he tells in *Chronicles* ("where I first heard Blind Lemon Jefferson, Blind Blake, Charlie Patton and Tommy Johnson"), and as a DJ in his radio show, he dwells on him more extensively:

"Along with Son House and Charley Patton, no one was more important to the development of Delta Blues than Tommy Johnson. And long before the stories about Robert Johnson, selling his soul at the crossroads, those same stories were told about Tommy Johnson. His live performances, where he would play guitar behind his neck, while hollering the blues at full volume, are legendary. Unfortunately, his addiction to alcohol was so pronounced, that he was often seen drinking sterno and even shoe polish, strained through white bread, when whiskey wasn't available."

... introducing "Cool Drink Of Water Blues", episode 23, *Water*. Dylan recalls the bizarre-appearing fact that Tommy even drank sterno and shoe polish to satisfy his alcohol addiction, but it does seem to be a true story; several sources report this disturbing biographical fact - not least Tommy Johnson himself:

Cryin', canned heat, mama
Sho', Lord, killin' me
Take alcorub to
Take these canned heat blues

... the opening couplet of "Canned Heat Blues" from 1928, in which Tommy complains that rubbing alcohol, the at least as poisonous isopropyl, is supposed to save him from the canned heat blues, from the sickly desire for that thoroughly toxic burning paste Sterno. Repulsive, but who knows - maybe it contributed to the emergence of immortal pillars of the blues, to monuments such as "Big Road Blues" that via Floyd Jones's "Dark Road" from 1951 eventually evolved into "On The Road Again".

"On The Road Again" (1968) is one of the biggest hits for the Californian blues rock band Canned Heat, the band that already honours Tommy Johnson in its choice of band name. And with this hit, the band contributes to the continuity of that image, of the image that *walking down the road* evokes;

Well, I'm so tired of crying
But I'm out on the road again
I'm on the road again
I ain't got no woman
Just to call my special friend

... the image of the pitiful, love sick dupe. The image carved by Tommy Johnson's "Big Road Blues" in 1928;

Cryin', ain't goin' down this
Big road by myself
A-don't ya hear me talkin', pretty mama?
Lord, ain't goin' down this
Big road by myself

But from that other monument, the song that DJ Dylan plays in the twenty-first century, "Cool Drink Of Water Blues", we hear echoes in Dylan's "Dirt Road Blues" as well; the simple blues lick that carries the song is a sped-up copy of Tommy Johnson's lick. Another song that reverberates for decades, by the way; Howlin' Wolf's 1956 hit "I Asked For Water" is Wolf's take on the same song.

... which the DJ knew all along, of course:

> "Cool Drink Of Water Blues" was amped-up in the fifties and became one of the great Chicago blues tracks when it was recorded by one of his biggest admirers, Howlin' Wolf, under the name "I Asked For Water, She Brought Me Gasoline"

Not an easy-going girl either, that one. "That's the troublingest woman, that I ever saw," as Howlin' Wolf says. Sooner rather than later, that boy shall go down the road too. But: by car, this time.

III But your brains are staying south

Gon' walk down that dirt road, 'til someone lets me ride
Gon' walk down that dirt road, 'til someone lets me ride
If I can't find my baby, I'm gonna run away and hide

For a quarter of a century, the Dutch author Arnon Grunberg has been bivouacking at and around the top of the literary Olympus in the Low Lands, and translations of his novels are read all over the world thanks to rave reviews in *The New York Times*, *Le Figaro*, the *L.A. Times* and the *Frankfurter Allgemeine*, among others. His output cannot be categorised; like Dylan, Grunberg jumps from one genre to another.

One of his greatest successes is the 2006 psychological thriller *Tirza*, a novel that reveals a soul connection to the spiritual father of songs like "Cold Irons Bound", "Soon After Midnight" and the 2021 rewrite of "To Be Alone With You". Lyrics with a brooding, lugubrious undercurrent that only comes to the surface at second glance.

In *Tirza*, we meet a somewhat dull, middle-class single father who idolises his youngest daughter in an almost unhealthy way. The farewell approaches; Tirza has finished her final exams and is on the threshold of an independent life. Before university life swallows her up, she and her boyfriend go on an adventurous holiday to Africa. Dad Jörgen brings them to the airport and then she is gone. And stays gone - there is no sign nor word from Tirza anymore, and the father, growing desperate and already instinctively suspicious of the boyfriend, decides to travel after her, decides to go look for her. He trudges over the dirt roads of Namibia, *he can't find his baby*, and gradually he takes the reader with him in his intention to stay here, never to return to Amsterdam, *to run away and hide*. In the meantime, he found a kind of surrogate daughter, nine-year-old Kaisa, and when he tells her his life story, the bomb hits; Jörgen tells Kaisa that months ago he killed his own daughter and her boyfriend, on the way to the airport.

It is a mind-boggling plot twist that hits with the force of a grenade, and makes the reader scroll back. Similar to mindfuck films like *The Sixth Sense* and *Shutter Island*: the plot twist forces the viewer to re-contextualise the entire story up until that point.

What did we miss, could we have seen this coming? And yes, the foreshadowing of the surprising catastrophe is usually hidden in small, unobtrusive hints that, on first sight, are at most a tiny bit unsettling.

Something like that, such a small, unobtrusive hint, seems to be hidden in this closing line of the first verse of "Dirt Road Blues". Up to and including *"If I can't find my baby"*, nothing is out of the ordinary; still a classic dirt road blues, a lament of a poor, lovesick sod. But then: *"I'm gonna run away and hide."* That, in twelve words, is the bewildering plot twist of *Tirza* - the protagonist who despairs of not being able to find his baby, and is then overcome by a run-and-hide urge. An urge that can only be explained by a preceding outrage, of course - either the protagonist is threatened and flees danger, or the protagonist has committed an atrocity and must now run-and-hide to avoid the consequences.

The second stanza does not clarify anything, but it does perpetuate the unease:

> *I been pacing around the room hoping maybe she'd come back*
> *Pacing 'round the room hoping maybe she'd come back*
> *Well, I been praying for salvation laying 'round in a one-room*
> *country shack*

... although it is a flashback, it is not a clarifying flash-back – the plot is still ambiguous. The narrator takes the listener back to a moment *after* the breaking point, to a moment when despair has already begun. And chooses reassuringly "ordinary" idiom to describe his despair, idiom as we know it from dozens of songs, from songs like Mel Tormé's "Comin' Home Baby";

I'm pressin' on, baby, now
And pacing up and down the floor
Oh, hear me holler, and hear me roar
Say you'll be with me
Gonna be with you ever more
I'm comin' home

... and from Muddy Waters' "All Aboard" (*"I'm hopin' and tusslin' she'd come back"*), or George Jones's monumental "He Stopped Loving Her Today" (*"He still loved her through it all / Hoping she'd come back again"*), or The Everly Brothers' "Chained To A Memory";

I get up in the morning
I'm pacing the floor
Like I'm expecting you to walk in the door
I keep forgetting I won't see you anymore
Guess I'm doomed to be chained to a memory

... and dozens of other songs from Dylan's personal jukebox in which pained protagonists are *pacing around* and are consumed by the desire that *she'd come back*. Just like the ending of this verse, *laying 'round in a one-room country shack,* does not raise any eyebrows; that too is a setting we know from plenty of blues songs, again a setting the conditioned listener has long associated with heartache and love affliction of an unhappy first-person chronicler. In Dylan's case, it probably got under his skin via Johnny Cash's version of Billy Joe Shaver's "Georgia On A Fast Train", or via Willie Nelson (who plays the song again at Farm Aid 2013) - although neither of these can match the raw charm of Billy Joe's 1973 original;

It's more likely, however, that the walking music encyclopaedia has a flopped single by Johnny "Guitar" Watson from 1958 in his record case: "Gangster Of Love b/w One Room Country

Shack", produced and accompanied by the man who is held in such high esteem by Dylan, Bumps Blackwell. Presumably Dylan was initially struck - again - by the sound, which is indeed close to the *Time Out Of Mind* sound. And is this décor an accidental by-catch;

> *I'm sittin' here, thousand miles from nowhere*
> *In this one room country little shack*
> *And my only worldly possession*
> *Is this raggedy old cotton sack*

On the other hand: given the subcutaneous suspense, the insinuated horror and the choice of scenery, it cannot be ruled out that Dylan was inspired by Louisiana Red's signature song "Sweet Blood Call", the lurid monologue of a psychopathic bad man, with the repulsive opening line "*I have a hard time missing you baby, with my pistol in your mouth*" and with, in the third verse, the scenery that Dylan will choose for his "Dirt Road Blues":

> *I see your eyes are rollin'*
> *Must mean your love for me has come back*
> *Must mean you're satisfied again*
> *With our little wooden country shack*
> *I have a hard time missing you baby, with my pistol in your*
> *mouth*
> *You may be thinking about going north woman, but your brains*
> *are staying south*

Not inconceivable, a line from "Sweet Blood Call" to Dylan's "Dirt Road Blues", and not only because of that in itself meagre similarity in scenery. Roughly since *Time Out Of Mind*, Dylan has developed a growing fascination for what, for the sake of convenience, can be called *murder-suggesting ballads*; ominous narratives surrounding sinister protagonists and macabre incidents, which are mainly diffusely, implicitly evoked - Dylan is not yet as explicit as in "Sweet Blood Call" or as in comparable bloody folk and blues songs ("Knoxville Girl", "Delia's Gone", "Crow Jane"). Here, it remains with that disturbing suggestion *I have been praying for salvation*; words that suggest the narrator is seeking deliverance from sin and its consequences.

But he apparently does not receive that salvation, in that remote one-room country shack. He is standing in the doorway, and then decides to go down the dirt road, decides to run and hide...

IV   Gross as beetles

Gon' walk down that dirt road until my eyes begin to bleed
Gon' walk down that dirt road until my eyes begin to bleed
'Til there's nothing left to see, 'til the chains have been shattered
and I've been freed

Apart from the very thin link some eccentrics try to see in "Paperback Writer"'s *based on a novel by a man named Lear*, The Beatles only once encounter *King Lear*, and that really is just a happy accident. In the chaotic final phase of "I Am The Walrus", we hear, with some difficulty, a dialogue from Act 4, Scene 5:

> "If ever thou wilt thrive, bury my body and give the letters
> which thou find'st about me to Edmund, Earl of Gloucester:
> seek him out upon the English party. O, untimely death! Death!"
> "I know thee well: a serviceable villain, as duteous to the vices
> of thy mistress as badness would desire."
> "What, is he dead?"
> "Sit you down, father: rest you."

... and not "Paul is dead", which is, by the way, one of the weakest arguments that the conspiracy-clowns put forward as "proof" of McCartney's death on 9 November 1966. By now we know for sure that there is no deep, hidden meaning behind the *King Lear* fragment. Studio engineer Geoff Emerick revealed that he and Lennon added some random radio chatter to the mix - and coincidentally, Emerick says, there was an integral *King Lear* broadcast on the BBC. Lennon confirms this in the famous radio interview with New York DJ Dennis Elsas, September 1974, and also reveals that he didn't even have a clue what it was:

> "I just heard a radio in the room that was tuned to some BBC channel all the time. We did about, oh I don't know, half a dozen mixes and I just used whatever was coming through at the time. I never knew it was *King Lear* until somebody told me, years later. 'Cause I could hardly make out what he was saying."

To what extent Dylan consciously incorporates his admiration for *King Lear*, or for Shakespeare at all, into his oeuvre is debatable. Associations are more common than in Beatles songs, in any case. From the Basement songs "Tears Of Rage" and "This Wheel's On Fire", lines to *King Lear* can be drawn, coincidentally or not, in the same scene Lear uses the expression *handy dandy*, the name of the protagonist of Dylan's nursery rhyme "Handy Dandy", coincidentally or not, and "time out of mind" is a *Romeo And Juliet* quote, coincidentally or not. And this third verse of "Dirt Road Blues" is, coincidentally or not, very similar to the dramatic low point in the dismantling of the poor Earl of Gloucester from *King Lear*. Gloucester, who after having his eyes gouged out, with bleeding eye sockets asks his son to lead him to a cliff, so that he will find freedom in a leap to his death.

Coincidence probably, but still, it *is* a remarkable and gruesome image, bleeding eyes. Usually used to freak out the audience, in horror films and films with supernatural stuff. And occasionally poetically - as at the end of Alfredson's magisterial 2011 adaptation of Le Carré's *Tinker Tailor Soldier Spy*. When, from a distance, Jim Prideaux shoots his close friend the traitor Bill Haydon in the head with a small calibre bullet just below the eye, a single drop of blood runs like a tear down the cheek of the dying Haydon - mirroring the one single tear running down the cheek of assassin Prideaux.

In the art of song, the image is less common. Alright, since the rise of trash metal and gothic punk, of bands with names like Anthrax and Primal Scream, eyes start to bleed a bit more often, but there the image seems to be derived from, and have the same function as in horror movies; to gross out the listener. "Tears of blood" or similar word combinations to express the horror of bleeding eyes are actually rarely used in the art of song, and, moreover, hardly unambiguous. Like in Sandy Denny's somewhat pathetic "Here In Silence";

> *Morning leaves a bed of echoes,*
> *Tears of blood in weeping meadows,*
> *Can you see me, can you hear me,*
> *Can you leave me here in silence?*

... and even when the grandmaster John Prine uses the image (in "The Hobo Song", 1978), he balances dangerously close to the edge of unbearable sentimentality. No, actually only the 1931 Mississippi Sheiks song "I've Got Blood In My Eyes For You" expresses approximately what Dylan also seems to want to express here;

> *I was out this mo'nin, feelin' blue*
> *I said-a, 'Good-lookin' girl can I make love with you?'*
> *Hey-hey-hey, babe*
> *I've got blood in my eyes for you*

Dylan's admiration for the Mississippi Sheiks is unquestioned. He records their "The World Is Going Wrong", "Sitting On Top The World" and "I've Got Blood in My Eyes For You", the DJ Dylan plays them three times on *Theme Time Radio Hour*, and in the liner notes to *World Gone Wrong* he is clear enough:

> "BLOOD IN MY EYES is one of two songs done by the Mississippi Sheiks, a little known de facto group whom in their former glory must've been something to behold. rebellion against routine seems to be their strong theme. all their songs are raw in the bone & are faultlessly made for these modern times (the New Dark Ages) nothing effete about the Mississippi Sheiks."

"I've Got Blood In My Eyes For You" is a heart-breaking song about a despondent, lonely john who in his misery tries to buy an emotional bond with a hooker but is rejected. The chorus line *I've got blood in my eyes for you* here seems to express either something like "extreme desire", "consuming yearning" or "extreme disappointment". Not a one-to-one congruence with Dylan's use of *bleeding eyes*, but at least in the same quadrant of the emotional colour scale; utter despair caused by love suffering. In "Dirt Road Blues", however, *Gon' walk down that dirt road until my eyes begin to bleed* and its continuation have the somewhat uncomfortable connotation that the protagonist doesn't *want* to see something or someone anymore. The postscript, after all, reveals that "blindness" will set him free, has the unsettling implication that the narrator is unbearably haunted by images of her in his mind's eye.

On a side note: in hindsight, it is a pity that Lennon and Geoff Emerick did not turn on the radio one minute earlier:

> *"The crows and choughs that wing the midway air*
> *Show scarce so gross as beetles"*

Now, *that* would have given the Paul-is-dead-conspiracists a field day.

V The purple piper plays his tune

'Til there's nothing left to see, 'til the chains have been shattered and I've been freed

Fans anyway, but there are some more serious music journalists and historians as well who consider *In The Court Of The Crimson King*, King Crimson's debut album from 1969, to be the big bang of prog rock. Which is debatable, of course, and ultimately mainly a matter of definition. The Moody Blues had already released *Days Of The Future Passed* two years earlier, and The Nice, with *The Thoughts of Emerlist Davjack* (1968), also deserve the label "Patriarchs of Prog Rock". But we can probably all agree that *In The Court Of The Crimson King* is a milestone, one of the Pillars Of Creation under the classical/symphonic rock that evolved from psychedelic rock.

The whole album consists of five marble songs, and the three crown jewels are "21st Century Schizoid Man", "Epitaph" with the beautiful, Rimbaudesque refrain *Confusion will be my epitaph / As I crawl a cracked and broken path* and as a finale the namesake of the album, the stately, overwhelming, mellotron-driven "In The Court Of The Crimson King". A monumental song, a crowd favourite to which King Crimson, in all its manifestations, always remains faithful and which, more than fifty years later (e.g. December 2021 in Japan), is still on the set list.

Robert Fripp, the genius who actually is King Crimson on his own, usually has a somewhat mythical story to tell about the song in interviews and retrospectives. "The name King Crimson is a synonym for Beelzebub, which is an anglicized form of the Arabic phrase *B'il Sabab*. This means literally *the man with an aim* and is the recognizable quality of King Crimson," he says in the booklet for *Frame by Frame: The Essential King Crimson Box Set* (1991).

The man who should know, the poet and songwriter Peter Sinfield, lyricist and sort of fifth King Crimson member on that smashing debut, dismisses Fripp's pompous interpretations. "It isn't the devil, it isn't Beelzebub, but it's… *arrogant*, and it's got a feeling of darkness about it, and Gothic." In the same fascinating Japanese TV documentary *Song To Soul* (2011), Sinfield recalls: "It was a sort of Bob Dylan song [*plays air guitar and sings "on soft grey mornings widows cry"*], it was like that." Composer Ian MacDonald confirms: "He had written it in a sort of folky, Donovanesque, early Bob Dylan style. A little folksy song. But essentially I threw out his music [*laughs apologetically*]." With which Sinfield can only agree: "It had to be better than what I had. Mine was three chords, not-very-good Bob Dylan, you know. Except the lyrics were interesting in their Gothic way." And elsewhere he characterises his lyrics as "a pastiche of images from Dylan, the Bible, and some of my favourite sci-fi and fantasy novels."

It is not the first time Sinfield mentions Dylan as a source of inspiration. In 2007, Sinfield is interviewed for *Louder*:

> "It was originally a sort of Bob Dylan song, if you can imagine that", says Sinfield. "Ian took it and rewrote the music. He'd studied harmony, he'd studied orchestration, so his references were not just The Beatles, but also big, sweeping things like Stravinsky, Mahler, things that were emotional. And that would come out. That track did take quite a while to pull together."

"In The Court Of The Crimson King" is a masterpiece that shines 2000 light years away from Dylan's oeuvre, but "a sort of Bob Dylan song" is perfectly understandable if you only look at the lyrics. "The purple piper plays his tune", "The cracked brass bells will ring", "The pattern juggler lifts his hand", "The yellow jester does not play / But gently pulls the strings"... the music archaeologists who, five hundred years from now, dig up this song will no doubt label it as *mid to late 20th century, probably B. Dylan*.

This is not only because of those Dylanesque images like *purple pipers* and *cracked brass bells*, but also because of Sinfield's perceptibility to sound, a sensitivity he shares with Dylan and which he developed through Dylan in the first place. He explains it, better than Dylan ever did, on the basis of the refrain-line *in the court of the Crimson King*:

> "What you have are the noises, the sounds of the words, like *crowds, queue, jokers*... 'k', 'k', 'k', do you see? You get this sharp cracking sound, and then it softens again...what is very important, even if you don't pick up on it, is the feel of these hard sounds, even if you don't understand the words, that there is something going on here - it was quite intentional to cause this effect - Bob Dylan admits to doing the same - it's like playing games, but the games you play with the noises, the sounds and the syllables, and especially the consonants in this example, should keep the listener right there, suspended - it's all in the way these are constructed."

... more clearly than Dylan put it in that famous "thin wild mercury sound" interview with Rosenbaum, 1977 ("It's the sound and the words. Words don't interfere with it. They... they punctuate it"), or during that wonderful 1965 press conference in San Francisco ("The whole total sound of the words, what's really going down is... it either happens or it doesn't happen, you know"). And similarly in *Chronicles,* Dylan doesn't get much further than saying *that* it may affect him like that ("you get tripped out on the sound of the words alone"), but he doesn't quite succeed in explaining it as vividly as Sinfield does.

However, the artistic congeniality is there. And we see it, for example, in the third verse of Dylan's "Dirt Road Blues", in that special word combination *shattered chains*, the combination Sinfield used in 1969 for the opening lines:

> The rusted chains of prison moons
> Are shattered by the sun.
> I walk a road, horizons change
> The tournament's begun.

"Shattered" is pretty much only used in songwriting for *shattered dreams* or a *shattered heart* anyway ("Confessin' The Blues", "The Curse Of An Aching Heart", "You Are My Sunshine", "There Goes My Everything", "One By One"... the list is endless, culminating in the Stones' 1978 "Shattered"). And "chains" are usually *chains of love*, and get *broken* or get *tighter*, or *can't loosen*, or *bind me*, or *have to be taken from my heart*, and are rarely *strong enough to hold me* - but shattered they never are, except by Dylan and his disciple Sinfield. Both poets undoubtedly being guided by the sound affinity of the palatal consonants *[sh]* and *[ch]*.

The difference, not surprisingly, lies in the poetic eloquence. Sinfield's pièce de résistance still breathes the influence of psychedelia and contents itself with quasi-deep images like "prison moons" and "I wait outside the pilgrim's door with insufficient schemes", with "a load of words that half mean something," as the British prog rock legend guitarist Richard Sinclair puts it.

Dylan, on the other hand, upholds the Holy Trinity of Rhyme, Rhythm & Reason; "I'm gonna walk down that dirt road 'til the chains have been shattered and I've been freed"... the yellow jester most certainly does not play. He walks a road and horizons change.

VI   Passion, on the other hand, is something no one wants

'Til there's nothing left to see, 'til the chains have been shattered and I've been freed

Friedrich Schiller himself was not too satisfied with it, with the work that is by far his most popular and most performed: "Ode To Joy" from 1785. The most performed, of course, because Beethoven used it for the choral finale of his *Symphony No. 9*, which in the twentieth century became the Anthem of Europe. In a letter from 1800 to his friend and patron, the freemason Christian Körner, Schiller judges that the long ode (originally 18 stanzas, 556 words) has little value, *"nicht für die Welt, noch für die Dichtkunst -* not for the world, nor for poetry". But that was way past the point of being able to stop it; immediately after its publication (in the magazine *Thalia*, 1786) it became popular, several artists set it to music and it was sung often and gladly, especially in student circles. The great composers were attracted as well; years before Beethoven adapted the poem, Schubert, Reichardt and others already had set it to music, and after Beethoven there were musical settings by Tchaikovsky and Johann Strauss, among others.

Schiller does try to intervene with a text revision. He deletes the last stanza and changes a few lines. In particular, the line that would become the most famous: *"Bettler werden Fürstenbrüder*, beggars become princes' brothers" from the first stanza was rewritten as the famous, nations-unifying *"Alle Menschen werden Brüder*, all men shall be brothers". The revision was published posthumously (Schiller died in 1805) and is the version used by Beethoven.

Incidentally, the most alienating demonstration of this unifying quality is provided by the Japanese glam metal band X Japan, the mascara collective that in the early years (around 1993) manifests itself as a living L'Oréal advertisement but does embellish, in between all the Formula 1 power rock, the hyper-neurotic songs with flawlessly executed Beethoven-on-speed interludes.

Friedrich's dissatisfaction is somewhat understandable, though. It really *is* a bit too pathetic, perhaps. "Whoever has succeeded in the great attempt / To be a friend's friend / Whoever has won a lovely wife / Add his to the jubilation!" and dozens of similarly sweet, naïve imperatives that call for a society of equal people, united by joy and friendship. Not really Schilleresque, and there are indeed indications that he originally wanted to ride his old familiar hobbyhorse *"Freiheit"* – so not *"An die Freude*, To Joy", but *"An die Freiheit*, To Freedom", actually.

Breaking chains, escaping, being freed from oppression... ninety per cent of Schiller's oeuvre can be summed up by this one line from Dylan's "Dirt Road Blues": *I'll go on 'til the chains have been shattered and I've been freed*. In his early work, they are often real, physical chains, prisons and oppressive tyrants; in his later work, the protagonists strive for what Schiller calls *"innere Freiheit, inner freedom"*, the goal also of Dylan's protagonist: real freedom is being freed from *"Leidenschaften und Trieben, passions and urges"*. Schiller does not need to adapt the language; "chains", "shackles", "prisoners"... the idiom is perfectly adequate as a metaphor as well.

The German poet is not the first and not the only one who is fond of its symbolic power. The metaphorical meaning of words such as "slave", "jail", "cuffs", etcetera, is in the Top 10 of Most Popular Metaphors in the eighteenth century. Not initiated, but at the very least scaffolded by the famous opening words of Rousseau's *Du Contrat Social* ("Man is born free, and he is everywhere in chains", 1762). And, even more fittingly for Schiller and Dylan, by Immanuel Kant: *"Leidenschaft dagegen wünscht sich kein Mensch. Denn wer will sich in Ketten legen lassen, wenn er frei sein kann?* - Passion, on the other hand, is something no one wants. For who wants to be put in chains when they can be free?"

It all may explain the classical, perhaps even somewhat archaic beauty of Dylan's words; the eighteenth-century ideal of inner freedom expressed with the eighteenth-century metaphor of *shattered chains*.

But as yet, the miserable runaway has not achieved that freedom, the freedom he expects from "nothing left to see":

I been lookin' at my shadow, I been watching the colors up
above
Lookin' at my shadow, watching the colors up above
Rolling through the rain and hail, looking for the sunny side of
love

... on the contrary; in every line of the following fourth stanza, the narrator explicitly stresses that he still has the capacity to see. "Lookin' at my shadow", for starters. Which, combined with the subsequent "watching the colours above", raises some concern about the man's mental state.

"My shadow" is still a relatively mundane image to illustrate the loneliness of the protagonist. It is perhaps most touchingly brought about in the classic "Me And My Shadow", which Dylan will appreciate in the versions of Bing Crosby, of The Mills Brothers, or in the most beautiful version, the one by Peggy Lee on one of her most beautiful albums (*Is That All There Is?*, 1969);

Me and my shadow
Strolling down the avenue
Me and my shadow
Not a soul to tell our troubles to
And when it's twelve o'clock
We climb the stair
We never knock
For nobody's there
Just me and my shadow
All alone and feeling blue

... just one example of the combination "*shadow - lonely protagonist*", which has been established in dozens of other songs long before Dylan's "Dirt Road Blues", of course. Johnny Cash's "To Beat The Devil" (*When no one stood behind me / But my shadow on the floor / And lonesome was more than a state of mind*); the Lovin'

41

Spoonful's wonderful "Six O' Clock" (*And now I'm back alone with just my shadow in front / At six o'clock*), written and sung by Dylan's confidant and occasional guitarist John Sebastian, on the last Lovin' Spoonful record to feature Sebastian (*Everything Playing*, 1967); The Monkees' "Early Morning Blues And Greens", on another highlight of the Summer Of Love, *Headquarters*... all songs that link *my shadow* to loneliness.

But only thanks to The Monkees do we know *which* colours Dylan's narrator and his shadow are seeing there, up above.

VII   The pale and the leader

I been lookin' at my shadow, I been watching the colors up above
Lookin' at my shadow, watching the colors up above
Rolling through the rain and hail, looking for the sunny side of love

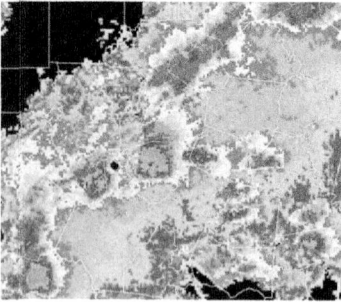

It is a meteorological interlude, all in all, this fourth verse. Sun, rainbow, rain and hail... probably all dug up from the archives by a lazy lyricist to arrive at the somewhat stale metaphor *the sunny side of love*.

It is not very likely, but still appealing to suppose that Dylan wanted to give Katie Webster an insider's wink with it, at her 1961 single "Close To My Heart b/w Sunny Side Of Love". When Dylan writes his song in 1997, Katie Webster is already a grand old dame, the Swamp Boogie Queen Of Louisiana. Dylan will certainly be impressed by the fact that Katie was Otis Redding's pianist, ever since a young Otis happened to see her perform in 1964, in Lake Charles, Louisiana. Reportedly, Otis was instantly hooked and demanded that she join his touring band immediately. In the 1980s, Mrs. Webster herself tells the story to radio host Louis X. Erlanger in New York, broadcast by *After Hours*:

> "Otis came out of his dressing room in his underwear. In this club, with all these people. "Stop that woman! Don't let her get off the stage! I gotta talk to her tonight!" So when I finished my song and did my encores and everything, I went back to the dressing room to talk to Otis, and he said, I've never in my life seen a woman work like that. He said, I have to have you as a part of my group. Can you go on the road with me and my band? I said, sure, I'd love to. He said, would you be ready to leave tonight? I said, no I couldn't leave tonight. But I could be ready for you very early in the morning."

So yes indeed, that is Katie Webster, on the brilliant *Live At The Whiskey A-Go-Go*, the gig Dylan also attends, April 1966, and at which he offers Otis "Just Like A Woman", in the dressing room afterwards. Maybe Katie was there too.

December 1967 Katie is heavily pregnant. She has to cancel the next Otis tour. And thus, on that fateful Sunday 10 December, she does not board Redding's Beechcraft H18 airplane to Madison, Wisconsin.

Otis' death hits Katie like a brick. She retreats from the spotlight for years, only to make a glorious comeback - especially in Europe - in the 1980s. The records she makes in those years are all wonderful (Dylan probably listened open-jawed to her goose-bumps inducing "Never Let Me Go"), but the walking music encyclopaedia Dylan undoubtedly has a soft spot for the obscure singles she released in the early 60s. Like the swinging "Close To My Heart b/w Sunny Side Of Love", which is released on Action Records in August '61. Both songs quite obviously show that Katie is the touring pianist for Ivory Joe Hunter at the time ("Since I Met You Baby"), but she still manages to put her own stamp on the sound. According to Bonnie Raitt, who assists Katie on her 1988 album *The Swamp Boogie Queen*, she even has "the voice of the century".

It's a nice scenario, the one where Dylan waves at a grand old dame two years before she dies. But a bit too romantic, probably. The Carter Family is much deeper under Dylan's skin, as is *keep on the sunny side of life*, the chorus line of their signature song "Keep On The Sunny Side", the song title that is inscribed in gold on A. P. Carter's pink marble tombstone at the country churchyard in Maces Spring, Virginia.

Dylan has always been quite outspoken about his love for The Carter Family. In *Chronicles*, he mentions them a few times; in interviews when the journalist asks him about his favourites and influences ("Odetta, The Kingston Trio, Harry Belafonte, The Carter Family. Guthrie only came along afterwards", for example); he considers them a point of reference ("There are a lot of spaces and advances between the Carter Family, Buddy Holly and, say, Ornette Coleman", Jerry Garcia's Obituary, 1995); in all phases of his career he plays their songs, and in the twenty-first century that doesn't change. He becomes even more explicit. "My songs are either based on old Protestant hymns or Carter Family songs or variations of the blues form," he says in the Robert Hilburn interview in 2003.

As a radio DJ (*Theme Time Radio Hour*, 2006-2008), he plays The Carter Family records four times, usually introduced with words of respect and admiration. He plays "Keep On The Sunny Side" from 1928 in his very first broadcast (Episode 1, *Weather*), and the next Carter Family record is in Episode 11, *Flowers*. When the DJ plays the monument "Wildwood Flower", he goes into great detail about the group and the song. As an introduction, he calls them "the most influential group in country music history" and praises A.P. Carter's approach, "enhancing the pure beauty of these facts-of-life tunes". After the last notes have sounded, Dylan goes on:

> "That was The Carter Family with "Wildwood Flower". The song was originally a written song from 1860 called "I'll Twine 'Mid the Ringlets". These songs were passed around, from person to person, over a long period. By the time the tune got to The Carter Family, many people claimed to have written it. And like a game of telephone, some of the words stopped making sense altogether:

>> *I will twine and will mingle my raven black hair*
>> *With the roses so red and the lilies so fair*
>> *The myrtle so green of an emerald hue*
>> *The pale emanita and the violets so blue*

> These lyrics are difficult to interpret. There is no flower named "emanita". Some hear it as *the pale and the leader*. Somehow, amidst the confusion, the song still makes sense."

... with which the DJ seems to allow himself a little dig at Johnny Cash. Who indeed does sing zappaesk nonsense, with almost frightening, very convincing solemnity:

> *O, I'll twine with my mingles and waving black hair*
> *With the roses so red and the lilies so fair*
> *And the myrtles so bright with the emerald dew*
> *The pale and the leader and eyes look like blue*

From the same LP that also contains three Dylan covers ("It Ain't Me Babe", "Don't Think Twice, it's Alright" and "Mama, You've Been on My Mind"), *Orange Blossom Special* (1965), which a proud Dylan must have heard more than once.

Anyway, in passing the DJ Dylan reveals how much value the songwriter Dylan attaches to semantics. A protagonist who walks in the sun, under a rainbow, rolls through the hail and rain, looking for the sunny side of love... *somehow, amidst the confusion, the song still makes sense*.

VIII You Ain't Going Nowhere

In 2004, Simon & Schuster publishes Dylan's third official song lyrics collection, *Lyrics: 1962-2001*. The previous edition ran until 1985, so this is the first with the lyrics of *Time Out Of Mind*, and thus also the first with the lyrics of "Dirt Road Blues".

Textual discrepancies in *Lyrics* are not uncommon. Words, half-sentences and, in extremis, even whole stanzas are different from what Dylan actually sings - which has been the case since the very first official release, since *Writings & Drawings* from 1973. In general hardly understandable, these changes, and puzzling in any case. We don't know if Dylan personally makes the changes, for example. Sometimes text differences seem to be due to careless transcriptions by a dyslexic secretary with hearing problems (*Ol' black Bascom, don't break no mirrors* as the opening line of "Tell Me, Momma" is famous), sometimes one suspects a teasing Dylan wants to play a prank (*I'll build a geodesic dome* in the transcription of "Santa Fe"), and sometimes it looks as if an embarrassed lyricist tries to cover up his own lousy poetry ("You Angel You").

None of the three options seem to apply to the rewritten last verse of "Dirt Road Blues". On *Time Out Of Mind*, Dylan sings, perfectly intelligible:

Gonna walk down that dirt road 'til everything becomes the same
Gonna walk down that dirt road 'til everything becomes the same
I keep on walking 'til I hear her holler out my name

Completely different from the lyrics published in *Lyrics 1962-2001*, in *Lyrics 1961-2012* and on the site:

Gon' walk on down that dirt road 'til I'm right beside the sun
Gon' walk on down until I'm right beside the sun
I'm gonna have to put up a barrier to keep myself away from everyone

Dylan will never perform the song, so we can't trace which one is meant to be the "actual" text. Normally, it would be plausible that the published text is the "definitive" one. *Lyrics 1962-2001* was released in 2004, seven years after *Time Out Of Mind*. It seems obvious that Dylan, in the meantime, went through the proofs with his red pencil, and made some changes here and there.

Against that scenario speaks the tip of the iceberg that producer Daniel Lanois offers, in a telephone interview with The Irish Times, 24 October 1997 (so three weeks after the release of *Time Out Of Mind*):

"In fact, when we first got together, he didn't play me any songs; he read me the songs. He read 12 lyrics back-to-back for an hour and it was like listening to someone reading a book. Then, later, in the studio, he modified the lyrics."

... which suggests that Dylan gave these very same written-out lyrics to Simon & Schuster, but forgot, or didn't bother, to incorporate the modifications that Lanois says he made later in the studio into the written-out lyrics. In that - somewhat more likely -

case the published text in *Lyrics* and on the site is the older text, the original text.

Debatable though it remains. Both in terms of content and stylistically, the "wrong", the published final couplet fits better with the rest of the song and with the overall colour of *Time Out Of Mind* at all;

Gon' walk on down until I'm right beside the sun
I'm gonna have to put up a barrier to keep myself away from everyone

... escapism pur sang. The whole of *Time Out Of Mind* is permeated with Dark Romanticism as it is; desire, Wanderlust, night, Evil, approaching death, decay, despair and melancholy - all the nineteenth century themes of Dark Romanticism can be found in every song. And the closing couplet is a textbook example of the romantic longing for an unattainable ideal: *right beside the sun* is, after all, just as unattainable as, say, "the horizon" or "the next mountain". A classic theme, but still an original way of putting it – "right beside the sun" does sound rather archaic, but is in fact an unknown image. Vaguely, we hear an echo of Kris Kristofferson's immortal classic "Sunday Morning Coming Down" (*I stopped beside the Sunday school*), but actually, it is an exclusively scientific word combination; to indicate the position of planets, for example, or to describe phenomena such as sun dogs.

We never hear the image in the art of song. Yes, across the border, though still hardly ever. With Francis Cabrel, the man who, with even more rights than Hugues Aufray, can be considered the French Bob Dylan. On his breakthrough album *Les Chemins de traverse* from 1979, the album with the hit "Je l'aime à mourir" and with the horrible cover, we find halfway through Side 2 the heartbreaking "C'était l'hiver", a Chronicle of a Suicide Foretold, with the final couplet:

> *Elle a sûrement rejoint le ciel*
> *Elle brille à côté du soleil*
> *Comme les nouvelles églises*
> *Mais si depuis ce soir-là je pleure*
> *C'est qu'il fait froid dans le fond de mon cœur*
>
> *(She has surely joined the sky*
> *She shines beside the sun*
> *Like the new churches*
> *But ever since that night I've been crying*
> *For it's cold in the depths of my heart)*

... so with a connotation completely different from Dylan's "beside the sun".

Just as Dark Romantic is the closing line. With, after that *lookin' at my shadow* from the previous verse, a second hint at the dark-romantic doppelganger motif; the narrator doesn't just want to keep away from everyone, no, he has to put up a barrier to keep *myself* away from everyone. As if there were a second I, which the first I must keep under control. Fitting with the earlier insinuations (*run away and hide, praying for salvation, chains*) that a second I has just committed an atrocity. An atrocity that leads the first I to close the barrier, flee to unreachable distances and hide beside the sun.

Again, a chilling image, and again quite original. But not entirely original; four years earlier, on their successful debut album *August And Everything After*, the Dylan disciples Counting Crows already sang in "Perfect Blue Buildings":

> *Gonna get me a little oblivion*
> *Try to keep myself away from me*

... but without the sinister connotations that linger under the skin of Dylan's song; singer Adam Duritz seems to be singing about the practical benefits of a drug or alcohol high. From the record with their breakthrough hit "Mr. Jones", the supposed ode to "Ballad Of A Thin Man" - and the predecessor of their catchy Dylan cover that concisely brings to the point the actual destiny of the fleeing "Dirt Road Blues" protagonist: "You Ain't Going Nowhere".

IX   And there will be nothing new in it

Gonna walk down that dirt road 'til everything becomes the same
Gonna walk down that dirt road 'til everything becomes the same
I keep on walking 'til I hear her holler out my name

The sung version, remarkably, offers a kind of opposite form of oblivion compared to the published final couplet. "Til everything becomes the same" is a terrifying prospect for the future, although it seems as if a sardonic David Byrne is trying to sell it as Paradise: "*Heaven is a place where nothing ever happens,*" says the refrain of one of his most beautiful songs, "Heaven" from one of Talking Heads' most perfect albums, *Fear Of Music* (1979). However, it turns out to be a multi-layered wordplay in the category of "My name is Nobody" and "Who's on first";

Everyone is trying to get to the bar
The name of the bar, the bar is called Heaven
The band in Heaven, they play my favorite song
They play it once again, they play it all night long

No, the place *where everything becomes the same* is in all cultures and story variants a poetic representation of Hell or else a diabolical punishment. The 49 daughters of Danaos are forever filling the bottomless barrel of the Danaids, Sisyphos has to push a boulder up a mountain in the Tartaros until the end of time, and a bit down the road Tantalos suffers perpetually from hunger and thirst while standing in a pond of crystal-clear water up to his chin. And that is just Greek mythology.

In Dante's Inferno it is not much different; most of the punished are in a loop of *everything is the same*, have to undergo an eternal repetition. The greedy and profligate constantly and aimlessly move the heavy stones that symbolise their former earthly possessions, the jealous helplessly suffer in an everlasting cold rain and hail, in the Fifth Circle the aggressive ones fight each other ceaselessly until the End of Time, and so on.

It all inspires Friedrich Nietzsche in August 1881 to write his famous Aphorism 341, "The Greatest Weight", which he publishes in *The Gay Science* in 1882:

> What if some day or night a demon were to steal into your loneliest loneliness and say to you: "This life as you now live it and have lived it you will have to live once again and innumerable times again; and there will be nothing new in it, but every pain and every joy and every thought and sigh and everything unspeakably small or great in your life must return to you, all in the same succession and sequence - even this spider and this moonlight between the trees, and even this moment and I myself. The eternal hourglass of existence is turned over again and again, and you with it, speck of dust!" Would you not throw yourself down and gnash your teeth and curse the demon who spoke thus?

... and which eventually inspires Harold Ramis to film the classic *Groundhog Day* (1993). Although, strictly speaking, not everything becomes the same there; the cynical weatherman Phil Connors (Bill Murray) does relive the same February 2 in a seemingly endless time loop, but he himself fills each day differently - he learns to play the piano, picks up foreign languages, commits thefts and has one-night stands, learns from his mistakes and becomes a different person. The denouement, however, does have a similarity to Dylan's plot. It will finally be February 3, Phil is finally redeemed: by the love of a woman.

Apparently, the narrator from "Dirt Road Blues" hopes for a similar redemption. He will keep walking until everything has become the same, and then keep walking *'til I hear her holler out my name*. Already quite classic; identical, for instance, to adaptations of *The Flying Dutchman*, such as Heine's fictional report in *Memoirs of the Herr von Schnabelowopski* (1833) and especially Wagner's opera (1843), in which the Dutchman is indeed cursed to try to round the Cape of Good Hope until the End of Time, but in which he can be redeemed: by a woman's love to the death. Which Wagner, of course, handles quite dramatically and literally; Senta tears herself loose from the arms of the men who try to stop her and throws herself off the cliff, hollering out:

> *Preis' deinen Engel und sein Gebot!*
> *Hier steh' ich, treu dir bis zum Tod!*
>
> *(Praise your angel and his words!*
> *Here I am, true to you till death!)*

Or the queen who can save her son if she says the name of Rumpelstiltskin, or all those other stories from different cultures that attribute magical powers to the mere knowing or mentioning of a name. Jehovah with the Jews, He-Who-Must-Not-Be-Named with Harry Potter, the many pseudonyms we invent to avoid having to pronounce the name of the Devil.

The Dark Romantic, Gothic version then suggests that Dylan's narrator is pursuing a slightly macabre afterlife experience, much like the aggressive climax on The Velvet Underground's *White Light/White Heat* (1968), in the trashy garage sale "I Heard Her Call My Name" (produced by Dylan producer Tom Wilson, by the way);

> *And I know that she's long, dead and gone,*
> *Still it ain't the same.*
> *When I wake up in the morning, mama,*
> *I heard her call my name.*

... in other words, the murder-ballad variant, the scenario in which the narrator has murdered his beloved in that one-room country shack, and is now doomed to be on the run forever *'til everything becomes the same*.

All in all, then, this final couplet of "Dirt Road Blues" offers an opposite plot to the published version; in *Lyrics*, the narrator opts for total isolation and oblivion, for a hideaway *right beside the sun*, a life behind *a barrier to keep myself away from everyone*. In this sung version, however, he can be rescued from the eternal sameness by communication, by interaction: when the woman he loves also loves him and calls his name.

Richard Wagner would undoubtedly have chosen this variant.

X   Sit down, Winnie

"But, on the other hand, with Dirt Road Blues *he made me pull
out the original cassette, sample 16 bars and we all played over
that."*

(Daniel Lanois, *Irish Times*, Oct. 24, 1997)

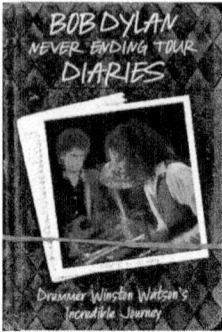

The hunt for the right sound seems to be
one of Dylan's greater concerns in all the
decades of his career, and especially in his
late work. More important than a chord
sequence, more important than semantics,
more important than the arrangement and
the key and the melody. Its importance to
Dylan is a refrain in the interviews,
speeches and self-analyses, and close
associates like studio staff, producers and session musicians
emphasise it again and again. Roughly from *Time Out Of Mind*
onwards, it even seems to become something of an obsession.

In the wonderful interview series published by Uncut in the
run-up to *The Bootleg Series Vol. 8 - Tell Tale Signs* (2008), this
fascination with sound is a theme with each of the interviewees.
Technician Mark Howard, for example, tells:

> "He'd tune into this radio station that he could only get
> between Point Dune and Oxnard. It would just pop up at one
> point, and it was all these old blues recordings, Little Walter,
> guys like that. And he'd ask us, "Why do those records sound so
> great? Why can't anybody have a record sound like that
> anymore? Can I have that?" And so, I say, "Yeah, you can get
> those sounds still." "Well," he says, " that's the sound I'm
> thinking of for this record."

... and he does find it eventually, that sound, with a slight detour.
Mark Howard explains it admirably. A few months before the studio

54

sessions, Dylan asks the technical guys whether they could record and mix a live show (House Of Blues, Atlanta, August 3 and 4, 1996). Dylan is peeping over Howard's shoulder as he mixes the recordings:

> "He says, "Hey, Mark, d'ya think you can make my harmonica sound electric on this one?" So I said, yeah, sure, and I took the harmonica off the tape and ran it through this little distortion box, and I played it, and he said, "Wow, that's great." So we're mixing away, and, after he stops playing harmonica, he starts singing into the same mic, and Dylan hears his voice going through this little vocal amp, and he gets really excited about it. "Wow! This is great!" And so I had to remix the whole record, putting this little vocal amp on all of his vocals for the whole show. And that sound became the sound of *Time Out Of Mind*."

As producer Daniel Lanois, not only in his interview with the *Irish Times*, but in Uncut as well, talks again about those "reference records":

> "Bob has a fascination with records from the Forties, Fifities and even further back. We listened to some of these old recordings to see what it was about them that made them compelling."

Lanois himself recalls old Al Johnson recordings, and in the 2001 interview with Mikal Gilmore for *Rolling Stone*, Dylan remembers yet another name:

> "I familiarized [Lanois] with the way I wanted the songs to sound. I think I played him some Slim Harpo recordings—early stuff like that. He seemed pretty agreeable to it"

Dylan's memory could be right. Slim Harpo has been a constant over the past half century. In interviews, he regularly cites him as an example of artists who fascinated the adolescent Bobby Zimmerman back in Duluth;

"Up north, at night, you could find these radio stations with no name on the dials, you know, that played pre-rock 'n' roll things — country blues. We would hear Slim Harpo or Lightnin' Slim and gospel groups, the Dixie Hummingbirds, the Five Blind Boys of Alabama. I was so far north, I didn't even know where Alabama was."

And Dylan remains faithful to Harpo. The throwaway "Seven Days" (1976) already seems to be a rip-off of Slim's "Mailbox Blues"; for *Down In The Groove* (1988) Dylan records an unreleased version of "Got Love If You Want It"; on this album *Time Out Of Mind*, the groove of "'Til I Fell In Love With You" is very similar to "Strange Love"; as DJ of *Theme Time Radio Hour* Dylan plays "Raining In My Heart" and "I Need Money (Keep Your Alibis)" in the twenty-first century; and in "Murder Most Foul" (2020) Slim drops by again: *play "Scratch My Back"*, the narrator asks Wolfman Jack.

Enough Slim Harpo traces, in any case, to go along with Dylan's claim that he is moved by this sound to such an extent that he wants to copy it for *Time Out Of Mind*. And indeed, the warm underwater sound of the bass, the tinny guitar sound and the metallic vocals with chilly reverb of, for example, "Strange Love" are quite similar to the sound of "Dirt Road Blues" - but still a bit warmer than the rest of *Time Out Of Mind*. Which can be traced back to that technical fact revealed by Lanois, that only this song used the basic tracks from that mythical demo session, presumably somewhere around that August 1996 live recording in Atlanta. Hence, this is the only song on which Winston Watson's drums can be heard; unusually, months before the actual studio recordings, Dylan had already been demo-ing new songs, searching for *the* sound, with members of his touring band. Of which Winston Watson, in Joel Gilbert's wonderful rockumentary *Bob Dylan Never Ending Tour Diaries: Drummer Winston Watson's Incredible Journey* (2009), has a vague recollection:

"So, at one point, he said actually something like to de facto: there's a sound I'm looking for and we're not getting it."

Winston remembers, with a pained face, how desperate he became when Dylan again and again stops rehearsals, unsatisfied, and how he sought to blame himself. When Dylan for the umpteenth time stops a song halfway through, Winston stands up and says ("I with my big mouth") that he can't take it any more.

"This is nerve-wracking. Obviously there's something you wanna hear from me that I'm not giving you. I wanna go home. I can't do this. This is... this is... I can't." So Dylan turns around to me, and he says: "Sit down, Winnie." I thought, oh my God, now I've done it, I've made Bob Dylan mad. And he puts his cigarette out and he stands up and he says: "Winston is here because he has a certain vibe. I want that vibe. I'm not getting that vibe. This whole room is full of complacency. So if you don't all wanna go home now, we're gonna start playing some music in here. Or everybody goes home."

The harsh pep talk seems to do the job. "Dirt Road Blues" most certainly has *a certain vibe*, in any case.

XI   I got to get back to the stage

After the recording of "Dirt Road Blues", the song is left behind. Left alone and lonely, even; all the other songs from *Time Out Of Mind* find their way to the stage, but "Dirt Road Blues" immediately disappears under the dust of the dirt road. And stays there. At least until 2003, when the song is dug up and dusted off, for just one single time. Not completely dusted, though. Just a little.

Malcom Burn, multi-instrumentalist and recording engineer on 1989's *Oh Mercy*, the "real" predecessor to *Time Out Of Mind*, tells a peculiar anecdote that plays out in the run-up to the recording sessions. In the days leading up to Dylan's arrival, when Lanois and he are busy preparing the recordings, they receive a music cassette in the mail. From Dylan.

> "And so Dan and I and Mark Howard, the other engineer, we sat down to listen to this cassette, and we put it in the machine – and this Al Jolson music started playing. And we were like, "What the Fuck? Al Jolson?" So, we fast-forwarded it, and it was just a whole tape of Al Jolson."

It also includes a note from Dylan. "Listen to this. You can learn a lot." Much later, halfway through the recording, Malcolm remembers this strange instruction, and now he understands at least something of it. During a break, Dylan tells us how important *phrasing* is. "You can have really great lyrics, but if you don't deliver them properly, they're not gonna mean a thing." And somewhere in that conversation Dylan says, "My two favourite singers are Frank Sinatra and Al Jolson."

Al Jolson was, of course, a great singer, and the "world's greatest entertainer", as DJ Dylan appreciatively agrees (*Theme Time Radio Hour*, Ep. 23, "California"), but survives - perhaps unfairly - as the most famous blackface singer ever. On Google's "images" page, for example, 8 of the first 10 hits are Jolson in blackface. And that's how he appears, as an apparition, as a blackfaced ghost, in one of the most memorable scenes from that remarkable Dylan film *Masked & Anonymous* (2003).

Towards the end of the film, Jack Fate stands in his trailer in front of the mirror shaving, while the irritating and pushy journalist Tom Friend tries to provoke him with suggestive questions. Fate remains silent and responds with an insipid look at best, until Friend touches him. Fate brusquely pushes the startled Friend away, who reproachfully says, "Hey man, I'm on your side." With that, Friend gets a first word out of Fate:

> Fate: That depends on your point of view.
> Friend: Hey, I don't want to be here any more than you do.
> Fate: I doubt it.

Fate steps out of the door as the single line "Tangled up in blue" sounds vaguely in the background, and walks onto the carnival-like set. Now, at 1:25:25, the soundtrack sets in "Dirt Road Blues". Not the Time Out Of Mind recording. This version doesn't have the Winston Watson vibe, but a distinct J.J. Cale vibe. "Mama Don't", "Anywhere The Wind Blows", "Okie", that vibe, sort of.

As we hear the first verse of "Dirt Road Blues", we follow Fate across the carnival. He climbs a scaffold and looks out over the set. Behind him, a blackface artist with a banjo descends the stairs and sits down on the steps. It does seem to be the ghost of Al Jolson, but he introduces himself as "Oscar Vogel" (Ed Harris). On the soundtrack, the music is mixed into the background, instead we now hear, softly and menacingly, the ghostly howl of the wind in the distance. The ghost's words are given a chilling reverberation, just as ghostly. Behind it still sounds, very vaguely now, a textless version of "Dirt Road Blues". Oscar tells us he is dead because he dared to criticise Fate's father, the dictator, from the stage.

> Oscar: They said it was an accident. [strums banjo] Some even said it was a suicide. Some people choose to die in all kinds of ways. Some people jump out of buildings And slit their wrists on the way down. Some fall on their own swords. I opened my mouth. Do you remember? My name is Oscar Vogel.
> Jack: Oscar Vogel. Well, I got to get back to the stage.
> Oscar: The stage - ah, yes - the stage. The whole world's a stage.

And then, as Jack descends the stairs, "Dirt Road Blues" swells again, still instrumental. Jack looks back one more time, up. The ghost of Oscar Vogel/Al Jolson is gone.

The song's connection to the film images is puzzling. "Something with Al Jolson" is the only thing that connects the Oscar Vogel scene with the somewhat circumstantial background story of the genesis of "Dirt Road Blues". Dylan doesn't seem to have any special feelings about it either; after this one-off reanimation, the dust settles over the song, and now for good.

The one-off resuscitation, this partly dusted off version of "Dirt Road Blues", was recorded with Dylan's touring band in July 2002, at the now demolished Ray-Art Studios film studio in Canoga Park, Los Angeles. On Variel Avenue, half an hour's drive from Dylan's home in Malibu. Just follow the dirt road and take Highway 101.

Standing In The Doorway

I   **He'll Have To Go**

I'm walking through the summer nights
Jukebox playing low

It is a select club, the guitarists who played in both the band of Living Legend John Fogerty and in the band of Living Legend Bob Dylan: members Billy Burnette and Bob Britt. Billy Burnette for a short while, replacing Charlie Sexton for eleven concerts Down Under. But Bob Britt, the guitarist who joined the Dylan ranks on *Time Out Of Mind*, has turned out to be a keeper; on *Rough And Rowdy Ways* (2020) he's back, and on stage he's been a remarkably unobtrusive, highly regarded force for a few years now. And with that knowledge, knowing Britt's concert performances, we can, with some certainty, pinpoint which notes he's playing in "Standing In The Doorway"; it must be those gliding, short licks in the intro and those short fills throughout the rest of the song. In any case, we hear a guitarist who has both Nashville and blues in his blood and in his fingers - and even the traces of his teacher, pianist Leon Russell. Russell who, in turn, learned the art from the ultimate Elvis pianist.

On YouTube, the charmingly enthusiastic grandson Jason Coleman explains his famous grandfather's trademark and demonstrates it with an obviously inherited talent: the "slip-notes" of the legendary Floyd Cramer. The keystrokes on the piano, where the finger slips off the adjacent key and in fact hits the wrong note at first, became a stylistic feature of the Nashville sound thanks to Floyd Cramer's thousands of recording sessions in the 50s and 60s, partly because Cramer declined Elvis' offer to go with him to the West Coast; he preferred to stay in Nashville.

By then, Floyd had already long secured his place in eternity; one of the most iconic piano parts in rock history, the piano part of "Heartbreak Hotel". Thereafter, he plays with all the greats, with Brenda Lee, The Everly Brothers and Roy Orbison, on "Crying In The Chapel" and on "Are You Lonesome Tonight?", with Chet Atkins and with Paul McCartney, and in the twenty-first century we even hear Dylan play Cramer's unmistakable slip-notes (in "Soon After Midnight" for example, Mankato, 2019). Remarkably, Cramer even influences, via a small diversion, Jimi Hendrix. Via Bobby Womack, that is. As a kid, Womack has taught himself guitar by imitating Floyd Cramer. Later, in 1964, het sits for hours and hours with Jimi on the tour bus:

> "I could tell what he was doing on the guitar, but he had no clue what I was doing. I was making up chords and all of them were unorthodox. I always played that way. It was a big joke with Jimi, who used to tell me, 'Man, you play some beautiful chords.'
> I told him about the piano player, Floyd Cramer, who I got my style from. Jimi didn't believe me. He said, 'But he's a piano player.' I said, 'Yeah, but imagine me hittin' the same notes on the guitar, playin' what you'd hear on a piano. It's different.' Sometimes me and Jimi used to sit backstage between shows and swap licks. That's how we became friends."
> (Bobby Womack - *My Autobiography - Midnight Mover*, 2006)

And sure enough, if you listen with that knowledge to (especially) "Little Wing", and even Jimi's "Like A Rolling Stone" (Monterey, 1967), you can hear Cramer's slip-notes.

And Floyd Cramer plays the indispensable part on one of the many stepfathers of "Standing In The Doorway", on "He'll Have To Go".

"Standing In The Doorway" is perhaps the ultimate illustration of that eclectic mash-up, of the recipe for the greatness of *Time Out Of Mind*. Dylan constructs both the music and lyrics from chunks of bluegrass, F. Scott Fitzgerald, blues, American Songbook, the Bible, folk, film noir and country. We hear snippets of Dock Boggs, reuse of "Moonshiner Blues", Big Joe Turner, "Bullfrog Blues" from 1928 (*I left you standin' here in your back door crying*), Jimmie Rodgers, and *I see nothing to be gained by explanation* from Willie Nelson's "Long Story Short (She's Gone)". That's just a small selection; almost every line of text can be found in one of the songs in Dylan's enormous working memory, in one of the novels in his bookcase, in one of the films in his home cinema.

Dylan's opening is an illustration the eclectic nature. "There was music from my neighbor's house through the summer nights" is the opening line of chapter 2 of F. Scott Fitzgerald's *The Great Gatsby* (1925), which could quite easily have been paraphrased into, say

> *I'm walking through the summer nights*
> *Music playing low*

But Dylan chooses "*jukebox playing low*" and thereby, by this simple intervention, tilts the atmosphere towards a tear-in-your-beer ballad, towards a country tearjerker, towards one of the greatest of all country tearjerkers;

> *Put your sweet lips a little closer to the phone*
> *Let's pretend that we're together, all alone*
> *I'll tell the man to turn the jukebox way down low*
> *And you can tell your friend there with you he'll have to go*

Jim Reeves' pièce de résistance from 1959. And Bob Britt seems to hear "He'll Have To Go" too; his fingers slip naturally from the adjacent note to the right one, just like Floyd Cramer's slip-notes in the intro of "He'll Have To Go" elevate the song to the stratosphere. Not on his own, by the way; the track was recorded by a Nashville A-Team. Elvis guitarist Hank Garland, Elvis and Dylan bassist Bob Moore, Elvis drummer Buddy Harman... Jim Reeves apparently already had some status, in 1959.

"He'll Have To Go" is less poetic and seemingly more one-dimensional than Dylan, but it is the same lament. One poor sap is discarded by telephone, and the other sod gets the door slammed in his face on the doorstep. Both wretches also seem to have lost the woman to a competing man. And both seek solace in the arms of another woman. By Dylan's narrator poignantly expressed with the words *"Last night I danced with a stranger, but she just reminded me you were the one"*; with Jim Reeves we only get that revelation in the sequel "He'll Have To Stay":

> *I can hear the jukebox playing soft and low*
> *And you're out again with someone else, I know*

... a good old fashioned answer song, in which Jeanne Black, over the same soundtrack and on the other end of the telephone, turns the whole plot around; Jim Reeves' narrator was apparently a notorious cheater who for years has been leading on his fiancée - and now she's had enough. *"You broke my heart too many times"*. And she has opened her heart and arms to a sweet, reliable rival. *"Now someone else is in your place, he'll have to stay"*.

"Buddy, you'll roll no more," she could have said just as well.

II   All these songs are connected

"I had to scramble around to find the right types of lyrics and basically moved lyrics around and put together the puzzle." Dylan gives three interviews in the week of 21 September 1997, all in an ocean-view hotel suite in Santa Monica, to John Pareles, Edna Gundersen and David Gates respectively. The above quote is from the interview with Gundersen and relates to "Highlands" - but, as we have seen especially thanks to the outtakes on *Tell-Tale Signs*, it is equally applicable to more songs from *Time Out Of Mind*.

Certainly to "Standing In The Doorway" too; of the 357 words, 83 were first in the outtake "Dreamin' Of You"; about a quarter of them therefore fall into the category "I basically moved lyrics around and put together the puzzle". And most of them are the "right type of lyrics" anyway, lyrics that Dylan found elsewhere, "by scrambling around". Without being too secretive about it by the way; like the insertion of a well-known line like *I'll eat when I'm hungry, drink when I'm dry* from the well-known "Moonshiner Blues", for example. After all, most people who buy *Time Out Of Mind* have been singing those words for decades, at the latest since the success of *The Bootleg Series 1*, which features Dylan's recording of it from the early 60s.

Not all borrowings are so well known, of course. A Rollins quote like *The light in this place is so bad* is only exposed by Scott

Warmuth many years later. The heartbreaking outcry *"Don't know if I saw you, if I would kiss you or kill you / It probably wouldn't matter to you anyhow"* is suspiciously similar to the text of a lobby card from the 1940s film with Humphrey Bogart, *Dead Reckoning*; "To kiss her or kill her... he's never quite sure!". A film noir, by the way, which is (naturally) mainly carried by Bogart, but even more so by his co-star, the irresistible Lizabeth Scott - who, for her performance of "Either It's Love Or It Isn't" alone, should at least have received an Oscar nomination.

A line like *"The last rays of daylight"* is of course not unique, but maybe Dylan just had R. L. Stevenson on his bedside table ("As the last rays of daylight dwindled and disappeared, absolute blackness settled down on Treasure Island"), and underlined this sentence. And a somewhat alienating interjection like *"Buddy, you'll roll no more"* may have been picked up by Dylan from the deeper shelves of his inner jukebox, from Bill Monroe's "Roll On Buddy, Roll On":

> *Roll on, buddy, roll on*
> *Roll on, buddy, roll on*
> *Wouldn't roll so slow*

Although it is more likely that he lovingly steals it from *The Rambling Boys*, the 1957 album by Ramblin' Jack Elliott and Derroll Adams, the album Dylan mentions in his autobiography *Chronicles*. "Roll On, Buddy" is the last song on that album, and in their version the men sing the verse:

> *Well I never liked no railroad man*
> *I never liked no railroad man*
> *Cause the railroad man will kill you if he can*
> *Drink up your blood like wine*

... the words Dylan will sing in "Stuck Inside Of Mobile With The Memphis Blues Again" (on a side note: in the verse before that, Elliott and Adams sing *"I slept in the pen with the rough and rowdy men"*). The rest of the track list does suggest that Dylan has played the album more than once: "Buffalo Skinners", "Danville Girl", "East Virginia Blues"... all songs whose echoes descend in Dylan's work over the years.

Both Bill Monroe and Ramblin' Jack Elliott sing *I got a home in Tennessee*, and Gillian Welch seems to notice that too.

In 2011, Gillian Welch releases her masterpiece *The Harrow And The Harvest*, an album that, very dylanesque, is bursting with borrowings, paraphrases and quotes. It becomes even more Dylan-like when Gillian takes most of her borrowings, paraphrases and quotes from Dylan. As in the moving "The Way The Whole Thing Ends", in which verse fragments such as *standing in the doorway crying* and *once you had a motorcycle but you couldn't ride it right* are explicit enough already, and the verse:

> *Momma's in the beauty parlor*
> *And Daddy's in the baseball pool*
> *Sister's in the drive-in movie*
> *Brother's in the old high school*

... winking pleasantly, unobtrusively at both "Tombstone Blues" and "Desolation Row". And just as charming Gillian incorporates a playful nod to "Sweetheart Like You" and to "Highway 61 Revisited":

> *Now what's a little sweetheart like you*
> *Doing with a bloody nose?*

The most subtle "Standing In The Doorway"-references are hidden in "Tennessee". A title she probably came up with because "Standing In The Doorway", in turn, references "Roll On, Buddy", as that song has the *"I got a home in Tennessee"* opening:

Back to Tennessee
It's beef steak when I'm working
Whiskey when I'm dry
Sweet heaven when I die

Now some will come confessing of transgressions
Some will come confessing of their love
You were there strumming on your gay guitar
You were trying to tell me something with your thumb

... the unobtrusive nod *"gay guitar"* (a somewhat unfortunate brand name, but it just so happens that its maker is called Frank Gay), and the witty reworking of *"I'll eat when I'm hungry, drink when I'm dry"*, the quote Dylan in turn had stolen from "Moonshiner Blues", to *"It's beef steak when I'm working, whiskey when I'm dry"*.

"All these songs are connected," Dylan says in one of his most beautiful and honest speeches, in the MusiCares speech, February 2015. He will have appreciated that Gillian Welch is incorporating his songs into the next link in the chain. Which is suggested by the tracklist of *Tempest*, which appears a year after Welch's *The Harrow And The Harvest*. Dylan seems to return the compliment. Track 6 is called "Scarlet Town"... exactly the same title as the opening song of Gillian's album. All these songs are connected.

4   Million Miles

I   The closer I get, the farther away I feel

"*I knew I should have taken that left toin at Albukoykee,*" Bugs Bunny usually says, when he has gone a million miles off course again and consults the map. Which tells us that Bugs certainly didn't intend to follow Route 66 – that one goes straight through Albuquerque and on to Los Angeles. A second claim to fame is the exceptionally successful TV series *Breaking Bad*, the saga about chemistry teacher Walter White who, in order to pay his hospital bills, becomes the most powerful drug dealer in the US Southwest. The success of the series seems to have given tourism to the city an enormous boost. And in Dylan circles, the city gets a third tick because of Scott Warmuth.

Goon Talk is the name of the wonderful blogspot of the admirable Scott Warmuth from Albuquerque. The site publishes results with academic quality of Warmuth's search for sources of Dylan's work and sparks for Dylan's inspiration, and describes those results in clear prose, always down to earth, avoiding sensationalism. Beyond this site, the New Mexican continues his work on Twitter; to this day Warmuth finds and publishes sources of verse fragments, of passages from Dylan's autobiography

Chronicles, and templates of Dylan's paintings (almost always film stills). These sources are as colourful as Dylan's oeuvre: a 1961 Time magazine, Baudelaire, revue texts from the nineteenth century, Coen Brothers films, Jack London, non-fiction travel guides and historical studies, Doc Pomus and Willie Dixon.

Warmuth's ground-breaking work is not applauded universally. There is a whole cohort of devout fans for whom it is intolerable that Dylan is *not* a divine genius who steadily manages to create something out of nothing. And then post unintelligent reactions to give vent to their indignation. With "counter-arguments" like *"C'mon!"* and *"This is all a bit silly"* and *"idiotic"*, and for some reason these displeased fans also have a tendency to write in capitals. Fortunately, it does not deter Warmuth.

A special chapter in *Goon Talk*'s fascinating series of articles concerns the remarkable multi-talented Henry Rollins. The all-round workaholic Rollins became famous as a punk rock singer, he is a successful and good actor, regular columnist for *Rolling Stone Australia* and *LA Weekly*, wins a Grammy Award for his autobiographical *Get in the Van* (1994) and publishes remarkable collections of poems or diary-like short stories. In these, in books such as *Black Coffee Blues* and *See a Grown Man Cry: Collected Work*, Warmuth finds a wealth of paraphrases, whole and half quotes, and sparks of inspiration for Dylan songs, mainly from the period 1997-2001, as well as for *Chronicles*.

Especially for *Time Out Of Mind*, Rollins seems to be a purveyor, as Warmuth demonstrates convincingly. Rollins traces can be found in no less than eight of the eleven songs, as well as in the outtakes "Mississippi" and "Dreamin' Of You". The only songs that seem to be Rollins-free (as far as we know) are "Love Sick",

"Not Dark Yet" and "Make You Feel My Love". All other songs contain similarities that transcend coincidence. Copied fragments like *You can't come back, not all the way* and *I have nothing for you, I don't even have a self for myself anymore* (transferred almost unchanged to "Mississippi"), or *"I think what I need might be a full-length leather coat / Somebody just asked me if I registered to vote"* from "Highlands", a sum of two parts found in two Rollins books. Or the sentences *Now if you think you lost it all, you're wrong. You can always lose a little more*, which Dylan slightly reworks for "Tryin' to Get To Heaven". *I hear voices when no one is around* that becomes the opening line for "Cold Irons Bound"...

Just a few examples. There are dozens, which is too many to be attributed to coincidence anyway, but usually also so idiosyncratic that any doubt about Rollin's significance as a source of inspiration can be ruled out. This also applies to the fragments Warmuth recognises from "Million Miles". In *Black Coffee Blues*, he first ticks off *I love dreamless sleep. Dreams tell me too much*, which takes him to the opening of the third verse:

> *I'm drifting in and out of dreamless sleep*
> *Throwing all my memories in a ditch so deep*

... which in itself is not too specific. But on the same page we also read: *Slowly I am forgetting them and their mind polluting words*. And that *is* quite specific;

> *Well, there's voices in the night trying to be heard*
> *I'm sitting here listening to every mind-polluting word,*

... far too specific, in any case, to ignore the connection with the opening of Dylan's last stanza - which, in retrospect, also elevates that *dreamless sleep* on the same page to "borrowing".

Fascinating, but ultimately these are merely idiomatic details. More serious is Warmuth's more daring observation. In that same *Black Coffee Blues*, he finds, twenty pages before that dreamless sleep and the mind-polluting words:

> "The next song I wrote was about the distance I felt when I thought about that girl. The song centered around the lines, "The closer I get, the farther away I feel." I was thinking that all the time I was with her, I worked hard to put that out of my mind. Romance passes the time."

Warmuth goes searching and does indeed find the song whose genesis Rollins describes here: "Down And Away", a trashy, riff-driven metal song on the Rollins Band's second album, *Hard Volume* from 1989. Rollins does indeed incorporate those key lines, in the second verse:

> *There's an ego followin' the way I feel*
> *The closer I get, the farther away I feel*
> *I can't get in and I can't get out*
> *Why don't you touch me so I can feel it*

Further on, that one *line The closer I get, the farther away I feel*, like a refrain, is repeated four times, then the band switches back to half-speed, and heavy and droning, mantra-like, Rollins shouts the line four more times. He is, apparently, quite content with its dramatic power. And Dylan might be too, Warmuth speculates. After all, the chorus line of "Million Miles", *I'm tryin' to get closer but I'm still a million miles from you*, expresses exactly the same thing in a similar idiom. Dylan chooses a poetic exaggeration (*farther away* becomes *a million miles*), but still: the sentiment is the same.

"I suspect," Warmuth writes, "that Dylan read that passage and considered that to be a good theme for a song, and that that passage very well may have been one of the sparks that led to *Million Miles*". And that is a proposition more exciting than all the paraphrases, quotations and borrowings put together; the proposition that one single sentence in Rollins' work can be the spark for an entire Dylan song suggests that we can see the workings of the creative mind of a Nobel Prize-winning poet. Which may actually lead us to hope for the answer to the Mother of All Questions: What's up, Doc?

II   They kind of write themselves

You took a part of me that I really miss
I keep asking myself how long it can go on like this
You told yourself a lie, that's all right mama I told myself one too
I'm tryin' to get closer but I'm still a million miles from you

True, in the *New York Times* interview with Douglas Brinkley from June 2020, there are some questionable passages. "Pretty Maids All-in A Row, that could be one of the best songs ever," Dylan declares on the hardly remarkable Eagles song. "Ruby, My Dear" by Thelonious Monk "inspired me as a songwriter" (Monk's ballad is one of his most beautiful, but: the song is an instrumental, the chords are off-centre, and progress quite unusual - if Dylan was inspired by it at all, it at most inspired him how to not write a song). But those strange passages pale into insignificance compared to the enlightening statements Dylan makes elsewhere. Especially about his working method, which he reveals in response to Brinkley's question about the song "I Contain Multitudes": "In that particular song, the last few verses came first. So that's where the song was going all along. Obviously, the catalyst for the song is the title line." And: "Most of my recent songs are like that."

Dylan has been a fan of it for more than half a century, of the antique ballad form inspired by François Villon (1431-1463), recognisable by the repetition of a single line at the end of each stanza. On *Blood On The Tracks* (1975), for instance, in five of the ten songs. On *Rough And Rowdy Ways* (2020) in three songs, six songs of *The Times They Are A-Changin'* (1964)... this specific form, in which "the catalyst for the song is the title line", is a constant in Dylan's oeuvre.

And here on *Time Out Of Mind*, it sets records; in eight of the eleven songs, the stanzas work towards the title line. Like in this "Million Miles", to the title line that, according to Scott Warmuth, is probably due to the inspiring Henry Rollins: "I'm tryin' to get closer but I'm still a million miles from you." The other verse lines in the eight stanzas should then be regarded, in this genesis scenario, as eight times the carriers of *where the song was going all along*.

The song poet does not make it too difficult for himself. Only three lines leading up to this title line, in the simplest rhyme scheme (*AABB*). Something like Blind Willie McTell's "You Was Born To Die", for example;

> *Don't want no woman that run around*
> *Stay out in the street and like a badfoot clown*
> *You made me love you and you made me cry*
> *You should remember that you were born to die*

... also four-line verses working towards a title line in the rhyme scheme *AABB*. And as in dozens of other songs, of course - but Blind Willie McTell's spirit seems to hover above the song anyway, and above the album altogether.

Not (yet) in the opening lines, though. The gentle, autumnal *You took a part of me that I really miss* is far too poetic for the he-man McTell, with his *boastful, manly kind of manner*, as Willie Dixon would say about Muddy Waters. Blind Willie McTell is a man who sings *Now looka here mama let me tell you this: if you wants to get crooked I'm gonna give you my fist*, and who sings *Mama, you'll never find another hot shot like me* - Blind Willie's machoism forbids vulnerabilities like *You took a part of me that I really miss*. That is something for heart-broken country heroes like Hank Williams or Hank Snow. Or, perhaps even more so, for Ferlin Husky:

> *When you walked out a part of me went with you*
> *My teardrops fell as you walked out the door*
> *Everything's gone wrong darling since you've gone*
> *And I'm not me without you anymore*

... "I'm Not Me Without You Anymore" from 1965. It's a drag of a song, actually, but the opening line is beautiful. And Dylan does have a thing for Ferlin too, as we know. In his autobiography, Robbie Robertson reveals that Dylan thought already back in 1967 of Ferlin Husky, wondering whether a Basement song would be suitable for the hit machine Husky:

> "The logic behind these recordings was to put together a collection of new Bob Dylan tunes that other artists might cover. After we would lay down a cut like "Too Much of Nothing", Bob might comment, "Okay, that one would be good to send to Ferlin Husky." He was only half kidding."

...as a DJ, Dylan plays him twice in *Theme Time Hour*, including Husky's biggest hit "On the Wings Of A Snow White Dove", the song Dylan will also quote in 2020, in "I've Made Up My Mind to Give Myself to You" (*If I had the wings of a snow-white dove / I'd preach the gospel, the gospel of love*).

So there are some Dylan-Husky lines, but actually too thin to promote *When you walked out a part of me went with you* to a trigger; at best it demonstrates an unlikely, artistic kinship with the song's author, Red "I'm A Truck" Simpson.

For the time being, Dylan the poet leaves it at that, and leans back after his beautiful opening line. The road to the title line, the next two lines, is filled with unspectacular cliché talk. *I keep asking myself how long it can go on like this* is a run-of-the-mill lament that we know, in variations, from dozens of country tear-in-my-beer songs, and undoubtedly also sung somewhere by Dylan's great hero George Jones. A bit more ambitious and original is the following *You told yourself a lie, that's all right mama I told myself one too*, although it does smell a bit like self-plagiarism; tone and content are very close to *I know you're sorry, I'm sorry too* from "Mississippi", which Dylan records during these same sessions.

The interlude *that's alright mama* seems too casual to be really meant as an Elvis-wink, but it does add to the eclectic nature of the song - like the previous line, it seems like a self-controlling intruder. "The songs seem to know themselves and they know that I can sing them, vocally and rhythmically," Dylan says in that same *New York Times interview*, "they kind of write themselves and count on me to sing them."

III   And thou didst commit whoredom with them

You took the silver, you took the gold
You left me standing out in the cold
People asked about you, I didn't tell them everything I knew
Well, I'm tryin' to get closer but I'm still a million miles from you

Jules (Samuel L. Jackson) considers it very cool and also makes a point of mentioning the source of the quotation; "There's a passage I got memorized, seems appropriate for this situation: Ezekiel 25:17." And then he quotes a big chunk of the Bible text (94 words), ending with the words *And you will know I am the Lord when I lay my vengeance upon you*, and usually he then blows his listener away. But today is different. "I been sayin' that shit for years," Jules says in the last scene (*Pulp Fiction*, 1994) to the petrified "Pumpkin", the robber who tries to take Jules' valuable briefcase,

> "… and if you ever heard it, it meant your ass. I never really questioned what it meant. I thought it was just a coldblooded thing to say to a motherfucker 'fore you popped a cap in his ass."

It *is* cool, indeed. Well, coldblooded even. And the fact that it is not actually an Ezekiel quote is not that important. It is in fact an insider's wink from director and scriptwriter Quentin Tarantino to one of his heroes from the 1970s karate films, Sonny Chiba, who paraphrases Ezekiel (in *Karate Kiba*, 1973). It does bring Ezekiel back into the spotlight, though.

In 2001, Dr Eric Altschuler, a neuroscientist at the University of California, San Diego, makes the BBC News. He diagnoses, some 26 centuries after the patient's death, a form of epilepsy in the prophet Ezekiel. *Temporal lobe epilepsy*, to be precise, a disease that can affect the functions of speech, memory and levels of awareness, and "in very rare cases people with the condition can develop symptoms such as hyper religiosity and hypergraphia." It is these symptoms in particular that lead Dr Altschuler to his provocative diagnosis; Ezekiel was indeed not only extremely religious but also rather verbose and, well, long-winded. His Bible book indeed is one of the longest, which is mainly due to the author's verbosity. So stylistically, it is not really a highlight. This *hypergraphia*, compulsive writing, does make the book really impenetrable at times. That, and presumably all those apocalyptic visions, may also explain why Jews were not allowed to read the book before their thirtieth birthday.

Throughout the ages it is nevertheless, despite its tiresome style, a popular book; Ezekiel's visions are bloodcurdling and breathtaking, his metaphors particularly evocative, and some of his adventures, such as those in the Valley of Dry Bones, have a pleasantly scary fantasy quality. The book is a constant in Dylan's oeuvre as well. Quotations, references and allusions can be found in "Blowin' In The Wind", in "Sad-Eyed Lady Of The Lowlands", in "This Wheel's On Fire", in "Angelina" and in "Dignity", and with some tolerance for what may be classified as "reference" or "influence", in even more songs.

Like in this second verse of "Million Miles";

"Thou hast also taken thy fair jewels of my gold and of my silver, which I had given thee, and madest to thyself images of men, and didst commit whoredom with them."

...says the pissed Ezekiel in 16:17, poetically railing against those naughty inhabitants of Jerusalem, who deceive God with all kinds of idols. Which has at most very indirectly something to do with "Million Miles", but *You took the silver, you took the gold* Dylan seems to take, including the narrative perspective, to his song. And then actually only based on that *thou hast taken / you took* similarity - the sole combination "gold and silver" we know, after all, from hundreds of stories, songs and poems. Including Dylan songs, by the way; "High Water", "Seven Curses", "10,000 Men", "Silvio", "Boots Of Spanish Leather", "You Changed My Life", "Unbelievable"... and those are by far not all the songs in which Dylan sings "silver and gold".

The *silver and gold* from the legendary "The Prisoner's Song" (1924) is not in this list, but it seems to be a song that keeps haunting Dylan's mind in these turn-of-the-century years. The status of "The Prisoner's Song", one of the greatest hits of the 1920s and indeed one of the greatest hillbilly hits ever, is undisputed. Dylan cites the song in his autobiography *Chronicles* as a benchmark, as an example of a song that has the power to elevate history to mythology;

> "Either one of those guys, Stevens or Roosevelt or even Morgan could have stepped out of a folk ballad. Songs like "Walkin' Boss," "The Prisoner's Song" or even one like "Ballad of Charles Guiteau." They're just in there somewhere, though maybe not in a specific way."

... and the short song (154 words) inspires him more than once to write his own songs. The first verse, for example;

> *Oh I wish I had someone to love me yes someone to call me their own*
> *Oh I wish I had someone to live with cause I'm tired of living all alone*
> *Please meet me tonight in the moonlight please meet me tonight all alone*
> *For I had a sad story to tell you it's a story that's never been told*

... doesn't seem too dazzling, but that one line *Please meet me tonight in the moonlight please meet me tonight all alone* apparently has enough impact to inspire Dylan to write an entire song, "Moonlight", in 2001;

> *The seasons they are turnin'*
> *And my sad heart is yearnin'*
> *To hear again the songbird's sweet melodious tone*
> *Meet me in the moonlight alone*

As we also hear the end of the song, *Now if I had the wings of an angel over these prison walls I would fly* returning, in variants, in dozens of songs. In "Watching The River Flow", for example ("If I had wings and I could fly I know where I would go"), in "Spike Driver's Blues" by Mississippi John Hurt and in Sleepy John Estes' "Sweet Mama", but which ultimately, of course, can all be traced back to one of the most beautiful songs of the twentieth century, to "Fare Thee Well", the song from Dink who complains that her lover seems to be a million miles away;

> *If I had wings like Noah's dove,*
> *I'd fly up da river to the man I love.*
> *Fare thee well, O Honey, fare thee well*

... "Dink's Song", as Alan Lomax calls the song when he writes it down in 1908. It is also part of Dylan's repertoire, and is an indestructible song that in every version has the power to move. Dylan played the song first in '61, and undoubtedly admired the versions of Pete Seeger, Harry Belafonte, Dave Van Ronk and whoever else. But the most beautiful twist the song receives in 2016, at the end of episode 20 of the eleventh season of the successful TV series *Supernatural*, when "God" reveals himself. It was Chuck all along. "God", Chuck, has given himself the skill to play guitar, and, lonely on the stage of a small-town café in front of a one-man audience, he performs a crushing "Dink's Song". Every word, in this context, sung by God, gets a new meaning.

More moving than all the visions of Ezekiel put together.

IV   What's it all coming to?

I'm drifting in and out of dreamless sleep
Throwing all my memories in a ditch so deep
Did so many things I never did intend to do
Well, I'm tryin' to get closer but I'm still a million miles from you

Within the Dutch literary landscape, Belcampo (1902-1990), with his remarkable, fantastic, magical-realist works, is an odd man out; he has no predecessors and no followers, and remains a separate movement on his own. Internationally, he is somewhat comparable to Roald Dahl, to Murakami perhaps, to Petrushevskaya in the distance... but above all: unique. A man accidentally cuts off his own index finger, doesn't know what to do with it, and finally decides on an impulse to bake it and eat it. "When I had eaten it, the discovery had been made, the discovery that no enjoyment on earth can compare to eating your own flesh." He becomes addicted to his own flesh, eats all his limbs in the following months and now needs the help of his friend the doctor to amputate and eat his last remaining limb, his right arm (*Page From The Diary Of A Doctor*, 1934). King Wurm forbids his people to dream. They are only allowed to *drift in and out of dreamless sleep*. His people revolt, behead him, but a surgeon manages to connect his head, the head of state as it were, to a device and keep it alive (*The Triple Combination*, 1934).

The Roller Coaster from 1953 is set in a near future, in 2050, in which science not only manages to erase memories, but even to transplant them; someone's memory, or selected parts of it, can be transferred to someone else's brain - which then integrates it as its own memories. A topic that Philip K. Dick will borrow for his story *We Can Remember It For You Wholesale* (1966), of which director Paul Verhoeven will then make the hit film *Total Recall* in 1990. In Belcampo's *The Roller Coaster* ("*De Achtbaan"*) a market of supply and demand soon emerges;

> "Now, for the first time, one could see how great the dissatisfaction with this life was that prevailed among people, and it also appeared that this dissatisfaction was due much less to the presence of happiness-inhibiting complexes than to the absence of gratifying and blissful images."

The story then centres on a couple who want to remove their memories of each other. Yes indeed, the same plot as in the brilliant 2004 film *Eternal Sunshine Of The Spotless Mind* by Charlie Kaufman - with an identical ending too, by the way.

Belcampo, Charlie Kaufman, Philip K. Dick, Paul Verhoeven... they all vary on the lament of Dylan's protagonist in "Million Miles", on the fantasy how liberating it would be to throw *all my memories in a ditch so deep*. Oblivion as a healer of the tormented soul, ignorance is bliss, or, as Alexander Pope put it in 1717, *the eternal sunshine of the spotless mind* (from "Eloisa to Abelard").

The mourning protagonist consciously seeks the ultimate state of denial, the first stage of any grieving process: he longs for a state in which he does not dream of her, cannot remember her... for the non-knowledge that she exists. But already in the third verse he seems to recognise the impossibility thereof; with the self-reproach *Did so many things I never did intend to do* he signals *guilt*, and thus already switches to the next phase of mourning. And immediately afterwards he shifts gear forward to the next phase:

> *I need your love so bad, turn your lamp down low*
> *I need every bit of it for the places that I go*
> *Sometimes I wonder just what it's all coming to*
> *Well, I'm tryin' to get closer but I'm still a million miles from you*

... to depression. For which the songwriter can blindly dig into the blues grab bag; after all, three quarters of all blues songs are about heartache - the canon offers an abundant choice of appropriate jargon. Dylan doesn't grab too deep. "Need Your Love So Bad", Little Willie John's immortal pièce de résistance from 1955 is somewhere at the front of the canon, especially after Fleetwood Mac's, or rather Peter Green's upgrade of the song in 1968. With indirect input from Little Willie, by the way; the string section for Fleetwood Mac's single was written by Little Willie's guitarist, the legendary Mickey Baker, at the request of producer Mike Vernon.

At least as famous is the next borrowing, *turn your lamp down low;*

> *Wake up, mama, turn your lamp down low*
> *Wake up, mama, turn your lamp down low*
> *Have you got the nerve to drive Papa McTell from your door?*

... Blind Willie McTell's "Statesboro Blues", which is perhaps even a few steps higher up in the Pantheon. Blind Willie recorded the song as early as 1928, Taj Mahal made it popular again in 1968, and with their live version from 1971, The Allman Brothers elevated "Statesboro Blues" to the canon once and for all. On *At Fillmore East*, with a Duane Allman, shortly before his death, at the top of his game.

The meaning of the phrase *turn your lamp down low* is somewhat diffuse, though. And Dylan, too, seems to prefer to keep it a bit vague. Blind Willie probably heard it from Bobby Grant, who a year earlier recorded his "Nappy Head Blues", with the opening lines *When you hear me walkin', turn your lamp down low / And turn it so your man'll never know* - in which "turn your lamp down" apparently means something like an invitation to adultery. But then, when Big Joe Williams takes the phrase in 1935 to the song that will also achieve such monumental status, to "Baby Please Don't Go", the meaning shifts to its opposite;

> *Turn your lamp down low*
> *You turn your lamp down low*
> *Turn your lamp down low, I cried all night long*
> *Now baby please don't go*
>
> *I begged you nice before*
> *I begged you nice before*
> *I begged you nice before, turn your lamp down low*
> *Now, baby please don't go*

... and seven more verses similar in content - the man begging his woman to remain faithful, to not let other men in; *turn your lamp down low* now meaning something like "keep your sexual urges under control".

In Dylan's "Million Miles" it can mean both. "*I need your love so bad*, let me in", or "*I need your love so bad*, don't give it to another". But the poet decides on playing with words, insinuating he needs both her love and her lamp: *I need every bit of it for the places that I go* - I'm entering a dark period, I may need some love and some light, so we have to be sparing with the lamp oil, something like that. Not too strong, but a signal that we are reaching the final stage of the mourning process: *acceptance*.

Yeah well. *Sometimes I wonder just what it's all coming to*, one would be inclined to think.

V   The sounds inside my mind

Well, I don't dare close my eyes and I don't dare wink
Maybe in the next life I'll be able to hear myself think
Feel like talking to somebody but I just don't know who
Well, I'm tryin' to get closer but I'm still a million miles from you

The hint of acceptance from the previous stanza evaporates again already in the fifth stanza. No, this narrator is still pretty upset, still in the penultimate stage of mourning, depression. Disregarding the context, the opening line would seem to be the mantra of a serious case of *FOMO*, of Fear Of Missing Out. Very serious, even: "I don't dare close my eyes and I don't dare wink"; this guy really doesn't want to miss anything. But within the context, and conditioned by a century of song tradition, we know what is really going on. Bing Crosby already warned about it:

85

Just when I think that I'm set
Just when I've learned to forget
I close my eyes, dear, and there you are
You keep coming back like a song
A song that keeps saying, remember

... in "You Keep Coming Back Like a Song" from 1946, with its truly beautiful title, which eventually inspired the heartbreaking album *You Come And Go Like A Pop Song* by The Bicycle Thief in 1999. In fact a project from the tragic hero Bob Forrest, whom Dylan fans know mainly from his contribution to the *I'm Not There* soundtrack, "Moonshiner", and who, on his '99 pièce de résistance, expresses with much more credibility the same suffering as Bing Crosby: "I can still see your face" (in "Everyone Asks").

As Sinatra, too, confesses in '55 on the unsurpassed heartburn album *In The Wee Small Hours* in "I See Your Face Before Me" (*I close my eyes, and there you are always*), as Dylan's fellow Travelling Wilbury Roy Orbison confided in "Afraid To Sleep" (*Can't close my eyes, afraid to sleep / Cause when I do I would only dream of you*, 1965)... we know by now what it means when a victim of Love says he dare not close his eyes.

The other distorted sense is less unambiguous. The narrator shares the inability to hear himself think with an earlier protagonist in Dylan's oeuvre, with the I-person from "One Too Many Mornings" (1964):

An' the silent night will shatter
From the sounds inside my mind

... at least, if we assume that he cannot hear himself think because of interfering noise. In any case, that is the scenario that a song's inspirator, Henry Rollins, invokes time and again in his work. *The choppers are so loud I can't even hear myself think*, for example (in "Art To Choke Hearts", 1986), or *I have the music cranking in my headphones so I can hear myself think over the caterwaul of my fellow masticators*. It is disturbing enough, the state of Henry Rollins' mind, but it is to be feared that Dylan's narrators are even worse off - there it is the inner chaos that makes following one's own thoughts impossible. In "Million Miles", a threatening inner chaos, even; an addition like *maybe in the next life* and the ultimate loneliness of *feel like talking to somebody but I just don't know who* suggest suicidal despair.

Seeing, hearing, feeling... his senses have been stripped, the poor soul. And apparently ready to fade too. But the cheerful, carefree connotation that Mr. Tambourine Man's friend communicates with those words is completely missing here. This is the fourth song on *Time Out Of Mind*, and the motifs begin to emerge. *Walking* is one (preferably *at night,* or so it seems), *world weariness*, or rather *life weariness* a second one, and the disturbed perception, like here in this stanza of "Million Miles", a third one. This motif returns in almost every song, with the devastating power of mental illness even. "Insanity is smashing up against my soul," says the narrator in the closing song "Highlands" - a superlative of the announcement "my brain is so wired" in the opening song "Love Sick". Prior to "Million Miles", in "Standing In The Doorway", we have already heard the narrator complain that he feels "sick in the head", and before that, in "Dirt Road Blues", concerns about mental health and the reliability of his sensory perceptions are justified as well.

After the first four songs on *Time Out Of Mind*, all three motifs keep returning. The weariness less pronounced, but unmistakable. They all walk, sometimes in combination with the third motif, the mental crisis: "I'm strolling through the lonely graveyard of my mind," says the pitiful wretch in song no. 10, in "Can't Wait". By then we have met his fellow sufferers one by one. Fellow sufferers whose *nerves are exploding* ("'Til I Fell In Love With You"), whose *nerves are vacant and numb* ("Not Dark Yet"), who *don't even know what "all right" means* ("Tryin' To Get To Heaven")... no, our narrator from "Million Miles" may be lonely, but he is not alone. Any one of those men is a suitable conversation partner for a guy who *feels like talking to somebody but just doesn't know who.*

Indeed. But then again, every one of those possible conversation partners is probably a million miles away, too.

VI   Like a wagon wheel

The last thing you said before you hit the street
"Gonna find me a janitor to sweep me off my feet"
I said, "That's all right, you do what you gotta do"
Well, I'm tryin' to get closer, I'm still a million miles from you

The song poet Dylan has a nice final couplet up his sleeve. But makes the discutable decision of going there by taking a detour; the two verses before that final couplet are undeniably the weakest links of the song. The penultimate verse even comes frighteningly close to being *filler* or even *lousy poetry*, and this sixth verse is unfortunately quite forgettable too. Mainly due, of course, to the corny pun with the janitor.

In itself, there is nothing wrong with a corny pun, every once in a while. Dylan indulges in it with some frequency, in fact in every decade of his sixty-year career. In the early sixties in songs whose form alone allows a cabaretesque approach, in talkin' blues songs like "Talkin' John Birch Paranoid Blues" and "Talkin' World War III Blues". Later in frenzied mercurial songs like "Tombstone Blues" (*The sun's not yellow - it's chicken*), it continues through to twenty-first century songs like "Po' Boy" (*Freddy or not here I come*) and culminates on *Rough And Rowdy Ways* (2020).

Here, however, there is something amiss. In a blues in which the protagonist is tossed to and fro between bitterness and despair, the cheap pun with "janitor" and "sweep me off my feet" is, well, inappropriate. All the more so, because the line catches the ear coming after the drama-promising opening line *The last thing you said before you hit the street* and before the eloquent but clichéd *That's all right, you do what you gotta do*. A verse line with a word combination, by the way, that is always attractive anyhow, as we can hear in Manfred Mann's "You Gave Me Somebody To Love", and in Santana's "Choose", but especially as demonstrated by the Grandmaster Jimmy Webb, who in 1968 wrote a whole song around it. "Do What You Gotta Do" sounds great in any version (B.J. Thomas, Nina Simone, The Four Tops, Clarence Carter, and more), but rarely as perfect as when Roberta Flack halves the tempo and pours a can of violins over it (1970, on the same record that features Roberta's heartbreaking "Just Like A Woman", *Chapter Two*); a beautiful song Jimmy Webb dashes off in 1968, sometime between "By The Time I Get To Phoenix", "MacArthur Park" and "Wichita Lineman" (to name but three landmarks).

Dylan himself seems to feel some dissatisfaction as well. After the recording, in January '97, he first ignores the song completely. Other *Time Out Of Mind* songs like "Love Sick", "Can't Wait" and "Cold Irons Bound" are immediately taken to the stage and performed over thirty times in their year of birth, "Million Miles" has to wait until January 1998. This verse is then sung, but the following one is skipped - and a year later, in 1999, this janitorial couplet is also discarded completely. After that, "Million Miles" is only performed occasionally. Three or four times a year, culminating in 2008, when the song is on the set list a mere eight times - leaving out even the last *three* verses.

The reservations about the penultimate verse are even more pronounced. In the studio, Dylan sings:

> *Rock me, pretty baby, rock me all at once*
> *Rock me for a little while, rock me for a couple of months*
> *And I'll rock you too*
> *I'm tryin' to get closer but I'm still a million miles from you*

... hardly earth-shattering, indeed. A friendly critic might qualify it as a reverence to one of the great blues foundations, to B.B. King's "Rock Me Baby", but Dylan's own fumbling with this verse suggests that he himself also sees it as a less successful improvisation product. In 1998, when the song is finally allowed to the stage, it is inexorably dropped. Only in 2003, in England, we hear the seventh verse return, but it has been rewritten in the meantime:

> *Rock me, pretty baby, rock me 'til everything gets real*
> *Rock me for a little while, rock me 'til there's nothing left to feel*
> *And I'll rock you too*
> *I'm tryin' to get closer but I'm still a million miles from you*

... rewritten to the version as it is published officially (in *Lyrics* and on the site). Dylan seems to think it's okay now; in 2004 and 2005 this rewritten *Lyrics* version is maintained - but in the dying year of the song, 2008, the stanza, together with the preceding and the concluding one, is removed again. The void is filled - rather un-dylanesquely - with long, somewhat rudderless guitar solos.

A pity, still. The rewritten version is superior; both *'til everything gets real* and *'til there's nothing left to feel* have the same colour, communicate the same emotional wound as "Cold Irons Bound" and "Dirt Road Blues", as *Time Out Of Mind* at all, actually. And the intentional or unintentional reverence to "Rock Me Baby", or rather, to its real father "Rockin' And Rollin'" by Lil' Son Jackson from 1950 remains intact. Not inconceivable, this reverence option; the song is one of the stepfathers of the unsightly snippet that a slightly bored Dylan shakes off in '73, during the recordings for the *Pat Garrett & Billy The Kid* soundtrack, and which is later polished up and promoted to a world hit by Old Crow Medicine Show and Darius Rucker, of the throwaway "Rock Me Mama (Like A Wagon Wheel)".

Colleagues have hardly problems with it, for that matter, with the skipped or rewritten *rock me* couplet. The two best-known covers, the one by Alvin Youngblood Hart (2002) and the one by Bonnie Raitt from 2012, simply stick to the discarded lyrics of the original studio recording, and unconcernedly rock *all at once*, rock happily *for a couple of months*.

VII   Songs that float in a luminous haze

Well, there's voices in the night trying to be heard
I'm sitting here listening to every mind-polluting word

Suddenly producer Tom Wilson is gone and replaced by Bob Johnston. In January '65, Dylan and Wilson passionately and harmoniously complete the first album of the mercurial trio, *Bringing It All Back Home*. When Dylan is over in England to be called *Judas*, Wilson is in New York doing overdubs for the intended single "If You Gotta Go, Go Now" (21 May 1965). And when Dylan returns, the men just get to work on the next masterpiece, on *Highway 61 Revisited*. Two days of recording, Wilson is still in the control room (15 and 16 June), the days when the final recording of "Like A Rolling Stone" is realised. No small feat either.

But still Wilson's swan song. On the third day of recording, 29 July, Bob Johnston is suddenly at the controls. Dylan acts like he doesn't know why, when *Rolling Stone* editor Jann Wenner asks him four years later about the producers change;

> BD: "Well, I can't remember, Jann. I can't remember... All I know is that I was out recording one day, and Tom had always been there – I had no reason to think he wasn't going to be there – and I looked up one day and Bob was there. (*Laughs*)"

Evasive and not very credible. It is not too plausible that Dylan, like a submissive wage slave, would let the Bosses Above Him decide with whom he must cooperate. Johnston doesn't know the ins and outs of it either, but he has an educated guess:

"His producer was Tom Wilson then. Gallagher called me in the office said, "We're getting rid of Tom Wilson." He didn't say why but maybe it was because Albert Grossman said he didn't like him, and I don't think Dylan liked him. I don't know, but he never said anything about it."

Wilson will never meet Dylan himself again, but indirectly, as a producer of other artists, still often enough, of course. In 1967, for instance, when he and Nico record one of Dylan's masterly throwaways, "I'll Keep It With Mine". And even more indirectly in 1970, when Wilson is the producer for the fifth LP of the infectious weirdos from San Francisco, for *CJ Fish* of Country Joe and the Fish. The final track of Side A will have taken him back in time;

> Hey Bobby, where you been ? We missed you out on the streets
> I hear you've got yourself another scene, it's called a retreat
> I can still remember days when men were men
> I know it's difficult for you to remember way back then , hey

… "Hey Bobby", the slightly awkward call for Dylan to return to the front, set to the same chord progression as "Like A Rolling Stone" is set, to "La Bamba".

In Dylan's 2004 autobiography *Chronicles*, it is a theme. In Chapter 3, "New Morning", Dylan looks back on a dark period in his life, the period around 1970, the years when Country Joe McDonald (among others) makes his pathetic appeal. The bard leaves no doubt about how enormously unpleasant he found it to be promoted "as the mouthpiece, spokesman, or even conscience of a generation". And how disruptive the consequences were. In Woodstock, he and his family were harassed by fans, followers and other nutcases, "goons were breaking into our place all hours of the night", in the press they kept portraying him as a kind of High Priest of Protest, colleagues like Robbie Robertson were waiting for his next move, waiting to show them where he's "gonna take it".

It is very, very unpleasant. "It would have driven anybody mad," Dylan writes. All the more so because he does not recognise himself at all in that image, nor does he have the ambition to be a spokesman of any kind. "I would tell them repeatedly that I was not a spokesman for anything or anybody and that I was only a musician," but that doesn't help, of course. It seems to frustrate Dylan still thirty years later, when he writes these words. "I really was never any more than what I was - a folk musician who gazed into the gray mist with tear-blinded eyes and made up songs that floated in a luminous haze."

And even more than Robbie Robertson's docility, even more than Country Joe's "Hey Bobby" or David Bowie's brilliant harangue "Song For Bob Dylan", he will have been irritated by the embarrassing "protest song" of his former life partner Joan Baez.

> "Joan Baez recorded a protest song about me that was getting big play, challenging me to get with it — come out and take charge, lead the masses — be an advocate, lead the crusade. The song called out to me from the radio like a public service announcement."

Dylan refers to Baez's open letter "To Bobby", the much-discussed song from the very mediocre album whose title also signals painful naiveté: *Come From The Shadows* (1972). In the self-written song, Baez does her best to wrap her appeal in Dylanesque rhyme patterns and eloquence. Like in the third verse;

> *Perhaps the pictures in the Times could no longer be put in rhymes*
> *When all the eyes of starving children are wide open*
> *You cast aside the cursed crown and put your magic into a sound*
> *That made me think your heart was aching or even broken*

... four lines that are "actually" six lines, judging by the *AABCCB*-rhyme scheme (*Times-rhymes-open / crown-sound-broken*), just like "Love Minus Zero" and "I Don't Believe You", Dylanesque assonant rhyme (*open-broken*, for instance) and a Dylanesque image like a *cursed crown*. Technically there is little wrong with that - but unfortunately Baez' faible for toe-curling melodrama, for kitschy images like the wide-open eyes of the starving children, is dominant. A faible she unfortunately also demonstrates in the possibly even more pathetic chorus, in

> *Do you hear the voices in the night, Bobby?*
> *They're crying for you*
> *See the children in the morning light, Bobby*
> *They're dying*

"Now listen," Dylan says in his 2015 MusiCares speech, "I'm not ever going to disparage another songwriter." And indeed, in this same speech, he does speak of Baez only with praise, with love and admiration ("A woman of devastating honesty. And for her kind of love and devotion, I could never pay that back"). Elegant. But probably no one in the audience, and not even Baez herself, would have blamed Dylan if, more than forty years after the fact, he had given his opinion about "To Bobby".

However, exactly halfway between Baez's 1972 song and Dylan's 2015 speech, he seems to be venting his opinion, subtly of course. In the last verse of "Million Miles", which Dylan recorded in January '97, he echoes the chorus of "To Bobby":

> *Well, there's voices in the night trying to be heard*
> *I'm sitting here listening to every mind-polluting word*

... in which, in this scenario, he expresses his opinion somewhat less elegantly (*every mind-polluting word*). Not unequivocal, however. The metaphor "voices in the night" is hardly unique (The Eagles' "Witchy Woman" comes to mind, and Joni Mitchell's "I Think I

Understand"), but it is still so unusual that it seems obvious that Dylan himself would think of Baez's whiny refrain. And apart from that, it fits perfectly on an album full of wandering protagonists with confused sensory impressions, on a record on which one protagonist confesses "I'm beginning to hear voices and there's no one around" ("Cold Irons Bound"), a second wonders if he hears *someone's distant cry* ("Love Sick") and a third, in "Not Dark Yet", sighs: "Don't even hear a murmur of a prayer".

But still. The expression *"voices in the night"* is just a bit too distinctive. And after all, "To Bobby" is, for all its awkwardness, one of those songs that float in a luminous haze.

VIII   Write twenty verses while you're in The Zone

I know plenty of people who would put me up for a day or two
Yes, I'm tryin' to get closer but I'm still a million miles from you

It is catalogued as "humorous fiction" and as "psychological fiction", Marni Jackson's *Don't I Know You?* from 2016, and other labels would also fit the charming collection of stories. The work consists of 14 short stories telling life chapters of the protagonist Rose McEwan, offering - chronologically - as many snapshots of Rose's life from age 17 to 60. The "gimmick", so to speak, of the story cycle are Rose's encounters - in each chapter Rose happens to meet a Famous Person, or a person who will later become famous, who is still in "the lobby of his life", as

Jackson calls it. At seventeen, she attends a writing class and attracts the attention of John Updike; a few years later, a holiday job as a waitress leads to a flirtation with a charming Bill Murray, Meryl Streep wants to be her friend at a weekend spa, and so it goes on until the final chapter, a canoe trip with Taylor Swift, Leonard Cohen and Karl Ove Knausgaard.

The fifth chapter is called *Bob Dylan Goes Tubing* and tells how Rose arrives with her then-life partner Eric at their holiday cottage by the lake. There is an unfamiliar Citroën parked in front of the house and Eric's nine-year-old son Ryan sees that someone is on the lake, lying on an air mattress.

> We shaded our eyes. A pale, small, but visibly adult figure was lying on the mattrass, slowly paddling with his hands toward the diving raft.
>
> "I need the binocs." Eric said, and went to get them. Standing on the deck he studied the figure.
>
> "This is really weird, but whoever that is looks exactly like Bob Dylan." He passed the binoculars to me. He was right. A pale little guy with a pencil mustache, in a Tilley hat, was on our air mattress.

We are probably somewhere in the early 1990s (although Jackson doesn't place too much value on historical accuracy, apparently; she suspects Dylan "is fragile right now" because *Empire Burlesque*, the 1985 album, is not a big seller - but he quotes "Everything Is Broken" and they sing along with Lucinda Williams' "Passionate Kisses", both songs from '89. Anyway: Dylan took a wrong turn on the way to Kashagawigamog Lake, and thought he was at his destination here, at Sturgeon Lake. And now he just stays here. Marni Jackson captivatingly and believably articulates how Rose and Eric, although finding this a little weird, take it for granted. The story unfolds charmingly and smoothly, without any dramatic plot twists. Dylan goes tubing with Ryan on the lake, has breakfast with Rose, oatmeal and syrup, philosophises with Eric about music standing in front of the record player, they play Monopoly, and one morning, after a week or two, Dylan is suddenly gone. And has then demonstrated an autobiographical truth behind this one line from "Million Miles": *I know plenty of people who would put me up for a day or two.*

"Million Miles" is not really a Very Great Dylan Song, but it does have, like many Very Great Dylan Songs, a somewhat alienating ending. We've had seven verses of lament, the wail of an abandoned lover mourning the loss of his beloved. Autobiographical interpreters with crypto-analytical ambitions might see something like "Dylan seeks his inspiration", the incorrigibly sentimental ones search in the Bard's love life, and stubborn Christian fans might put an evangelical spin on it ("Dylan suffers from a crisis of faith and seeks his God", or something like that), and sure enough, with some creative acrobatics many verses and images can be turned into metaphors supporting one interpretation or the other.

All of them, however, will have trouble squeezing this final couplet, and especially this final line, into a comprehensive interpretation. In the twenty-first century, Dylan changes the line to "There must be somebody who would put me up for a day or two" (London '03, for instance), but that doesn't open up any vistas either - it is still out of character. This is not love sickness or related misery, but pure, desperate, existential loneliness, no longer words directed outwards, to a *you*, but rather words from a desperate inner monologue, addressed to oneself.

In the *Consequence Podcast* of 9 March 2022, Mike Campbell reveals Dylan's writing routines, which may explain why Dylan's lyrics sometimes seem to wander off. Campbell is a founding member and mainstay of Tom Petty And The Heartbreakers, and Dylan's guitarist both on stage and in the studio, so he has some expertise and some right to speak. As a songwriter, he is not unsuccessful (co-credits on Petty hits like "Refugee" and "Here Comes My Girl", for example, as well as on Don Henley's world hit "The Boys Of Summer"), but he still gratefully recounts the writing tips he received from Bob Dylan:

> "He told me once, which was a really good tip, he said, when you're writing a song, you know, you got your verses, your bridge and your chorus, he said, don't stop there. Write twenty verses while you're in The Zone. You know, the last ones might be better than all the stuff you had."

Campbell's revelation is in line with what Dylan himself says in *Chronicles* about the creation of the song "Dignity". Long enough, that song, but there were many more couplets;

> "There were more verses with other individuals in different interplays. The Green Beret, The Sorceress, Virgin Mary, The Wrong Man, Big Ben, and The Cripple and The Honkey. The list could be endless. All kinds of identifiable characters that found their way into the song but somehow didn't survive."

Speculation, of course, but it seems that the lyrics for "Million Miles" were also written in "The Zone", also had twenty verses "with other individuals in different interplays", the majority of which "somehow didn't survive". And that after the deletion of ten or twelve stanzas, the text became unbalanced - hence perhaps a melodious, but essentially strange stanza as the seventh, the "rock me" stanza. And in the last stanza the introduction of a narrator who seems to have a different state of mind than the previous one. The state of mind in which you desperately yearn for human company.

The state of mind which makes you crash other persons' holidays at a cottage at Sturgeon Lake.

IX   Shall we roll it Jimmy?

It has an irresistible, voyeuristic appeal, the gimmick that Dylan and his producers have used many times over the years. Before the song actually begins, the listener hears shuffling, clinking glasses, studio chatter, a single stray guitar chord, a false start perhaps. Before "Bob Dylan's 115th Dream" begins, we hear an acoustic, broken-off start and laughter, and in 1969 Dylan asks producer Bob Johnston "Is it rolling, Bob?", to name just two examples.

The best-known messy intro of all time is probably The Beatles' "Get Back". By now, there must be billions of people who can playback along with McCartney's enigmatic "Rosetta..." and Lennon's warm-up exercise "Sweet Loretta thought she was a cleaner...", can hit an imaginary piano key in sync as Billy Preston and George Harrison are still tuning up, and know every single swirling note of that first twenty-one seconds by heart.

Roxy Music's first album (1972) opens with babbling and buzz and glass clinking - it sounds like there's a vernissage going on, and it takes twenty-five seconds for Bryan Ferry's piano "Remake/Remodel" to pop over it - an opening that is copied over thirty years later on Razorlight's debut album in the song "Which Way Is Out", with the same exhilarating effect. Led Zeppelin's "Black Country Woman" is introduced with Robert Plant's question "Shall we roll it Jimmy?", we hear a plane fly over disturbingly, Jimmy Page wants to wait a little longer, Plant laughs and says "Nah, leave it, yeah." And Slade's Noddy Holder insists to this day that his shouted "Baby baby baby" was not part of the song at all, but that he was just testing whether the microphone was on. In vain; the iconic scream has long since been integrated, and is also sung again when Oasis cover "Cum On Feel The Noize" in 1996. Without irony, by the way; the Gallagher brothers are devout Slade fans, as the documentary *It's Slade* (1999) also shows, in which Noel solemnly declares:

> "People just think when they listen to Slade, they think of *Cum On Feel The Noize* and *Mama Weer All Crazee Now*, but: *How Does It Feel* is easily one of the best songs ever written. Ever. Such a brilliant song. Go on buy it if you're watching this. It's on the Greatest Hits. Track 13."

Lanois and Dylan are evidently aware of the particular charm of a messy intro; *Time Out Of Mind* opens with six seconds of unstructured studio sounds before Augie Meyer's staccato organ strikes start "Love Sick"; the first two seconds of guitar rumble on the following "Dirt Road Blues" may remain; Lanois is still looking for a riff and someone (Tony Mangurian, probably) takes his place behind the drums at the start of "Highlands"; and the record is set by "Cold Irons Bound": fourteen seconds of rudderless guitar and piano notes before bassist Tony Garnier gives the starting signal.

That's already four of the eleven *Time Out Of Mind* songs with such a chaotic beginning - and the fifth is "Million Miles". Eight seconds of fumbling and haggling, you can almost *hear* Tony Garnier giving the nod, and then it starts. Again, a deliberate choice; after all, it's no trouble at all to cut the unstructured studio seconds from "Love Sick", from "Cold Irons Bound", from each of the five songs. In the case of "Highlands" and "Million Miles", one might even suspect that the opening seconds were artificially added to suggest some kind of studio spontaneity. At least, that's what Lanois' account in *Uncut* implies:

> "Tony and I played along to those records, and then I built some loops of what Tony and I did, and then abandoned these sources; which is a hip-hop technique. And then I brought those loops to Bob at the teatro. And we built a lot of demos around them, and he loved the fact that there was a good vibe on those. Some of the ultimate productions ended up having those loops in them. Songs like "Million Miles" and, uh, is it "Heartland"? [*he means "Highlands"*] – those long blues numbers have those preparations in their spine."

Lanois is referring to the homework Dylan had given, those "dusty old rock'n'roll records" from artists like Charley Patton, Little Walter, Slim Harpo and "guys like that", as technician Mark Howard says. So, for the studio recording of "Million Miles", Dylan and the band play along with a loop already recorded by Lanois and Tony Mangurian; pressing the start button should be the natural starting signal of the song - and not the nod of the bandleader on duty.

Meanwhile, the source, that loop, is intriguing. All the guitar parts are too casual, too loose, to trace back to an old recording of, say, Charley Patton or Lightnin' Hopkins. Not as obvious, anyway, as for instance the lick from Little Walter's "I Can't Hold Out Much Longer" that we hear back in 2020's "Crossing The Rubicon".

"Million Miles" may have a similar structure and stomp as, say, Little Walter's "Sad Hours", but the searching, seemingly improvised guitar parts, the swirling licks and the near stumbling sooner lead to the coolness of Lightnin' Hopkins, to records like *Texas Blues Man* (1968), to records that Hopkins so casually fills all on his own, without a band.

Still, "Million Miles" doesn't have much status. It's generally dismissed as one of the lesser songs (by the same fans and critics who condemn "Make You Feel My Love", typically), although often enough with the comment that on an album full of Great Songs there are of course Very Great Songs and Less Very Great Songs. Dylan himself seems to share the sentiment. After all, all through 1997 he ignores the song, and even after the stage debut in January '98, it does not receive much love either: 25 performances in a whole year of 111 concerts is a bit disappointing. Especially compared to other *Time Out Of Mind* songs like "Cold Irons Bound" (82 times), "Can't Wait" (64) and "Love Sick" (104 performances).

Noteworthy then is Susan Tedeschi's report, following her invitation to the MusiCare event in 2015, when Dylan accepts the MusiCares Person of the Year 2015 Award and surprises everyone with a long, fascinating speech. Tedeschi, along with husband Derek Trucks, is one of the artists invited to grace the festive evening with a Dylan cover:

> When Susan Tedeschi found out that Bob Dylan had personally requested that she perform his song "Million Miles" with her husband Derek Trucks, her reaction was short and sweet: "Holy crap! I don't care if it's Super Bowl weekend, we're there."
> (Ryan Cormier, The News Journal, 13 February 2015)

Charming, but of course the most remarkable thing is not so much that Dylan personally requested Tedeschi, but that he specifically requested "Million Miles" - the song to which he himself never gave too much love and which he has already more or less dropped from his setlist. The last performance, well, kind of performance anyway, was in July 2014 in Greece, where he played only the first verse, and then let the song flow into "Cry A While".

Tedeschi and Trucks's rendition does not lead to a reappraisal. After the well-known cover by Bonnie Raitt and the somewhat lesser known one by Alvin Youngblood Hart (for the successful Dylan tribute album *All Blues'd Up* from 2002), there are hardly any artists who put the song on the repertoire anymore. Wynonna Judd does it once - and beautifully - in 2016, at the Dylan Fest Nashville, celebrating Bob Dylan's 75th Birthday, but the best one is again from Bonnie Raitt, when she performs the song together with Keb' Mo' in 2019, at the fifth edition of Eric Clapton's Crossroads Guitar Festival. Bringing it all back home; Raitt plays country blues licks like Lightnin' Hopkins, Keb' Mo' contributes vocals like Elmore James and plays a B.B. King-like solo - and it takes 28 messy seconds before the song starts.

5   Tryin' To Get To Heaven

Among the many pearls glittering on one of his most beautiful albums, *Hunky Dory* from 1971, shines the remarkable "Song For Bob Dylan", a beautiful song with a striking text, of which the often quoted *a voice like sand and glue* are the perhaps most memorable words.

Bowie's song doesn't fall from the sky. With the partly idolising, partly reproaching ode, the British chameleon shakes off the Dylan feathers he has worn for a year or two: on his playlist are the Dylan covers "She Belongs To Me" and "Don't Think Twice", for a while he performs in a Dylan-1963 look, including proletarian cap, the first two albums are filled with half and full Dylan references and the word *dylanesque* is a constant in the (mostly positive) reviews of those LPs.

In an interview for *Melody Maker* ('76) the singer looks back on "Song For Bob Dylan":

> "It was at that period that I said, OK, if you don't want to do it, I will. I saw the leadership void."

But he remains faithful to his idol in the following decades. In this same *Hunky Dory* period Bowie records another unreleased nod to Dylan, "It's Gonna Rain Again", with the hobby project Tin Machine he releases "Maggie's Farm" on a single, in between with the band of Bryan Adams he records a heavy but attractive "Like A Rolling Stone" and most of all: in 1998 he takes a shot at "Tryin' To Get To Heaven". Officially released only in 2021, five years after Bowie's death, although it is a superb, mesmerizing version.

It is a very well-chosen cover. With its despondent, dark verses full of mysterious imagery and expressive metaphors, the monumental masterpiece is situated exactly at the intersection of Dylan's and Bowie's repertoire - even the title fits both Bowie's first hit "Space Oddity" (1969) and his last, his swan song "Lazarus" (2016).

In reviews, the song is often mentioned in the same breath as that other monument on *Time Out Of Mind*, "Not Dark Yet". Understandable: apart from the music both songs are also thematically comparable. The narrator despairs, the end of life approaches inevitably.

Tryin' is still slightly less desolate. Where "Not Dark Yet" does not even offer the prospect of redemption in an afterlife ("I just don't see why I should take care"), at least the gate to heaven is open here - still, anyway. Though it is far from a consoling, cloudless counterpart of "Not Dark Yet", obviously. Predominant is an identical worn-out languor, embedded in a same structure: both lyrics are cast in Dylan's beloved François Villon format, songs without a chorus but with recurring refrain lines that end every verse.

And the song is more accessible. Dylan opts for the well-known, almost archaic *life path* metaphor, as it has been worded for centuries, by poets such as Emiliy Dickinson, Pablo Neruda, Paul McCartney and Robert Frost:

> *Two roads diverged in a yellow wood,*
> *And sorry I could not travel both*
> *And be one traveler, long I stood*
> *And looked down one as far as I could*
> *To where it bent in the undergrowth*
>
> (The Road Not Taken, 1916)

In every couplet the narrator travels, the protagonist is literally on his way and in a figurative sense trying to reach the gate of heaven. The I-person roams from the *middle of nowhere* to Missouri, follows the Mississippi down to the estuary, as far as New Orleans and thus roughly following Highway 61. On the way, he plucks to his heart's content from the blues idiom. "Trying To Get To Heaven" Dylan already hears in 1962, at a concert by Reverend Gary Davis in Gerde's Folk City, and he is probably familiar with Al Kooper's variant, with the chorus *"Tryin' to get to heaven in due time / Before the heaven doors close"* ("Wake Me Shake Me", The Blues Project, 1966).

Just as classic and extremely effective is the trick with which the poet sets the mood in the first two lines: the threatening, dampening silence preceding a summer thunderstorm.

> *The air is getting hotter*
> *There's a rumbling in the skies*
> *I've been wading through the high muddy water*
> *With the heat rising in my eyes*

Inspired, no doubt, by one of the song's many mothers, the old gospel "Wade In The Water" (from which Dylan also borrows for the outtake "Marchin' To The City");

I heard a rumblin' up in the sky
Must a-been Jesus passin' by...
Wade in the water, wade in the water, children
Wade in the water, God's gonna trouble the water!

As in many of Dylan's finest works, the lyrics reach lyrical and poetic heights through that combination: the mixing of fragments of blues clichés and half-quotes (*When I was in Missouri, they would not let me be* and *muddy water* are both from Furry Lewis' "Turn Your Money Green"), with paraphrase (the Biblical *lonesome valley* comes from Psalm 23, though Dylan probably prefers to sing along with the old gospel song *You've Got To Walk That Lonesome Valley*) and with catachresis, the innovative word combinations ("The heat rising in my eyes").

"You can seal up the book and not write anymore" is another great find, such an elegant variant of the Closed Book as a metaphor for the end of a relationship. Found in the Bible, (the phrase is found in both Daniel and Revelation), but Dylan must have copied it from a song in his inner jukebox, "John The Revelator":

Seal up your book, John,
An' don't write no more

And like this, almost every verse in Dylan's song can be found in the Bible, in old gospel songs, in blues classics, in Woody Guthrie songs (*Some trains don't pull no gamblers* is from "Bound For Glory", for example).

Teasing are the nostalgic references to drug consumption. Mary-Jane is an almost antique pseudonym for marijuana, but Dylan's first association is the whore madam from the old folk song "Ridin 'In A Buggy, Miss Mary Jane", which he probably knows in the performance of Pete's half-sister Peggy Seeger (1958) :

Oh, Miss Mary Jane.
Sally's got a house in Baltimore,
in Baltimore, in Baltimore.
Sally's got a house in Baltimore,
and it's full of chicken pie.

Thanks to Nancy Sinatra's "Sugar Town" (1966) and especially the frank explanation by songwriter Lee Hazlewood, we know that *Sugar Town* is sugar cubes drenched in LSD. In a few reviews of *Tryin'*, it is partly therefore concluded that the entire song is a tribute to the deceased Jerry Garcia - and also because it is possible, with some kung-fu acrobatics, to filter fragments of Grateful Dead song titles from the song. It is a hardly sustainable thesis with thin evidence. And anyway: whenever Dylan writes an admiring in memoriam, he is far from vague or ambiguous: "Lenny Bruce", "Roll On John", "Blind Willie McTell", "High Water (For Charley Patton)".

No, that *Sugar Town* also penetrates Dylan's song via an old folk song, as we can read on Eyolf Østrem's invaluable site *dylanchords*. Half a platoon of eminent Dylanologists, including the distinguished professor Richard Thomas, puzzle together all references in "Tryin' To Get To Heaven", and Jim Jenigen from Richmond, Virginia, points out an ancient folk song from Alabama, "Buck-Eye Rabbit":

I wanted su-gah ver-y much,
I went to Sug-ah Town,
I climbed up in that sug-ah tree
An' I shook that sug-ah down

The literary peak is in the middle, as it should be. The third verse portrays in a masterful, stifling way the meaninglessness of existence, by observing a platform full of commuters: "*I can hear their hearts a-beatin' / Like pendulums swinging on chains.*"

The next lines are different from the published lyrics on *bobdylan.com*. The official site states:

I tried to give you everything
That your heart was longing for

In the studio it does, apparently, not feel right. The lines are moved to the last verse (replacing the mysterious "Some trains don't carry no gamblers"-line, which seems like a debatable decision). Morten Jonsson has also given it some thought and finds a fascinating explanation for the operation:

"It does seem a shame to lose those lines, but the revision is more than just a cliché. It's from "The Streets of Baltimore", written by Tompall Glaser and Harlan Howard and best known in the recordings by Bobby Bare and by Gram Parsons and Emmylou Harris: "*A man feels proud to give his woman what she's longing for / And I kind of liked the streets of Baltimore*." Perhaps Dylan is simply giving a nod to that song, prompted by the mention of Baltimore in his own song. But I suspect it was on his mind when he wrote "Trying to Get to Heaven". Perhaps it even provided the pattern he followed. Both songs are made up of four-line stanzas (though Dylan's lines are split into two on the page, making eight), ending with a refrain. And the refrains – "*the streets of Baltimore / Trying to get to heaven before they close the door*" – rhyme with each other. You could even see Dylan's song as a kind of sequel: after the singer left his woman walking the streets of Baltimore, he never did make it back to Tennessee. He's been wandering the world ever since, trying to get to heaven before they close the door. But that's going a little far."

Or maybe Dylan just stumbles over its too clichéd nature. Anyway, he improves it by replacing the lines at this point in the song to the much more powerful, much more desperate lines:

When you think that you've lost everything,
You find out you can always lose a little more.

... possibly thanks to Henry Rollins' *Now if you think you lost it all, you're wrong. You can always lose a little more*

Lucinda Willams' cover (on the Amnesty project *Chimes Of Freedom*, 2012) is appreciated, in general. Overappreciated, perhaps. It is true that the instrumentation is beautiful, but Williams' singing is weird, overacting like a Nicholas Cage in a ten a penny action movie (with a similar diction too, by the way) and Lucinda is so busy groaning and gasping, that the question arises: does she know *what* she is singing?

Then the reading by veteran Peter Rowan, a bluegrass musician from a lower division, is much more attractive. With the Czech backing band Drúha Tráva, he records a dreamy, sultry version for the album *New Freedom Bell* in 1999. And the interpretation by loyal Dylan disciple Robyn Hitchcock, with the cooperation of renowned Dylan interpreters Gillian Welch and David Rawlings, is very attractive too (on *Spooked*, 2004).

But towering far above them all is the gothic cathedral Bowie constructs from "Tryin' To Get To Heaven". Bowie's respect is almost tangible, but it doesn't paralyze him. An artist of his calibre dares to deviate from the original, an artist with his qualities knows how to enrich the original. Bowie's tendency to the theatrical is of course much more pronounced than Dylan's tendency to dramatize, fitting this work very well. Unlike in the parent song, a sharply rising tension curve is constructed here, which, very dramatically, collapses halfway. The intensity with which Bowie then sings the last two verses is chilling.

It is a magnificent cover by an unforgettable artist.

6   'Til I Fell In Love With You

I   The Day Before You Came

Rolling Stone dismissed them, or rather their album *Arrival* (1976, the album with "Dancing Queen" and "Money, Money, Money") as "muzak mesmerizing in its modality", their already "vapid lyrics" being reduced to "utter irrelevance". More than 40 years later, Björn nods in recognition and grins: "I mean, they were harsh, those critics." "Yeah," Benny adds, "we had the wrong clothes and the wrong image overall – but I have to say: I didn't care much. I don't think anyone did." (*CBS Sunday Morning*, October 2021).

The opinion of a few conceited music journalists should indeed hardly matter when you have such a massive fan base and score such astronomical sales figures. And the opinion of the *real* connoisseurs and professionals, successful musicians, will probably weigh more heavily too. Led Zeppelin recorded their last studio album, *In Through The Out Door*, at Abba's Polar Studios, and in between Robert Plant painted Stockholm red together with Björn and Benny. Elvis Costello never disguises his admiration, borrows the triumphant grand piano lick of "Dancing Queen" for his biggest hit "Oliver's Army", bases the Bacharach collaboration "This House Is Empty Now" on a line from "Knowing Me, Knowing You" (on *walking through this empty house, tears in my eyes*), and goes on to reveal in his autobiography that they listen to *Arrival* on the tour bus and "our Abba cassettes, even early recordings in Swedish that I proudly purchased at the service stations and listened to faithfully."

Even more unlikely but convincingly documented is the Abba love of Nirvana's Kurt Cobain (he adored the Abba cover band Björn Again), and of the Sex Pistols. In his 1994 autobiography *No Irish, No Blacks, No Dogs*, Johnny Rotten admits that "Pretty Vacant" was based on "SOS".

> "Glen [*first bass player Glen Matlock*] was a closet Abba fan, and funny enough, so was Sid [*Sid Vicious, Matlock's successor*]. We got rid of one Abba fan and got another one in its place. Once Sid ran up to the girls from Abba in the Stockholm airport to ask for their autograph. Sid was completely drunk and stuck his hand out. They screamed and ran away."

Nevertheless, we have to agree, reluctantly, with one point being made by those sour critics: the "vapid lyrics" of "I Do, I Do, I Do, I Do, I Do", "Mamma Mia", "Fernando" and all the other million sellers do not have much depth or poetic brilliance. With one, extraordinary, brilliant exception: the poetic masterpiece "The Day Before You Came".

It is, perhaps tellingly, the last song Abba wrote and recorded, and in more ways than one (lyrically, arrangement, the sparse melody line) is a break from the trend. It does seem to be a first step towards the next career of "the unmolested masterminds behind ABBA" (Costello) Benny and Björn, a step towards musicals. The lyrics tell, in stripped-down prose but still with fascinating, Dylanesque vagueness, how a banal, uneventful life of the female protagonist is definitively and irrevocably capsized by - presumably - a brief, sweeping love affair that is already over. *I was all right 'til I fell in love with you*;

Must have left my house at eight, because I always do
My train, I'm certain, left the station just when it was due
I must have read the morning paper going into town
And having gotten through the editorial, no doubt I must have frowned
I must have made my desk around a quarter after nine
With letters to be read, and heaps of papers waiting to be signed
I must have gone to lunch at half past twelve or so
The usual place, the usual bunch
And still on top of this I'm pretty sure it must have rained
The day before you came

What Agnetha veils or at best insinuates in "The Day Before You Came" is expressed by Dylan's "'Til I Fell In Love With You" in baroque multicolour. The dazed lady from Abba's song acknowledges that until *The Day* she "had no sense of living without aim", and "at the time I never even noticed I was blue", thus merely insinuating that now her state is the dramatic opposite. Dylan's narrator is not insinuating. On the contrary:

Well, my nerves are exploding and my body's tense
I feel like the whole world got me pinned up against the fence
I've been hit too hard, I've seen too much
Nothing can heal me now, but your touch
I don't know what I'm gonna do
I was all right 'til I fell in love with you

... but the emotional state of the protagonist is, of course, exactly the same: total despair after a devastating love affair. Just as the structure chosen by both Dylan and Björn Ulvaeus is identical. In Abba, four interchangeable stanzas tell the same story four times; the mind-numbing monotony in which the protagonist floats through life, culminating in the recurring refrain line *the day before you came*. In Dylan's song, five interchangeable stanzas describe the same story five times: the inner battlefield of the crushed protagonist, culminating in the recurring refrain line *I was all right 'til I fell in love with you.*

Stylistically, the lyrics (obviously) differ enormously. Ulvaeus' lyrics have the couleur of a to-do list, deliberately of course, brilliantly blurred by that endless row of *I must haves*. Eloquent - again, deliberately - it is not. Dylan, on the other hand, is far from restrained. To describe the state of his protagonist, he plunders his inner jukebox, the books on his bedside table, his meandering, associative brain, Henry Rollins and the Bible. Naturalism versus expressionism, to put it a bit more academically.

This guy is one of the few sparked-up protagonists on *Time Out Of Mind*, one might be inclined to think after the explosive opening line. All the other men are burned-out, world-weary, sometimes even zombie-like creatures, but this man seems quite over-stimulated, tormented by smothering, suffocating oppression. The image, however, does not last; already in the third line, the line borrowed from Henry Rollins *I've been hit too hard, I've seen too much*, the numbness descends again - this sucker, too, is stricken and defeated.

It looks like a core line. The lines around it are filled with echoes from other songs, or so it seems. Dylan has sung *"against the fence"* a few times on stage with Van Morrison, in Van The Man's beautiful "And It Stoned Me" (*"We just stood there gettin' wet / With our backs against the fence"*), although the word combination is not too distinctive.

Nor is her "healing touch". John Hiatt's "Through Your Hands" has a similar image, and in recent years has been sung by Don Henley, by David Crosby, and by others - the song may have entered Dylan's ears as well. The appeal for Dylan, however, will lie mainly in its evangelical connotation. "*Nothing can heal me now, but your touch*" is, evidently, a messianic image, and archaically and biblically expresses the salvation sought by the poor protagonist of Dylan's song.

And Agnetha's too, of course.

II   Burning Down The House

"Whoever does the words has a very hard job. That's the sharp edge of the music. Whatever else the music is doing, if there are words there, you know that is going to be the focal point of the music for so many listeners. And you can really fuck it up with words. If they're not good, you can totally wreck the whole thing," Brian Eno says in an interview with Michael Engelbrecht for the German magazine *Jazzthetik* (March 1996).

The statement seems atypical of the grand master of soundscapes, of the artist who, early in his career, increasingly moved away from songs with vocals and made mainly instrumental records. Ten years earlier, in the fascinating account of Eno's conversation with John Cage in *Musician* (September 1985), he is quite unambiguous:

> "But I have the same feeling about lyrics. I just don't want to hear them most of the time. They always impose something that is so unmysterious compared to the sound of the music they debase the music for me, in most cases."

... but is very much in line with his statements ten years later; Eno loves language, or rather vocals, but not the "de-mystifying" effect that its content can have. "I cut the language up," he explains, "a few words will come out - space - another word - another six words - space - another two words. So the language really keeps falling apart. In a way, it's like using language and trying as hard as possible to break the meaning down, and see what's left. See where the meaning still comes out of it."

Which does sound very much like William Burroughs' cut-up technique, and is:

> "What I did is, I took little tiny phrases, pieces of sentences from a magazine describing Serbian torture in Bosnia, a porno magazine, and an article about homeless people in London. I took these phrases, then I have a randomiser, so that I can start to throw them together in new ways."

In fact, a copy of Burroughs' working method, so to speak. And of the writing process that Dylan already imitated in the sixties, and according to writing partner Larry Charles still practices in the twenty-first century, around *Time Out Of Mind* as well. Charles, who co-wrote the script for the Dylan film *Masked And Anonymous* in 2003, reveals that the Bard literally has a box full of slips of paper and torn-off scrap sheets, full of one-line ideas, loose metaphors and whatnot. During the writing process, the box is placed on the table, Dylan turns it over and starts moving snippets back and forth;

> "He takes these scraps and he puts them together and makes his poetry out of that. He has all of these ideas and then just in a subconscious or unconscious way, he lets them synthesize into a coherent thing. And that's how we wound up writing also. We wound up writing in a very 'cut-up' technique."

Explicitly, Eno words his philosophy in the opening track of the wonderful 1975 album *Another Green World*, in "Sky Saw";

All the clouds turn to words
All the words float in sequence
No one knows what they mean
Everyone just ignores them

Over which Eno then sings contextless strings of words like *"Open stick and delphic doldrums / Open click and quantum data"*. But with hindsight, the technique has been recognisable since his first solo album *Here Come The Warm Jets* (1973). And apparently, Eno also converts David Byrne. The second Talking Heads album produced by the prodigious Briton, *Fear Of Music* (1978), opens with the song Eno and Byrne wrote together to an adapted text by Dadaist Hugo Ball, "I Zimbra". The lyrics consist of meaningless strings of words like *"A bim beri glassala glandride / E glassala tuffm I zimbra"*. The lyrics of the songs on their collaborative project, the 1981 successful *My Life In The Bush Of Ghosts*, are entirely construed of sampled sound fragments from radio sermons, talk shows and Lebanese singers.

David Byrne can manage without Eno after that, and has learned a valuable lesson: the next world hit "Burning Down The House" is constructed by Byrne, very Dylanesque, from collected scraps, fragments and scribbles. "I [would] just write words to fit that phrasing... I'd have loads and loads of phrases collected that I thought thematically had something to do with one another, and I'd pick from those," as he reveals in an interview on NPR's *All Things Considered* (December 1984). In which he also gives a glimpse of what else can be found in his box: word combinations that were originally included in "Burning Down The House" but were rejected again. *"I have another body"*, for example, and *"Pick it up by the handle"*.

It demonstrates, all in all, a funny art fraternity of Brian Eno, David Byrne and Bob Dylan. Thanks to the release of the outtake "Marchin' To The City" on *The Bootleg Series Vol. 8: Tell Tale Signs* (2008), we know that Dylan also used scissors and glue to create "'Til I Fell In Love With You". Apart from the chorus line, the second verse features two lines from that rejected outtake too;

> *Well, my house is on fire, burning to the sky*
> *I thought it would rain but the clouds passed by*
> *Now I feel like I'm coming to the end of my way*
> *But I know God is my shield and he won't lead me astray*
> *Still I don't know what I'm gonna do*
> *I was all right 'til I fell in love with you*

The first two lines, that is - lines of verse that no doubt emerged from that legendary "very ornate, beautiful box" as well. Which also suggests an unimportant, but again amusingly similar thematic fascination. Eno's box seems to contain a disproportionate number of word combinations with "fire" and the likes (which is demonstrated in the titles alone; "Baby's On Fire", "The Paw Paw Negro Blowtorch", "Here Come The Warm Jets", "Burning Airlines Give You So Much More", "Over Fire Island", "St. Elmo's Fire", "Lava"...). The same applies to the first time David Byrne starts cutting and pasting:

> *Ah, all wet*
> *Hey, you might need a raincoat*
> *Shakedown*
> *Dreams walking in broad daylight*
> *365 degrees*
> *Burning down the house*

"He takes these scraps and he puts them together and makes his poetry out of that"... Larry Charles' testimony about Dylan's methods seems to apply one-to-one to Byrne's "Burning

Down The House". The coincidental similarities in content with "'Til I Fell In Love With You" are meaningless, of course. On the other hand: "Take something that is all accidents and chance events," Eno teaches in that same 1996 interview, "and then make it all happen again."

III   Ballad Of A Small Town Boy

Neon Park (1940-1993) was a colourful and versatile illustrator, cartoonist and designer, whose clients included Playboy and DreamWorks, but his lasting fame is mainly due to the beautiful album covers he drew for Little Feat - apart from the 1971 debut album, Park provided every Little Feat album up until his death, i.e. up to and including 1991's *Shake Me Up*, with great, often witty covers. Apart from his technical craftsmanship, Neon Park distinguishes himself by his playfulness; the men of Little Feat usually let him do what he wanted, which resulted in covers full of hidden allusions, obvious persiflages, winks and Hieronymus Bosch-like frenzies. Like the cover of *Sailin' Shoes* (1972): a pie with women's legs, swinging on a tree swing, watched by both a giant snail and Mick Jagger dressed as Thomas Gainsborough's *Blue Boy* from 1770.

A running gag throughout his career are duckfaces; Marilyn Monroe, Humphrey Bogart, Marlene Dietrich... he paints them in iconic, recognisable poses, but replaces body and face with enlarged, humanised Donald Ducks. And Little Feat did not escape this either; the last album with Lowell George, *Down On The Farm* (1979), is decorated with one of Parks' most perfect covers: a sexy Duck posing as one of Gil Elvrgen's famous pin-ups from the fifties: "The Finishing Touch".

It is a brilliantly chosen template to illustrate the title song of Little Feat's album:

> *They all asked about you*
> *Down on the farm*
> *The cows asked, the pigs asked*
> *The horses asked, too*
> *All want to know why to the city*
> *You moved, changed your name to Kitty*
> *What's come over you?*
> *It ain't true; it ain't true, Linda Lou*
> *Say it ain't true, Linda Lou*

... the classic story of the local beauty who tries to satisfy her lust for wealth and fame in the Big City, and goes down with it. For Neon Park, the exceptional opportunity to place its running gag in a narratively correct context; this one time, the banality of something as mundane as a duck, placed in an alienating, glamorous setting, does actually make sense.

The plot is over-familiar and has been milked in dozens of films, novels and songs. Usually rather kitschy and moralistic. The one-hit wonder John Collins Cunningham scored a hit with "Norma Jean Wants To Be A Movie Star" in 1974 ("She died in L.A. in a lonely room"), Elton John's brilliant, enchanting ballad "Cage The Songbird", Bob Seger's compelling "Hollywood Nights"... kitschy or not, the theme often brings out the best in artists.

For this third verse of "'Til I Fell In Love With You", Dylan borrows clichés and motifs from all those identical, doomed fame-chaser stories;

> *Boys in the street beginning to play*
> *Girls like birds flying away*
> *When I'm gone you will remember my name*
> *I'm gonna win my way to wealth and fame*
> *I don't know what I'm gonna do*
> *I was all right 'til I fell in love with you*

... where in Dylan's mind there are probably no Elton John or Bob Seger buzzing around, but one of the pillars of all those lonely-at-the-top songs: Johnny Cash's corny "Ballad Of A Teenage Queen" from 1958, recorded for his first compilation album *Sings The Songs That Made Him Famous*. Certainly not a highlight of Cash's discography, this ballad with its hard-to-enjoy penny novelette content and its supersweet happy ending, but it provides a motif and some jargon for a Dylan song - and that's worth something. And a No. 1 hit in the Country Charts it was as well, nonetheless;

> *Then one day the teenage star*
> *Sold her house and all her cars*
> *Gave up all her wealth and fame*
> *Left it all and caught a train*

Though with Dylan too, as with Cash and unlike Elton and Seger and Cunningham, the motif of the hollow pursuit of wealth and fame does not bring out the best. This central stanza of "'Til I Fell In Love With You" falls a bit out of tune. These four lines are the only lines that don't emotionally connect with the chorus lines *I don't know what I'm gonna do / I was all right 'til I fell in love with you*; they are the only lines in which the narrator's tone is not defeated and despondent, but rather one of venom and revenge. Childish, that *just wait, you'll be sorry* wailing of verses three and four, and not fitting for the state of mind of the main character as we get to know it in the other four stanzas.

Still, apparently its inclusion was a well-considered decision by the songwriter. After all, the lines come from the preliminary study of "'Til I Fell In Love With You", from the outtake "Marchin' To The City #1" that we know from *Tell Tale Signs: The Bootleg Series Vol. 8*. Thanks to that wonderful Bootleg Series episode, we also know that Dylan himself initially had some reservations about these trite lines: in #2 of "Marchin' To The City", the version that also musically resembles the final product "'Til I Fell In Love With You"; these lines have been deleted and replaced by the admittedly very sentimental, but thematically more appropriate *"Sorrow and pity through the earth and the skies / I'm not looking for nothing in anyone's eyes"*. However, somewhere between the recording of this version and the final recording of "'Til I Fell In Love With You", these lines are also deleted and Dylan returns to that *just wait, you'll be sorry* wail of "When I'm gone you will remember my name / I'm gonna win my way to wealth and fame".

A rather incomprehensible intervention. But then again, it is the literary intervention of a small-town boy who left home to pursue wealth and fame and a Nobel Prize for Literature in the Big City, and who, as we all know, has succeeded incomparably -

> *All want to know why to the city*
> *You moved, changed your name to Dylan*
> *What's come over you?*

... is a question no one will ever ask Robert Zimmerman.

IV   It Keeps Rainin'

Junk is piling up, taking up space
My eyes feel like they're falling off my face
Sweat falling down, I'm staring at the floor
I'm thinking about that girl who won't be back no more
I don't know what I'm gonna do
I was all right 'til I fell in love with you

"He soon got used to the various changes in his room. It had become a habit in the family to push into his room things there was no room for elsewhere, and there were plenty of these now." The family treats Gregor more and more as what he, in fact, is: an annoying insect. At first, Grete, the sister who has taken on the care, still has a loving urge to give "*him as wide a field as possible to crawl in and of removing the pieces of furniture that hindered him,*" but after the painstaking process of habituation and the growing irritation, Gregor's room degenerates into a junk room. *Junk is piling up, taking up space.*

Dylan communicates in this fourth verse the same claustrophobic feeling as Kafka in *Die Verwandlung* ("The Metamorphosis", 1912), but we may assume that in "'Til I Fell In Love With You" it is meant purely metaphorically - to express a panic-stricken state of mind of the protagonist. He feels, just like the narrator in "Mississippi", *trapped* and *tight as the corner that I painted myself in*, and

Time is pilin' up, we struggle and we scrape
We're all boxed in, nowhere to escape

An identical state of mind, very similar word choice (*Time is pilin' up* versus *Junk is piling up*; *thinking about Rosie* versus *thinking about that girl*; *my eyes go blind* versus *my eyes feel like they're falling off my face*)... starts to look like "'Til I Fell In Love With You" is one of the reasons for Dylan's unforgivable decision to discard "Mississippi" from *Time Out Of Mind*.

Might even be the same narrator, one might think after hearing the last two stanzas. In the last verse of this song, the narrator considers going "Dixie bound", the narrator in "Mississippi" *has* meanwhile arrived in the South, coming from the North ("*I got here following the southern star*"). And seems to be haunted by a similar unspeakable something that is insinuated in this song now, at the end.

The narrator's panic-stricken claustrophobic attack in "'Til I Fell In Love With You" is followed by a bizarre emotion that is hard to fathom: "*My eyes feel like they're falling off my face*". Either he is crying very, *very* hard, or his subconscious has a very strong need to stop seeing something. In the canon, we recognise at most a half-resemblance of the latter option to the gruesome climax in *Oedipus Rex*, when Oedipus is so shocked by the crimes he has unknowingly committed that he gouges out his eyes. And furthermore, we only know about eyeballs popping out from Spongebob and Tex Avery's whistling wolf in *Little Red Walking Hood* - but it is highly unlikely that Dylan is trying to drive the listener's associations towards Looney Tunes. No, apparently there is something particularly shocking there, so shocking that the eyes want to leave their owner. But what?

The lyrics are, as we can reconstruct thanks to the outtakes on *Tell-Tale Signs*, largely pasted together from scraps of the rejected "Marchin' To The City" (57% of the 277 words come from that outtake), making it less obvious that Dylan had a narrative in mind when he sat down for "'Til I Fell In Love With You". It's more likely, as in many Dylan songs, Dylan gets inspired by his own words while he's writing, arrives at a hint of a scenario, and then doesn't worry about plot holes or incongruities - it's lyrical poetry, after all.

He seems to want to build in a hint of a murder ballad now, about halfway through the song's lyrics. The opening, with its claustrophobic panic attack, is then retroactively given a kind of logical underpinning; *Sweat falling down, I'm staring at the floor / I'm thinking about that girl who won't be back no more* suggests the aftershock of a dramatic climax, of a man who, panting, stands bent over the corpse of the woman he has killed to his own dismay - *she won't be back no more, I don't know what I'm gonna do*. In which, incidentally, Dylan incorporates a nod to Fats Domino, to his 1961 hit "It Keeps Rainin'", probably out of playfulness. At least, the way Dylan, especially in live-versions, sings *"she won't be back no more"*, is very much à la Domino's *"she won't be back no mo'ah'"* - also as a rhyme word for the preceding *"floor"*, by the way;

> She left me reelin' an rockin'
> Walkin' the floor
> She lef' a note last night
> She won't be back no mo'

Reasoning back, the preceding stanzas are then something like fragments of a bitter quarrel, fragments of scenes, echoes of reproaches back and forth. A sentence like *I'm gonna win my way to wealth and fame* is, in that scenario, not spoken by the protagonist, but by his female counterpart while she is packing her suitcase. *"I feel like the whole world got me pinned up against the fence"*, the second line, expresses the strangling panic attack that overwhelms the narrator when she says she is going to leave him.

And so, with some adjustments, each line of the text can be interpreted as a non-chronological account of a murder and the run-up to it.

A facile interpretation, of course. Well, lazy even. All exaggerations, incongruities and untruths in the text would then be explained by the stressed, and therefore unreliable, state of mind of the narrator in the first minutes after a traumatic event. But then again - still more conclusive than the interpreters who get no further than "a pretty nasty song" (Heylin), "reflections of a man who still trusts in God" (Beckwith), a lost love (Weir) or "dull and pointless" (Kevin P. Davis in *Judas!* #19). By far the most commentators and Dylanologists ignore the song.

Still, everyone does agree that he is in some kind of trouble, this narrator. He should leave. And go South, for some reason...

V   Still among the living, all of them

Well, I'm tired of talking, I'm tired of trying to explain
My attempts to please you were all in vain
Tomorrow night before the sun goes down
If I'm still among the living, I'll be Dixie bound
I just don't know what I'm gonna do
I was all right 'til I fell in love with you

"South Bound Blues", which Ma Rainey recorded with her Georgia Jazz Band in April 1924, is actually a non-blues, but no less influential; the lyrics offer a sampling of phrases, one-liners and word combinations that generations of songwriters will use gratefully. "*You caused me to weep and you caused me to moan*" from the refrain, for example. Pete Seeger copied and pasted it into his version of "Goodnight Irene", Blind Blake took it, also in Chicago, into his immortal "Black Dog Blues" (1927), and somewhere in the 1930s the verse even infiltrated the granite monument "In The Pines". At least; the first commercial recording of it (Dock Walsh, 1926) doesn't have the line yet, Lead Belly, the moral owner of the song, recorded several versions and sometimes smuggles in "*You caused me to weep, and you caused me to moan*", and in 1941 Bill Monroe records his version with "*You caused me to weep, you caused me to mourn*". Although Monroe probably stole it from The Carter Family's "Foggy Mountain Top" from 1929, to complete the circle to Dylan.

Anyway, just one example of the fertility of "South Bound Blues". The author, the legendary Tom Delaney, has struck dozens of such piles under the blues canon in his career. In this "South Bound Blues" alone, templates like "*my time ain't long*" (a pillar under Robert Johnson's monumental "Dust My Broom"), "*low-down, dirty ways*" ("Thank you," say Sonny Boy Williamson, Son House, Alberta Hunter and all the others), "*you done me wrong*" , and one that Dylan, too, respectfully steals:

> *Yes, I'm mad, my heart's sad*
> *The man I love treats me so bad*
> *He brought me out of my hometown*
> *Took me to New York and throwed me down*
> *Without a cent to pay my rent*
> *I'm left alone without a home*
> *I told him I was leavin' and my time ain't long*
> *My folks done sent me money, and I'm Dixie bound*

"*I'm Dixie bound*", then. Not that its use sheds much light on the plot of Dylan's song. In this last verse, there is no shift like in other semi-narrative Dylan songs, there is no hint like in songs like "Desolation Row" or "Red River Shore" that turns the lyrics around or sheds a new light. We still hear an abandoned, resentful lover á la "Don't Think Twice". That moaner complained 35 years ago *"You just kinda wasted my precious time,"* this one whines; *"My attempts to please you were all in vain."* Or like the hurt suitor in "Idiot Wind" who snarls at his lover that she's too stupid to breathe, this one is equally spiteful and misguided when he growls *"I'm tired of trying to explain."* Not a change in trend, all things considered, from the previous choruses.

Just like Dylan continues to make quasi-lurid allusions, still blurred and ambiguous, in this final couplet. The rather melodramatic *"If I'm still among the living"* is as unclear as the *"girl who won't be back no more"* from the previous verse, for example. Although the addition that he has to leave here, will flee to the South, at least confirms that something has happened, Something, in any case, that forces him to leave. After all, he is not sent away; the *you* has either left or is dead. Plus, that theatrical *"If I'm still among the living"* provides, again not for the first time in this song, a Biblical connotation; not only through the mere use of the word "among", but especially thanks to *Anyone who is among the living has hope* (Ecclesiastes 9:4).

Well, it may not be too clear what is bothering the narrator or what is driving him - but still, a blues it is.

That also applies to one of the pillars under the musical accompaniment: Slim Harpo. "What's the point in listening to us doing *I'm a King Bee* when you can listen to Slim Harpo doing it?" Mick Jagger asks rhetorically in the *Rolling Stone* interview with Jonathan Cott in 1968. Slim Harpo, the name Dylan himself mentions when he tells in the interview with Mikal Gilmore (2001) which "reference records" he played to producer Lanois at the time, is a benchmark for Dylan, these years. And he remains so; the Grammy Award-winning "Someday Baby" from 2006, for instance, is a rip-off of Slim's "Shake Your Hips" from 1966 (also covered by The Stones), and the melody of the hit "Got Love If You Wanted" (which, incidentally, is not only on - again - The Stones' set list, but also on Dylan's), moves to Dylan's "It's All Good" in 2009.

For "'Til I Fell In Love With You", the reference record was probably one of Slim's particularly beautiful gems: the hypnotic, brooding "Strange Love" from 1958, the B-side of the second single "Wonderin' And Worryin'". Songs, which James Moore aka Slim Harpo recorded just like his first single and hit "I'm A King Bee", all in 1957, all in the same little studio of producer J.D. Miller in Crowley, Louisiana, all with the same musicians - then and there, with those men, the sound Dylan so diligently searches for is created.

Forty years later, January 1997, when Dylan does his thing at Criterion Studios in Miami, they are all still alive; Gabriel "Guitar Gable" Perrodin, his brother John "Fats" Perrodin on bass and Clarence "Jockey" Etienne on drums. The studio in Crowley, Louisiana, also still exists, and is run by J.D. Miller's son Mark Miller. Even Lovell Moore, Slim's widow who came up with the name "Slim Harpo" for her husband James, and - uncredited - had written and co-written most of his hits, is *still among the living*. She is 72 then, and very much alive and kicking. "Slim wrote a bunch of his songs with his wife, Lovell...boy, do I wish I had a wife like that to help me write songs," says DJ Dylan in May 2006, in episode 1, "Weather", of *Theme Time Radio Hour*, announcing "Rainin' in My Heart".

So, Dylan could have saved himself a lot of searching for the right words and a lot of experimenting with the right sound if he had followed his own advice. If he had made a phone call to Mark Miller and visited Lovell with some flowers. If he, in short, had decided to be *Dixie bound*.

James "Slim Harpo" Moore & Lovell Moore

7   Not Dark Yet

I   Mehr Licht

Shadows are fallin' and I've been here all day
It's too hot to sleep and time is runnin' away
Feel like my soul has turned into steel
I've still got the scars that the sun didn't heal
There's not even room enough to be anywhere
It's not dark yet but it's gettin' there

We owe it to Dr. Carl Vogel that we know Goethe's last words, or, more specifically: the revised reconstruction of that finale: "*Mehr Licht* (More light)".

Vogel, Goethe's physician, was in the room next door during the last minutes on March 22nd, 1832. Other persons, who were present in the bedroom, report something like "Open the other hatch, so that there be more light," or correct the quotation to the equally romantic variant "*Mehr nicht* (No more)". And Goethe's daughter-in-law Ottilie, also present, later revealed that the old poet, very profane, in his last moments asked his servant Friedrich Krause for the "*Botschampfer*", the chamber pot.

All more realistic and more likely, but a year later, in 1833, Dr. Carl Vogel publishes his *Journal der practischen Heilkunde* ("Journal of practical medicine") containing the words that would become famous:

"More light", are said to have been, while I had left the death chamber for a moment, the last words of the man who hated darkness in every respect.

"The last words of the man who hated darkness in every respect"... being, obviously, far more attractive than something as banal as *I have to pee*. Dr. Vogel's intervention is defensible.

The court physician's poetic instinct is admirable. Approaching darkness as a metaphor for dying has been a popular image among artists for centuries. Especially in literature (*Heart Of Darkness, Voyage Au Bout De La Nuit*, "Do Not Go Gentle Into That Good Night", to name but three relatively recent examples), but just as popular with painters, of course. David's "Death of Marat", the dark skies of Carel Willink, and Morbelli's painted impression of Goethe's time of death is striking as well: on *Goethe Morente* (1880) the light falls on Ottilie, the great poet's head fades into darkness. Not dark yet, but getting there.

Goethe himself was also receptive to the dramatic power of darkness; Werther commits suicide on 21 December, the shortest, i.e. darkest day of the year, at midnight. *Faust I* ends in a dark cell with the death of Gretchen, at the end of the night - the darkest hour right before the dawn.

Although the metaphor is too universal to draw a line from Goethe to Dylan's "Not Dark Yet", the artistic congeniality with Goethe and, as Professor Ricks passionately argues, with Keats but especially with later generations of poets in the heart of the Old Continent is unmistakable - Rilke and Trakl, in particular.

The Marilyn Monroe of the European fin-de-siècle lyricism is Rilke's early masterpiece "*Herbsttag*" ("Autumn Day", 1902). It's a rather short poem that, unlike most poems in the canon, does not survive because of an unforgettable opening (like "April is the cruellest month"), or one memorable, quotable verse ("Two roads diverged in a wood"), but rather because of its overall perfection, from the superb opening line to the supreme last line.

Not only in that respect, "Herbsttag" is comparable to Dylan's dark pearl "Not Dark Yet". Rilke's opening, and with it the theme, is identical too:

> Herr: es ist Zeit. Der Sommer war sehr groß.
> Leg deinen Schatten auf die Sonnenuhren,
> und auf den Fluren laß die Winde los.

> Lord: it is time. The summer was immense.
> Lay your shadow on the sundials
> and in the fields let loose the winds.

Identical imagery (the shadows depicting the approach of death), the same observation regarding the passage of Time without the narrator, and the withdrawal from the world, the loss of Space - great minds think alike, apparently.

However, it is not limited to Rilke, the kinship of "Not Dark Yet" with the decadent grandeur of the dying days of the Danube monarchy. If one of Dylan's works, in terms of elegance, choice of words and visual power, fits into a Vienna of roughly 1910, into the downfall melancholy of the Austro-Hungarian Empire, it's this song.

With another giant of those days, from that part of the world, the kinship is at least as demonstrable and just as remarkable; with the Austrian poet Georg Trakl (1887-1914), one of the most important poets of Expressionism. Immortalized by his last poem, the terrifying war memorial "Grodek", which he wrote just before his (presumed) suicide, but the congeniality with Dylan is evident in many more of his works. The majestic "Psalm" (1912) for example, which in itself already looks like a preliminary study for "A Hard Rain's A-Gonna Fall", and of which on a detailed level the synesthetic images, the melancholic tone and the trench jargon echo in songs like "Gates Of Eden", "Jokerman" and "Not Dark Yet":

> *Auf silbernen Sohlen gleiten frühere Leben vorbei*
> *Und die Schatten der Verdammten steigen zu den seufzenden*
> *Wassern nieder*

> *Former lives glide past on silver feet*
> *And the shadows of the damned descend to sighing waters.*

"Former lives glide past on silver feet"... the beauty, visual power and autumnal melancholy of such a verse paints in seven words the same Great Emotion as Dylan's "Not Dark Yet"; the cocktail of feelings, insights and stillness on the threshold of death, the musings of an old man at the end of his life. As Trakl's next line, "And the shadows of the damned descend to sighing waters", summarizes in one line the content of Dylan's masterpiece.

Producer Daniel Lanois does not make that connection with the Austro-Hungarian Dual Monarchy of a century and a half ago, but is close - by acknowledging an ancient trench feeling:

> There's always going to be a sense of discovery with Bob because, at the last second, without warning and as the "record" button is pressed, he'll change the key and time signature! Then musicians will just look at themselves and dribble in and often Bob will say "that's it". That happened in at least half the tracks on this album. Not Dark Yet had a radically different feel in the demo we did, which I loved and still miss. It was quicker and more stripped down and then, in the studio, he changed it into a civil war ballad.
>
> (interview *Irish Times*, 24 oktober 1997)

"A civil war ballad"? It's hard to tell wherein Lanois does hear that or of what he is thinking. "Dixie"? "When Johnny Comes Marching Home"? "John Brown's Body"? None of the standard civil war ballads seem to have a link to Dylan's "Not Dark Yet". Perhaps Lanois is hearing an echo of "New River Shore", the civil war ballad from 1864 from which the words *she wrote me a letter and she wrote it so kind* are indeed copied by Dylan.

Lanois explicitly doesn't mean the lyrics though, but rather the musical accompaniment. However, the feel of civil war ballads is not discernible there either; they are usually faster and more stripped down - like for instance Dylan's own civil war ballad, "John Brown". At best, the "feel" corresponds with the war ballad "'Cross The Green Mountain", which Dylan will write a few years later for the film epic about the American Civil War, *God And Generals* (2003) - but obviously, Lanois does not know that song yet at the time of the interview.

No, presumably Lanois' association is driven more by the Walt Whitman-"feel" of the lyrics after all, rather than by the slowing down of the musical accompaniment, which apparently was more up-tempo originally.

Still, "Walt Whitman" is hardly more than an instinctive link. Very demonstrable influence of the great American poet there is not in this "Not Dark Yet", at least not as tangible as a quarter of a century later in "I Contain Multitudes" (2020). The album title could have been inspired by Whitman's "Song Of The Broad-Axe" ("Served those who, time out of mind, made on the granite walls rough / sketches of the sun, moon, stars, ships, ocean-waves"), and from Whitman's continuous preoccupation with Time and Space, lines can also be drawn, just like from his weak-spot for *shadows* (undoubtedly in the Top 10 of Whitman's most used nouns, along with *soul*), but that's about it.

In the end the choice of words is, just like the theme at all, too universal to lead back to one admired work or one admired poet. If so, then Paul McCartney would be an even better candidate:

> *Suddenly, I'm not half the man I used to be*
> *There's a shadow hanging over me*
> *Oh, yesterday came suddenly*

II   Lucy

> *Well, my sense of humanity has gone down the drain*
> *Behind every beautiful thing there's been some kind of pain*
> *She wrote me a letter and she wrote it so kind*
> *She put down in writing what was in her mind*
> *I just don't see why I should even care*
> *It's not dark yet, but it's getting there*

It is an ineradicable but fertile myth, the myth that we only use a small percentage of our brains. It does inspire often amusing advertisements, books, comics and films - in which, incidentally, usually thanks to a drug, the "other brain areas" are unlocked, after which the protagonist acquires extreme perception and intelligence (*Limitless*, 2011) or superhero powers, usually psychokinesis.

The most successful, and perhaps the most philosophical adaptation of the subject is released in 2014: the film *Lucy* by the French filmmaker Luc Besson. Lucy accidentally is exposed to an absurd dose of a new synthetic drug, gradually unlocking larger and larger parts of her brain. In addition to all kinds of more and less spectacular abilities, this also leads to what we, with our limited insight, would call "inhumanity"; for example, Lucy realises that we never "really" die - and can therefore kill completely insensitively. Besson, through Lucy, defines it as a loss of *humanity*:

> *Lucy*:
> I don't feel pain, fear, desire. It's like all things that make us human are fading away.

Dylan's protagonist in "Not Dark Yet" has reached a similar state of detachment, and Dylan suggests that this is due to advancing insight as well. Fortunately, not by something as childish as a fictional, brain-unlocking drug, but by life experience.

The narrator begins with his conclusion, *my sense of humanity has gone down the drain*, followed by the brilliant, melancholy aphorism *behind every beautiful thing there's been some kind of pain* - a poetic variant of the ancient wisdom that an unhappy childhood is the artist's goldmine, that behind every great work of art there is a Great Suffering.

The examples of artists giving witness to this are numerous. Frida Kahlo, Vincent Van Gogh, Kafka, W.H. Auden... all of them are artists who claim with some right to a say that only suffering can produce Art. From The Kinks' Ray Davies is the quote "I call it suffering and pain, they call it entertainment" and that is practically the same as Dylan's own observation, in the radio interview with Mary Travers, 26 April 1975.

MT: And one of the things I enjoyed about *Blood On The Tracks*, as an album, was that it was very simple.
BD: Hm, hm. Well that's, you know, that's the way things are really, they are basically very simple. A lot of people tell me they enjoy that album. It's hard for me to relate to that. I mean, you know, people enjoying the type of pain, you know.

Yes, indeed - *behind every beautiful thing there's been some kind of pain*. Granted, the message is not too earth-shattering, but is beautifully, poetically expressed.

However, the true brilliance of the song poet Dylan only begins to shine now, in the next line: *she wrote me a letter* - and suddenly the song is tilted.

Until this ninth verse line we listened to the farewell words of a reflective, resigned narrator on the threshold to death. The choice of "one day" as a metaphor for the whole of life, although old-fashioned, remains moving. These first eight lines also neatly follow the classical composition from personal (*I've been her all day*) to universal (*behind every beautiful thing*), so that the very intimate, very personal outpouring in verse 9 contrasts all the more sharply: the narrator has apparently just received a so-called Dear John letter, the letter in which his lover puts an end to the relationship.

The tone of the letter is well chosen. He is "*kindly*", lovingly, dumped - the Dylan fan involuntarily thinks back to the tone of "If You See Her, Say Hello". It may soften the blow, but it remains crushing; with the loss of her, the narrator loses all zest for life (*I just don't see why I should even care*) and, as we understand now, the light of his life - it is getting dark when she disappears from his life.

It is a classic stylistic tool to which Dylan often resorts, contrasting the private with the universal. Usually very successful, such as in "The Groom's Still Waiting At The Altar", "Slow Train", "Changing Of The Guards", but rarely as crushing as in the exceptional masterpiece "Not Dark Yet".

The prop *letter* to force a plot twist is not new either. In "Boots Of Spanish Leather" the narrator receives such a Dear John Letter, but there, the attentive listener had already seen it coming. In "When The Night Comes Falling From The Sky" and "Where Are You Tonight?" the letters are indeed not much more than props, they don't tilt the plot, but in "Desolation Row" we see a similar impact and a similar change of perspective as here in "Not Dark Yet" – although in *Desolation* it doesn't seem to be a farewell letter.

Here it is. The blow robs the narrator of his *sense of humanity*, time runs away from him, his "soul turns into steel", he can't sleep and just sits there staring, the poor soul. *I don't feel pain, fear, desire. It's like all things that make us human are fading away.*

III   Gaîté Parisienne

Well, I've been to London and I've been to gay Paree
I've followed the river and I got to the sea
I've been down on the bottom of a world full of lies
I ain't looking for nothing in anyone's eyes
Sometimes my burden seems more than I can bear
It's not dark yet, but it's getting there

Cole Porter wondered as early as 1953: "Who Said Gay Paree?", next to the immortal "It's All Right With Me" and the classic "I Love Paris" one of the stand-out songs from the hit musical Can-Can. The link with Jacques Offenbach is obvious; Porter was an admirer and incorporated in his musical winks at the work of the great German-French composer of the nineteenth century.

Offenbach himself, ironically, has never heard his most famous work. Manuel Rosenthal (1904-2003) is the French composer and conductor whose claim to fame is a kind of Best Of: *Gaîté Parisienne* is a suite composed of highlights from operettas by Jacques Offenbach. Rosenthal premiered it in 1938 in Monte Carlo, and its success definitively established Offenbach's *Can-Can* (originally the "Galop Infernal" from the operetta *Orphée aux Enfers*, 1858) as *the* soundtrack for Gay Paree, or as standard background music to cheerful, exuberant scenes at all.

Despite the very French concept of *gaîté*, the expression *gay Paree* seems to be of Anglo-Saxon origin, and much older than 1938. Cole Porter is looking the wrong way. In 1919 Jim Europe's 369th Infantry Band scores a huge hit in America with the song of the returning American soldiers from World War I: "How You Gonna Keep 'em Down On The Farm (After They've Seen Paree)?". The expression itself has turned out to be a keeper (as in *The Big Lebowski*, where The Dude says: "How you gonna keep 'em down on the farm once they've seen Karl Hungus?"), just like the naughty-meant spelling of "Paris". In Nathanael West's debut, *The Dream Life Of Balso Snell* from 1931, for example, can be read:

> He claims that the only place to commit suicide is on Chekov's grave. The Seine is also famous for suicide: "'midst the bustle of `Gay Paree'—suicide." "She killed herself in Paris." There is something tragic in the very thought. French windows make it easy; all you have to do is open the window and walk out. Every window over the third floor is a door into heaven.

This in itself intriguing fragment is an exception; *Balso Snell* is a rather adolescent, rudderless work, by no means as successful as *Miss Lonelyhearts* and *The Day Of The Locust*, the two works that have elevated Nathanael West to the pantheon of Great American Writers. But we do know that Dylan uses *Balso Snell* as a source. In *Chronicles*, Dylan even copies almost literally from West's novella:

> I'm like an old actor mumbling Macbeth as he fumbles in the garbage can outside the theatre of his past triumphs,

... is in *Chronicles* paraphrased into*:*

> The mirror had swung around and I could see the future — an old actor fumbling in garbage cans outside the theater of past triumphs.

In songs, "Gay Paree" has been a twoness since the nineteenth century. For example, "I've Been To Gay Paree" from 1893, "The Tips Of Gay Paree" from 1900, "Sammy In Gay Paree", "When The Robert E. Lee Arrives In Tennessee, All The Way From Gay Paree"... in the sheet music section of the Library Of Congress there are quite a few humorous songs with the frivolous location indication.

For the *Gay Paree* in "Not Dark Yet", however, the inspiration comes neither from Cole Porter, nor from Nathanael West, nor from any of those pub songs. The best candidate is another antique song: "My Heart Goes Back To Dear Old

Pendleton". It's a rather obscure song that was sung somewhere around 1910 in the saloons of Pendleton, Oregon, and is included in Norm Cohen's anthology *American Folk Songs*. The opening lines inspire Dylan:

> *Now I've sailed the sea, I've seen gay Paree,*
> *I've seen the sights of old London.*

"Not Dark Yet" differs from this song, and from all the others, for that matter - obviously - in poetic value; in all those songs the protagonist really, physically, goes to the capital of France, to Paris and then refers to it with a boyish oh-la-la-la wink. The poet Dylan, however, uses it metaphorically; the narrator has not really been to Paris, but expresses in this verse the emotional ups and downs of his life in general and of his recent love drama in particular.

The poet Dylan likes to use the topographical metaphor to express an emotional "very far" or "very much", ever since his very first songs, actually. Initially, a quarter of a century before this *London and gay Paree*, he thinks *from Washinton Heights to Brooklyn* is quite enough (hardly an hour's walk, from "Hard Times in New York City"), in "Down the Highway" we have to walk about 5000 km from the Golden Gate Bridge to the Statue of Liberty and the well-known simplification thereof (*from the west unto the east*) he uses in "I Shall Be Released".

The search for more original variants began in the 1970s. *From the heavens to the ground* in "Never Say Goodbye", *from the Grand Coulee Dam to the Capitol* in "Idiot Wind" and *from Mexico to Tibet* in "We Better Talk This Over" - which would be beyond the 10.000 km limit.

In "Slow Train" the poet slows down a bit (*from Amsterdam to Paris*), but in the different versions of "Caribbean Wind" he is back at it again; first the wind blows *from Mexico to Curacao*, which changes into *Tokyo to the British Isles* and when the song finally reaches the shore, it's *from Nassau to Mexico*, so still 2000 kilometers. In "Union Sundown" Dylan then reaches the superlative: *from Broadway to the Milky Way*, although a less poetically inclined know-it-all will object that it actually says 'from here to here" - after all, our earth is part of the Milky Way.

In terms of content, we shouldn't look for anything in *London and gay Paree*. The metaphor stands for something like *good times, bad times* of *ups and downs*. With the archaic frivolity of *gay Paree*, the poet, just like with the introduction of that very earthly letter, prevents the lyrics from getting stuck in the stately, untouchable tone of the first stanza, "so lofty they sound as if they shit marble," as Mozart says in Shaffers *Amadeus*.

London then bubbles up thanks to the encyclopaedic song knowledge of the poet Dylan, thanks to that "Dear Old Pendleton" and is skilfully processed; with Nobel Prize-worthy brio, the poet processes the assimilating *o-o* in every next line (*London - followed - bottom - for nothing*). These lines further express, in one lyrical direct hit after another, the weariness and disillusionment of the narrator. He has followed the river and has now reached the sea - the end, that is. He has seen the worst of the world and has no further desires - contained in the bluesy, ungrammatical double negation *I ain't looking for nothing*, an echo of the *I ain't got no*'s from Nina Simone's "I Got Life".

The stately, marble verse lines the lieder poet saves for the last verse.

IV   A languid lizard

I was born here and I'll die here against my will
I know it looks like I'm moving, but I'm standing still
Every nerve in my body is so vacant and numb
I can't even remember what it was I came here to get away from
Don't even hear a murmur of a prayer
It's not dark yet, but it's getting there

Majestic is the word that often comes up in the reviews of "Not Dark Yet", mainly due to the music, rather than the words. The lyrics are not really "majestic". The words are dark and gloomy, the words of an old man who sees that the end is nigh, with no hope of a better world in an afterlife. The old man quotes from the Jewish *Pirké Avot*, the *Proverbs of the Fathers* (*"for against your will you were created, against your will you were born, against your will you live, against your will you die"*) but he does not quote the last words *"and against your will you are destined to give an account before the Supreme King of Kings, the Holy One Blessed be He"* - precisely the words that give a life purpose, promising an afterlife. The I-person does not see that light; *I just don't see why I should even care*, he doesn't *even hear a murmur or a prayer*.

And in between, between that Jewish proverb and the hopelessness that is so deep that even the murmur of a prayer can no longer be heard, are the three verses that most heartbreakingly express the desolate state of the narrator.

The first two are fascinating enough. *"It looks like I'm moving, but I'm standing still"* is a surprisingly intimate, moving way of expressing the detachment that the main character is now beginning to feel. Seen from the outside, he still seems to participate, still feel pain, fear, desire, but inside he is "standing still", nothing touches him anymore. By the way, the protagonist here seems to be close to the lieder poet Dylan:

> "I'll be playing Bob Nolan's *Tumbling Tumbleweeds*, for instance, in my head constantly — while I'm driving a car or talking to a person or sitting around or whatever. People will think they are talking to me and I'm talking back, but I'm not. I'm listening to the song in my head. At a certain point, some of the words will change and I'll start writing a song."

...from the interview with Robert Hilburn in 2003, six years after the recording of "Not Dark Yet".

Robbie Robertson, who has been inspired by Dylan songs since "The Weight", takes the image with him to the first record on which he sings autobiographical songs, to *How To Become Clairvoyant* from 2011. In "This Is Where I Get Off" he talks about the breakup of The Band. The song opens with:

> *The Earth keeps on shaking but I'm standing still*
> *The chances I'm taking against my will*

Incidentally, a rather tasteful song, including a nice guitar duet with Clapton halfway.

The depressing gloom of the physical diagnosis *every nerve in my body is so vacant and numb* is just as unusual in song lyrics. After "Not Dark Yet" it does penetrate to the rock idiom, though. In "Letter To Myself" by the short-lived rock band Mad At Gravity from California, for example ("My mind is mute / My nerves are numb"), in a song by the Beagle Boys of Quiet Riot ("Critical Condition"), the English starlet Diana Vickers sings "I feel numb, my every nerve has lost its feeling")... but it's all far removed from the poetic shine and existential extinction of Dylan's narrator. The only one who can measure up to that is the giant Vladimir Vysotsky, the Russian Bob Dylan, Russia's greatest song artist of the twentieth century.

Vysotsky's own "Not Dark Yet", the masterpiece "Песня готового человека" ("The Song of a Man at His End") from 1971, as well as similar poems by Rilke and Trakl, reveal Dylan's artistic soul affinity with the True Greats:

> *И НЕ ПРИХВАТЫВАЕТ ГОРЛО ОТ ЛЮБВИ,*
> *И НЕРВЫ БОЛЬШЕ НЕ В НАТЯЖКУ, - ХОЧЕШЬ - РВИ, -*
> *ПРОВИСЛИ НЕРВЫ, КАК ВЕРЕВКИ ОТ БЕЛЬЯ,*
> *И НЕ ВОЛНУЕТ, КТО КОГО, - ОН ИЛИ Я.*

> *Love no longer grips my throat in a fit;*
> *My nerves are numb, you can rip them off, if you will;*
> *My nerves like washing lines are hanging loose,*
> *And I don't care who it is – him or me.*

The song opens with the brilliant metaphor *A languid lizard crawls in my bones* and elsewhere the listener is struck by Dylanesque, despondent verse fragments like *Wounds do not ache, and scars do not hurt* and *I'm not looking for a philosopher's stone anymore* - Vysotsky's I-person is as exhausted, beaten man as Dylan's protagonist and the Russian has a similar talent for expressing that.

The most beautiful verse line, also the longest of the whole song, closes this trio: *I can't even remember what it was I came here to get away from*.

It is a brilliant line, which unites poetry, song tradition, and a philosophical paradox. In the mind of the walking music encyclopaedia Dylan undoubtedly buzzes around the song he played in '67 with the men in the basement of the Big Pink House; "I Forgot To Remember To Forget", Elvis' first country hit.

That song varies through the antithesis *forget/remember* on the otherwise not too revolutionary theme unforgettable love. Classics like Hoagy Carmichael's "I Get Along Without You Very Well" (sung by the entire premier league, but Frank Sinatra's version is inviolable - at most Chet Baker can stand next to it) and Dylan's own "Most Of The Time" (1989, *Oh Mercy*), which are based on that same theme, derive their lyrical power from the reversal; the main character emphasises line after line that he doesn't miss his ex-lover at all, but makes it increasingly clear line after line that he can't forget her;

> *I've forgotten you just like I should,*
> *Of course I have,*
> *Except to hear your name,*
> *Or someone's laugh that is the same,*
> *But I've forgotten you just like I should.*

The in itself already attractive paradox *I've forgotten you* (if you've *really* forgotten her, you don't remember that you've forgotten her), Dylan deepens with this one line *I can't even remember what it was I came here to get away from*. His poetic instinct tells him to avoid the word *forget* - that would make it an Elvis or Sinatra paraphrase in one fell swoop. Rhythmically it would fit better, though. An obvious alternative like *I can't even remember what I needed to forget* has fourteen syllables, thus following the structure of the song; the other verses all have between eleven and fourteen syllables.

Dylan's intervention stretches this verse line by 150 %, which doesn't have to be a problem for a Grand Master of phrasing, of course. The singer Dylan does tackle bigger challenges (his record being the twenty-two syllables he squeezed into one verse line of "Summer Days": *She says, "You can't repeat the past". I say, "You can't? What do you mean, you can't? Of course you can"*).

Nevertheless, despite his unequalled phrasing, the musician Dylan intervenes; the slowing down of the tempo, mentioned both by producer Lanois and guitarist Duke Robillard ("the version we recorded in Miami was slowed down") probably has a lot to do with this very line. By switching back to long, languid melody lines, the singer Dylan doesn't have to "cram" the line here, thus saving its shine - like a black pearl in the semi-darkness.
It *is* a majestic verse line.

V   The music and the covers

Despite the despondent lyrics "Not Dark Yet" is not a jeremiad, thanks to the music - and just as much to the production and arrangement of Lanois. Over a carpet of guitars, the song unrolls in a pleasantly languid cadence, the music goes up when the lyrics descend, and the key remains mostly major, so not minor. But that does not yet explain the secret, magical power of the accompanying music. A musician like Tony Attwood can identify this magical power very well:

"*Not Dark Yet* is in standard 4/4 time – meaning four crotchet beats in each bar. So, you hear four beats with the heaviest accent on the first beat. You are counting 1-2-3-4, 1-2-3-4.

The first oddity is that the band plays the first beat, but Dylan starts singing on the second beat. That's not unknown but still quite rare. So if you were saying the beats when there are no words you would say

one *Shadows are falling...* **four one** *and I've been here all day….* **four**

… with "*falling*" and "*day*" held on so that they go over two beats.

But then at the end of the line the band put in two more beats in the music. There are no lyrics at this point, just two extra beats.

So you have two bars of four beats (which have the words sung) and then one bar of two beats which is music only. This pattern continues through the whole song.

To try and explain this further here below are the opening lines with the beats written above. Obviously, every beat is of equal value, so you count them slowly at a standard pace. If you make each beat one second, that is about right. A classical musician would call this "Crotchet equals 60", meaning 60 crotchet beats a minute, one a second.

Writing this music out you would have four crotchets in each bar, except at the end of each line of lyrics the musicians play an extra bar of just two beats.

Here are the opening lines with the beats indicated – the additional two beats at the end of each line are in bold

1	2	3 4	1	2	3 4	**1 2**

Shadows are falling   and I been here all day

1	2	3 4 1		2	3 4	**1 2**

It's too hot to sleep   and time is running away

1	2	3 4	1	2	3	4	**1 2**

Feel like my soul has   turned into steel

… and so on throughout the song, even in the instrumental verse.

It gives a sense of timelessness, because we cannot automatically count out the beats (unless one is used to doing this as a musician). It is a brilliant idea to give that feeling that time is just passing – without it a huge amount of impact would be lost."

The unorthodox choice to leave one verse without vocals "empty", so not to fill it with a guitar solo, works excellent. Although the poet does not use words of consolation or resignation, the music lifts the whole song up to: melancholy. It is the melancholy of Rilke's Herbsttag, the film music of Schindler's List, the paintings of De Chirico.

It is mastery - music that goes beyond simply supporting or enhancing the poetry; as a matter of fact, it is only the music that brings the light that cannot be found in the words, giving the in itself bleak poem a much deeper colour.

Failed covers of this work hardly exist, although this time Dylan is rarely surpassed. The notes are in the right place, apparently - even with the artists who lack the age or conviction to play this song, it remains a beautiful piece of art. Many covers rightly adopt the slow, long lines of the original, but the versions of the inevitable ukulele girls on YouTube are also fun.

Slowhand

Anton Fig drummed with all the Greats of the Earth. As a regular drummer of David Letterman's house band, the CBS Orchestra, he is in the enviable position of accompanying superstars like Bruce Springsteen, James Brown and Miles Davis, but he is also a much in demand session musician. Jagger, Joan Armatrading, Madonna, Joe Cocker... the list is long and dazzling.

They are not always the easiest employers, and in June 2002 journalist Robyn Flans asks Anton Fig how he survived such a notoriously demanding, eternally dissatisfied and passionate bandleader as Ray Charles.

TIME OUT OF MIND

MD: Ray Charles has a reputation for chewing up and spitting out players.
Anton: I've played with him on the show and at the Rock 'N' Roll Hall Of Fame, and I've never had a problem. First of all, you have to watch his feet. He conducts with them. I remember the first time I played with him on the Letterman show. I couldn't see his feet, so I actually got a camera monitor so I could.

Watch his feet. The trick will have helped Anton Fig again when he has to show up at Dylan's, for *Empire Burlesque* and for *Knocked Out Loaded*. Dylan has the same tell, as producer Don DeVito reveals to a desperate Eric Weissberg during the bizarre, hallucinatory first recording session for *Blood On The Tracks*, September 16, 1974 in New York.

Until midnight Dylan overwhelms the musicians with (fragments of) "Simple Twist Of Fate", "Call Letter Blues" (which turns into "Meet Me In The Morning" without warning at the second take), "Idiot Wind", "You're Gonna Make Me Lonesome When You Go" and "Tangled Up In Blue". While listening back to one take, Dylan already plays another song right through it, he gives absolutely no clues, doesn't even reveal in which key he's playing (or that his guitar is in the unusual open D-tuning) or starts another song halfway through the recording.

Any other session Weissberg would have walked out, he says. But this is *Dylan*. "Remember, Eric," he says to himself, "this guy's a genius. Maybe this is how geniuses work."

He's being rescued by Don DeVito, the producer who already has some experience with Dylan. In his book *Making Records. The Scenes Behind The Music* (2007), Phil Ramone, the recording engineer on duty, devotes an entire chapter to *Blood On The Tracks*, and describes DeVito's intervention:

"There were no charts and no rehearsals. The musicians had to watch Bob's hands to figure out what key he was playing in. Don DeVito also gave them a suggestion: "To stay in the groove, you've got to watch his feet," Don explained. "It's something I learned from [producer] Bob Johnston, and that I witnessed on earlier sessions with Dylan."

And Eric Clapton, who had similar disconcerting experiences during the Desire recording sessions, shares a comparable revelation. Clapton probably saw a kindred spirit: Slowhand himself moves feet and even the whole leg with spasm-like convulsions when he is in the groove.

The recording of Clapton's performance of "Not Dark Yet" in the Royal Albert Hall, May 2009, nicely demonstrates this peculiarity, also because he's playing there sitting on a kitchen chair - left foot tapping the beat, suddenly his heel swings away, the knee swings out and in extremis the entire left leg - the contrast with guitarist Andy Fairweather Low and bassist Willie Weeks, who flank him, also on kitchen chairs, is beautiful; both accompanists tap conservatively along, left foot only, with the beat.

The song's execution is magnificent. Not substantially different from the original, which is no objection, of course. Clapton has a deep respect for the song and its author. Ever since '99, when he accompanies his guest Bob Dylan at the *Eric Clapton & Friends To Benefit Crossroads Centre Antigua* concert in Madison Square Garden. Dylan sings and plays the guitar, of course, but on this evening it's especially remarkable that the moderate guitarist Dylan takes on almost all guitar solos - while standing next to one of the world's best blues guitarists, he fumbles through *Slowhand*'s solo in the blues classic "It Takes A Lot To Laugh". Not every note is right on spot, to put it mildly. But Clapton is a gentleman and, moreover, does have respect. He politely steps back - even at the finale "Crossroads", the Robert Johnson monument of which Clapton has been the main curator for over thirty years, since his glory days as Cream guitarist.

No matter. The pure, boyish pleasure of both men in their fifties makes up for everything.

"Not Dark Yet" remains on Clapton's playlist, that spring 2009 tour, and his autobiography reveals how the song is under his skin.

He talks about his childhood. His mother, who later turns out to be not his mother but his grandmother, has a deformed face, "a massive scar underneath her left cheekbone that gave the impression that a piece of her cheek had been hollowed out". It doesn't affect her self-awareness, Eric says, quite on the contrary:

> In his song "Not Dark Yet," Dylan wrote, "Behind every beautiful face there's been some kind of pain." Her suffering made her a very warm person with a deep compassion for other people's dilemmas. She was the focus of my life for much of my upbringing.

Granted, he does not quote entirely correctly (it's beautiful *thing*, not beautiful *face*), but certainly his mate Dylan won't mind. Live, on stage, Eric always sings it properly. Foot-swinging, knee-twitching and leg-jerking.

Jimmy LaFave

When he is told in early 2017 that he has only a few months left to live at most, Jimmy LaFave does not consider that an excuse to shy away from action. He continues to perform, he remains committed to the Woody Guthrie Foundation, he continues to record songs and he continues to honour his other great hero, Bob Dylan. He performs until three days before his death (May 21, 2017), but his intention to record another hundred of his favourite songs doesn't materialize - the counter remains stuck at twenty.

These recordings are released July 13, 2018, more than a year after his death, one day after his sixty-second birthday. The double CD *Peace Town* is arguably his most beautiful album, a crushing testament of a great musician, who audibly fights the approaching death. The tumours in his chest are already pressing against his windpipe, which makes his emotional, hoarse voice even more poignant. The three Dylan songs are, as always with this great, great Dylan interpreter, breath-taking and now, in this context, get a new charge: "What Good Am I", "My Back Pages" and, number 18, "You're Gonna Make Me Lonesome When You Go".

The well-chosen final, a cover of Tim Easton's "Goodbye Amsterdam", with the now heartbreaking opening line *Goodbye Amsterdam, I didn't want to leave just yet* and the beautifully sad last words, literally the farewell words:

When there's no destination
You just keep going 'til your time runs out
If it is to be then it's up to me
Now goodbye Amsterdam

"Not Dark Yet" would have been appropriate, obviously. But LaFave already recorded it, for his album *Cimarron Manifesto* in 2007. The perfection of that particular recording, LaFave wisely concludes, cannot be improved. The unique phrasing of the hoarse, high-pitched voice he achieves is matched in his latest live performances (Grollo 2015 is on YouTube and is brilliant), but the production, the arrangement, the organ sound and the tantalizing slide guitar solo... no, that's unmatchable. We have to put this recording on LaFave's posthumous farewell album *Peace Town* ourselves. As the opening number, perhaps.

Tuva, Cherie & Severa

In general, nine out of the ten most beautiful covers are made by ladies. A cover of the untouchable "Tangled Up In Blue" is actually only tolerable when it is done by the Indigo Girls (live, on *1200 Curfew*), the unsightly Basement ditty "Clothes Line Saga" is polished to eighteen carats by The Roches, nobody sings "I Believe In You" as heart-breaking as Sinéad O'Connor, Barb Jungr has been building a breath-taking Dylan catalogue of dozens of covers for decades now and she delivers the most beautiful "Is Your Love In Vain?", Emmylou Harris ("Every Grain Of Sand"), Mary Lee's Corvette's smashing song-for-song cover of *Blood On The Track*, Norah Jones' "Heart Of Mine", the "Mississippi" by the Dixie Chicks... we could go on and on.

The ladies enrich, in short, Dylan songs more often than the gentlemen.

The same goes for "Not Dark Yet". Without wishing to give offence to Jimmy LaFave or Eric Clapton, but they are of course more or less in the same corner as Dylan's original is: same cadence and same tempo, a carpet of guitars and (LaFave) remarkable phrasing.

More ladies dare to step off the beaten track.

Rightly praised is the charming performance by Shelby Lynne & Allison Moorer. The accompaniment is beautiful, but not too spectacular (resounding *Bridge Over Troubled Water* grand piano and two acoustic guitars). The magic is provided by the ladies' singing together - a similar marvellous harmony as The Roches and The Everly Brothers.

They miss the Top 3 by a few inches, though.

A sober, superb rendition can be heard in the Swedish film *Små mirakel och stora* ("All It Takes Is A Miracle", 2006). The film is only moderately successful, but halfway there's the scene where "Love" (a supporting role of the actress Tuva Novotny) sings "Not Dark Yet". In a café, very lonely with just a guitar. Afterwards, the filmmakers realize that this is the real highlight; the song is chosen to embellish the credits.

Novotny sings it herself. Technically she's not a great singer, on the contrary, but certainly with Dylan songs that is hardly important; it's all about the emotion, after all. Which Tuva Novotny provides excellently. All the regret, resignation and fragility that even a Dylan can only bring at his best moments.

Even further away from the world of professional artists is the unknown nonprofessional Cherie Girard, who uploads her special, somewhat Massive Attack-like trip-hop songs to Soundcloud. Girard's "Not Dark Yet" is accessible. Cheap electronics, minimal production and chilling vocals - and a brilliant dramatization after two minutes and eight seconds on London and gay Paree (and again after four minutes, in the coda); it's actually quite staggering how much suspense can be evoked by crackling electronics, a clinical drum machine and Cherie's inventive, echoing vocal arrangements.

However, the most dazzling cover comes from Slovenia: Severa Gjurin contributes a perfectly produced "Not Dark Yet" to a charity project on the occasion of Dylans seventieth anniversary: *Projekt Bob Dylan Postani Prostovoljec* (2011).

Again minimally dressed up, in a classic, slow-flowing arrangement, and the simple bass drone is a great enrichment for the melancholy atmosphere, but the real driving force, the anchor is Severa. Subterranean, veiled voice that she apparently can fully control; a slight vibration in a last syllable, then again threatening to break, and in the wonderful finale a subdued, controlled suite of three or four restrained Severa vocals.

Severa does bring *mehr Licht.*

8   Cold Irons Bound

I   Dear Dr. Ralph

"It was a really great band. And I'm sorry not to be in it today. I miss Bob and I miss that band." Drummer David Kemper does open the doors to his heart, in Uncut's wonderful interview series surrounding the release of *Tell Tale Signs* (2008), number 8 in *The Bootleg Series*. For the thirteen-part interview series, Uncut talks to men like engineer Malcolm Burn, drummer Jim Keltner, guitarist Mason Ruffner and producer Daniel Lanois, men who were directly involved in the making of albums like *Oh Mercy, Time Out Of Mind* and «*Love And Theft*», of records Dylan made between 1989 and 2006.

It provides a wealth of amusing anecdotes, inside information, and intimate glimpses into Dylan's working methods. Like the story of David Kemper, Dylan's drummer from 1996 to 2003, about the making of "Cold Irons Bound". Kemper remembers the recording day, January 1997 at Criteria Studios in Miami. He's earlier than the appointed time, he's alone in the studio and starts drumming - a variation on a pattern he heard on his way here, "this disco record with a Cuban beat".

> "So I was playing this drum beat, and then Bob snuck up behind me and said, 'What are you playing?' I said, 'Hey Bob, how are you today?' He said, 'No, don't stop, keep playing, what are you playing?' I said, 'It's a beat, I'm just writing it right now.' 'Don't stop it. Keep doing it.' And he went and got a yellow pad of paper and sat next to the drums, and he just started writing. And he wrote for maybe ten minutes, and then he said, 'Will you remember that?' And I said, yeah, I got it. And then he said, all right, everybody come on in, I want to put this down."

A "disco record with a Cuban beat" can indeed be heard in it. Miami Sound Machine's "Bad Boy", for example. But despite the not-so-subtle addition "I'm just writing it right now", neither David Kemper nor Gloria Estefan get any credit.

Anyway, Kemper suggests that the drum pattern inspires Dylan so much that he hears a song in it and in ten minutes comes up with the complete lyrics for "Cold Irons Bound". In line with more anecdotes from other witnesses who tell how amazingly fast Dylan can produce lyrics, anecdotes we've heard before, but fascinating it remains still. And, as far as possible, insightful; at the very least, it gives a glimpse into the workings of a Nobel Prize-winning poet's creative mind.

After the first two lines, it is already clear what the inspired Dylan has in mind today;

> *I'm beginning to hear voices and there's no one around*
> *Well, I'm all used up and the fields have turned brown*
> *I went to church on Sunday and she passed by*
> *My love for her is taking such a long time to die*

... "The Fields Have Turned Brown" is quite a giveaway. By The Stanley Brothers, Dylan's bluegrass heroes who we encounter more than once here on *Time Out Of Mind* (on the *highway of regret* in "Make You Feel My Love", for example). This particular song seems to be haunting him - it's also the song Dylan quotes in the congratulatory telegram he sends to the jubilee Dr Ralph Stanley two months earlier, on 9 November 1996. Dylan is often mentioned in the autobiography *Man Of Constant Sorrow* (written with Eddie Dean, 2007) - Stanley is, rightly, proud of the fact that Dylan admires him so much. He mentions that telegram from 1996 twice, and the second time he reveals its contents:

> "They had a big celebration for me in Nashville in honor of my fiftieth anniversary as a professional musician. There was a fancy reception at the Country Music Hall of Fame, with all kinds of friends from down through the years and former Clinch Mountain Boys there to greet me. Then I played a show with my band at the Grand Ole Opry. During the show, Opry host Del Reeves announced to the crowd he had a telegram "a special fan" had sent from New York City. The telegram said:

> > "DEAR DR. RALPH.
> > THE FIELDS HAVE TURNED BROWN.
> > NOT FOR YOU, THOUGH.
> > YOU'LL LIVE FOREVER.
> > BEST WISHES, BOB DYLAN."

> That was something I didn't expect, and it was a wonderful surprise. I know what Bob meant in his message, and it really touched my heart. I know he meant my music would be around long after I'm dead and gone."

And just as gladly (also twice), he recalls that "we sang together on *Lonesome River* for the Clinch Mountain Country album", and that "Bob Dylan told me it was the highlight of his career when he sang with me on *Lonesome River*." That duet was recorded on Sunday, 30 November 1997, ten months after the recording of "Cold Irons Bound". Remarkably then is the first half of the sound check for the concert in Atlanta, the next day (Monday, December 1):

1. *Unidentified Blues*
2. *Cold Irons Bound*
3. *The White Dove (Carter Stanley)*
4. *The White Dove (Carter Stanley)*
5. *Cocaine Blues (trad.)*

... apparently Dylan still feels the strong connection of "Cold Irons Bound" with The Stanley Brothers. Which goes beyond "The Fields Have Turned Brown". The third line, *I went to church on Sunday and she passed by*, comes almost literally from the Stanley's version of "Handsome Molly", the old folksong Dylan himself also played in '61 and '62, but back then always skipping this verse:

> *I'd think of Handsome Molly*
> *Wherever she may be*
> *Well I saw her at church last Sunday*
> *She passed me on by*
> *I knew her mind was changing*
> *By the roving of her eye*

... an omission that Dylan makes up for almost forty years later in "Cold Irons Bound".

All in all: "The Fields Have Turned Brown", "Handsome Molly", the theme and tone of Stanley Brothers songs like "If That's The Way You Feel", "The Lonesome River" and "The Memory Of Your Smile"... it seems very likely that on his way to the studio Dylan had the compilation album *Stanley series: Vol. 3, no. 4* in the CD player. And that the chorus of "I'll Fly Away" could be buzzing through his head next: *No more cold iron shackles on my feet*. However, Mark T., an alert *Untold* reader, recalls an old folk song in which the peculiar expression *in cold irons bound* is sung verbatim: "The Banks Of Inverness".

This old folksong has many variants, and this particular line is also sung in many variants. John Healy sings "For he's bound in iron chains along a foreign shore", Julie Mainstone sings "For he's bound in irons along some distant shore", and variants such as "For he's bound in irons strong upon a Turkish shore" and "For he's bound up in irons strong all on fair Turkey's shore" can also be found. A recording with the words *in cold irons bound* cannot be found, but researchers from California State University, Fresno report in their *Ballad Index*:

> "The sailor sees a girl sighing on the banks of the (Inver)ness. He asks her if she is available. She says she is engaged to Willie. He declares that Willie is **"in cold irons bound"** and will not return. She says she will remain faithful. He reveals himself."

... which is far too specific to be a coincidence.

By the way, we don't have to feel too sorry for David Kemper, who misses drumming in Dylan's band so much. He has an enviable career, playing with all the greats, was in the Jerry Garcia Band for eleven years, drummed in Holland with Focus, in Nashville for ex-Eagle Bernie Leadon, in Malibu with Beach Boy Dennis Wilson and in London he recorded perhaps his most beautiful drumming: his session work for Joan Armatrading's masterpiece *Show Some Emotion* (1977). In the many highlights, in masterful songs like "Willow" and the title track, but especially in "Peace Of Mind", we can hear why an Eagle, a Beach Boy, the supreme Deadhead Jerry Garcia and the living legend Bob Dylan are so charmed by Kemper's superior drumming; understated, elegant, all-round, tasteful and with that special, mesmerising Mick Fleetwood quality of playing just microseconds behind the beat.

David Kemper will live forever, too.

II To live is to be alone

I'm waist deep, waist deep in the mist
It's almost like, almost like I don't exist
I'm twenty miles out of town in cold irons bound

The Fog (1980) is a low-budget horror film by John Carpenter which, despite poor reviews, was well attended at the time and has since become somewhat of a cult classic in the twenty-first century. The story is simple enough: exactly one hundred years after a ship has been lured onto the rocks by evil-doers using false light signals, a strange, luminous fog creeps into a Californian coastal town, and this fog brings with it the vengeful spirits of the drowned sailors. Not too imaginative, but Carpenter is a craftsman who impresses with lighting, music and almost poetic tableaux - such as the sheer iconic image of the ghosts, the non-existent, emerging from the fog: *waist deep in the mist, almost like they don't exist.*

Apparently Dylan also recognises its poetic power, and he explores its metaphorical potential for the chorus of "Cold Irons Bound". Inspired, he sits with his yellow pad of paper next to the drumming David Kemper, echoing in his mind are the songs of *Stanley series: Vol. 3, no. 4,* and presumably he has already fixed the refrain line *I'm twenty miles out of town in cold irons bound*;

> "In that particular song, the last few verses came first. So that's where the song was going all along. Obviously, the catalyst for the song is the title line. It's one of those where you write it on instinct. Kind of in a trance state."

That's what Dylan says in 2020 about the creation of "I Contain Multitudes", with the addition *most of my recent songs are like that* (New York Times interview with Douglas Brinkley). The outpouring seems to apply one-to-one to the creation of "Cold Irons Bound". The last line, *I'm twenty miles out of town in cold irons bound,* is probably there before the previous one. Kemper's drum pattern inspires. It just so happens that today The Stanley Brothers are buzzing through Dylan's mind, and via "The Fields Have Turned Brown" and "Handsome Molly" the stream of consciousness flows to "I'll Fly Away", to *cold iron shackles on my feet,* which perhaps awakens *in cold irons bound* from an obscure variant of "The Banks Of Inverness".

Strong metaphor, the poet thinks, to express *bound-against-your-will*, to express the state of mind of his protagonist; an I-person who is love sick, standing on the doorway, about to hit the dirt road. The musician Dylan's particular choice of words is then, as so often, sound-driven - not *on the road in iron shackles*, and not like the worried man in "Worried Man Blues" *twenty-one links of chain around my leg on the Rocky Mountain line*, but a superior assonant triplet around the *ou*-sound: *out - town - bound.*

The bridge to that refrain line is not fixed. The poet is inspired, trusts the richness of the stream-of-consciousness and will choose different images and different words in each of the five refrains to express the loneliness and the quiet desperation of the unhappy protagonist. Here, in this first refrain, is the desolate image of disoriented people wandering through the fog. The symbolic power of this, of course, has been recognised by artists for centuries. Who knows, maybe Dylan has also browsed through the works of fellow Nobel Prize winner Hermann Hesse:

TIME OUT OF MIND

Seltsam, im Nebel zu wandern!
Leben ist Einsamsein.
Kein Mensch kennt den andern,
Jeder ist allein.

Strange, to wander in the fog,
To live is to be alone.
No man knows the next man,
Each is alone.

(Hesse, *Im Nebel,* 1911, transl. *In the Fog* Scott Horton, 2007)

Although - on a side note - this cinematic image conveying alienation and sadness probably has never been used in such a goosebumps-inducing way as in the most gorgeous "mist-song" ever, in Gene Clark's "In A Misty Morning" from 1972;

Running through my thoughts
Were the memories of the days that I had left behind
Way down in my soul were the hopes
That better days were always there to find
The fog rolled in and the lights grew dimmer
And the sound of the city streets seemed amplified
In the misty morning when it had just been pouring
Like the clouds above the storm just had to cry

The unusual repetitions in these two chorus lines give some credence to Kempers' story that Dylan wrote the lyrics in ten minutes. "Ten minutes" is probably more or less true, but it is likely that Dylan, the compulsive scribbler and note-taker, had already got a few one-liners up his sleeve. A refrain line like *I'm twenty miles out of town in cold irons bound* and a couplet line like *My love for her is taking such a long time to die* have a polished perfection that suggests they were already a while in the making, the marble elegance of the coming "decaying beauty" aphorism doesn't seem to have come out of the blue either.

Still, the atypical repetitio in these couplet lines (*waist deep, waist deep* and *almost like, almost like*) is the stopgap solution of an inspired poet who does not want to lose his flow, who wants to keep the momentum going and quickly fills in the empty syllables with repetition. Atypical for the eloquent Dylan, but a ten-a-penny style characteristic of The Stanley Brothers;

> *Everybody I met, everybody I met, seemed to be a rank stranger*
> *No mother or dad, no mother or dad, not a friend could I see*
> *They knew not my name, they knew not my name, and I knew*
> *not their faces*
> *I found they were all, I found they were all, rank strangers to me*

III   He who is alone now, will long so remain

> *The walls of pride are high and wide*
> *Can't see over to the other side*
> *It's such a sad thing to see beauty decay*
> *It's sadder still to feel your heart torn away*
>
> *One look at you and I'm out of control*
> *Like the universe has swallowed me whole*
> *I'm twenty miles out of town in cold irons bound*

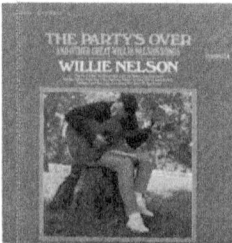

"The walls of pride" is not too remarkable an image; any given Sunday there must be a preacher somewhere in the world who reads from Ezekiel, Acts or Isaiah and then warns the congregation of the *walls of pride*. Dylan, as we know, is not necessarily averse to an evangelical connotation either - but in this context, in "Cold Irons Bound", it is more likely that the slightly worn-out metaphor has surfaced in Dylan's stream of consciousness via the heartbreaking "No Tomorrow In Sight";

In our efforts to break through
The thick walls of pride
With harsh words that burned to the core
The walls still remain
But the words broke inside
And strengthened the walls even more

... on *The Party's Over and Other Great Willie Nelson Songs* from 1967, from the time when Willie still had short hair and at least had one foot firmly planted in the Nashville clay. But also a record that demonstrates from start to finish what Dylan admires so much in Willie: "No one writes a bitter song like Willie Nelson" (Robert Hilburn interview, 1992). There is a line to "Cold Irons Bound" in there too, but still: too generic to put the "influential song" stamp on "No Tomorrow In Sight".

All the more radiantly, after that clichéd opening, shines the most elegant aphorism of the song, and one of the most poignant of the album at all: *It's such a sad thing to see beauty decay / It's sadder still to feel your heart torn away.*

Its perfection suggests that Dylan had the oneliner already up his sleeve. "It was hotel stationary, little scraps like from Norway, and from Belgium and from Brazil, you know places like that. And each little piece of paper had a line," as Larry Charles reveals in 2014 about Dylan's working methods in the 1990s. The isolation of the line within this song seems to confirm this; in terms of content, the first part, the decaying beauty, does not match the emotions that the protagonist conveys. *One look at you and I'm out of control* he sighs after this, and at the end of the song *looking at you and I'm on my bended knee...* heartfelt sighs and choice of words that at least suggest that there is no question of *decaying beauty*, but quite on the contrary, of radiant beauty.

The line must have been inspired by Keats, by the indestructible *A thing of beauty is a joy for ever* from "Endymion" (1818), and presumably its continuation (*its loveliness increases*) also triggered Dylan. Keats' opening line has gained proverbial status and is quoted all over the place - by Willy Wonka, by physicists admiring the elegance of a beautiful formula, in adverts, by Mary Poppins, in songs (ABC's "Never More Than Now", for example) and by Woody Harrelson in *White Men Can't Jump*... by everyone and everything, actually. In an ironic way, often enough, but just as often to express genuine admiration.

Keats' figurative meaning is clear, of course. The *memory* of beauty can provide lasting, *for ever*, happiness, comfort or poignancy - Keats does know and acknowledge that beauty in itself is impermanent, (as "Ode To A Nightingale", the poem in which Professor Ricks sees the template for "Not Dark Yet", demonstrates). In 1882, Oscar Wilde argued pretty much the same thing, in *The English Renaissance Of Art* ("Beauty is the only thing that time cannot harm"), and Wilde was no fool either, obviously. Yet, strictly speaking, all beauty is indeed perishable, indeed does decay - even the stars above eventually fade away, after all. Which is the root of all melancholy, and thus an inexhaustible source of inspiration.

Melancholy is probably, after Love, inspiration No. 2 in the Arts since Homer, and the combination, the melancholy caused by a lost love, has also animated poets and songwriters for centuries. Usually clichéd and superficial ("Bye Bye Love", "I Still Miss Someone"), as the emotion itself is big and recognisable enough to communicate without much poetic artifice. Exceptional talents, such as Tim Buckley, do manage to deepen it, though;

So tell me darlin' if the feeling's wrong
Don't waste another day
Lord, the saddest thing I've ever known
Was to watch it die away
("Love from Room 109 at the Islander (On Pacific Coast Highway)", 1969)

The Very Greats still know how to avoid every cliché and avoid all mushiness - and thus still manage to move with melancholy. The template being, obviously, François Villon's "Ballade des dames du temps jadis" (*Où sont les neiges d'antan? – "Where are the snows of yesteryear"*, 1461). Dylan's "Not Dark Yet" on the same album is another perfect example, John Williams' film music for *Schindler's List*, De Chirico's paintings, and a poetic masterpiece like Rilke's "Herbsttag" (1902), with whom Dylan, not for the first time, demonstrates an artistic kinship;

Lord: it is time. The summer was immense.
Lay your shadow on the sundials
and let loose the wind in the fields.

Bid the last fruits to be full;
give them another two more southerly days,
press them to ripeness, and chase
the last sweetness into the heavy wine.
(transl. "Autumn Day" - Edward Snow)

... and to that list of extraordinary works of art belongs the sepia-coloured aphorism *It's such a sad thing to see beauty decay / It's sadder still to feel your heart torn away.*

The second part of the aphorism, *heart torn away*, fits in well with the desperate tenor of the song, and is also in line with the famous last part of Rilke's "Herbsttag". (*He who has no home now, will build one never / He who is alone now, will long so remain*).

The beauty of Dylan's aphorism shines through all the more strongly because of the relative weakness of the surrounding lines. The introduction, with its *walls of pride*, is not very spectacular. And the continuation, the varying "transition lines" to the refrain line *I'm twenty miles out of town in cold irons bound*, again underpin the credibility of David Kemper's testimony that Dylan dashes off the lyrics in ten minutes;

> *One look at you and I'm out of control*
> *Like the universe has swallowed me whole*

... first a run-of-the-mill cliché, and then a sonorous, neatly rhymed, but in fact incomprehensible, inconclusive metaphor. Apparently, the poet wants to express something like "struck by lightning" or perhaps "on cloud nine". The eloquence of "the universe has swallowed me", however, is rather polluted by its absurdity - you don't have to be too scientifically literate to realise that we are all already "in the universe". To understand how you can be swallowed by something you are already in requires an imagination that even a Kafka or a Charlie Kaufman would not dare to presume in the audience.

Well, in his defense: the poet *is* out of control, after all.

IV   Little Boy Lost

> *There's too many people, too many to recall*
> *I thought some of 'm were friends of mine, I was wrong about 'm all*
> *Well, the road is rocky and the hillside's mud*
> *Up over my head nothing but clouds of blood*
>
> *I found my world, found my world in you*
> *But your love just hasn't proved true*
> *I'm twenty miles out of town in cold irons bound*

Dylan remains in Villon mode for a while, in *Où sont les neiges d'antan* spheres. Or, to stay close to Paris, in the Georges Moustaki mode. More precisely: in the theme and colour of one of Moustaki's loveliest songs, "L'Homme Au Coeur Blessé" from 1971, the formidable translation of a song by the Greek legend Mikis Theodorakis. Also, like "Not Dark Yet", "Tryin' To Get To Heaven", Rilke's "Herbsttag" and this "Cold Irons Bound", the dismal retrospective of a man in the autumn of his life, disillusioned and melancholy. With, as in "Cold Irons Bound", the depressing image of the man who wonders where the friends of the past have gone;

> *Les quatre murs de sa maison*
> *N'abritent que l'absence*
> *Où sont partis les compagnons*
> *Avec leurs rires et leurs chansons ?*

> *The four walls of his home*
> *Contain nothing but absence*
> *Where have the companions gone*
> *With their laughter and their songs?*

... and whose heart-breaking opening line alone, *Jour après jour, les jours s'en vont, laissant la vie à l'abandon* ("Day after day, the days go by, leaving life behind"), already has such a strong *Time Out Of Mind*-vibe, of course.

Just as conventional as the image of the friends dissolved in the mists of time is the subsequent *rocky road* on which the beaten narrator finds himself - but then the fast-rhyming artist finds his inspiration again. A *muddy hillside* is already a fresh inversion of the cliché. For centuries, in songs, novels and poems, hillsides have been the backdrop of blooming flowers, of carefree summers in love, the background of a setting sun, and wild roses often grow there too. Or, quite on the contrary, the sad location of the grave of a loved one – in which case it is usually misty.

Dylan chooses the conventional setting for an unconventional scene: to reinforce the protagonist's Sisyphean state of being. Not only does he trudge along in cold irons bound, but the road is rocky and the hill he climbs muddy - he is truly not to be envied, this mirror image of Jeff Beck's insufferably optimistic *Hi-Ho Silver Liner* ("Going down a bumpy hillside, in your hippy hat"). To be fair, songwriter Scott English later confessed he tried to write "the most unusable, stupid lyric he could think up, about flies in pea soup and beach umbrellas" to scare off Beck's producer Mickey Most; Scott actually wanted to keep the song himself.

The pitiful scene is spanned by *clouds of blood*. Like *hillside*, not necessarily an original décor, but like hillside, alienating here - this time, however, mainly through the choice of words. *Red skies* in themselves are not all that uncommon in the Arts. In painting, it is already so commonplace that any artist who paints the sky red risks getting the label "kitsch". And in songs, it has been around long enough. Usually to express menace. Like in Ry Cooder's "Poor Man's Shangri-La" (*It's a red cloud over Chavez Ravine*), in "Johnny, Kick A Hole In The Sky" by the Red Hot Chili Peppers (*The red cloud rains and the black horse rides*), in Fisher-Z's "Red Skies Over Paradise". Or to frame idyllic scenes, like Tom Petty's "California" (*Sundown, red skies*), U2 in "Even Better Than the Real Thing" (*We're free to fly the crimson sky*) and like in "Galbraith Street", Ron Sexsmith's nostalgic childhood memory.

There are many more examples, and Dylan himself has been using the expressionistic value of a *red sky* at least once in every decade of his career. The corpse of Emmett Till is disrespectfully rolled away *amidst a bloody red rain*, the narrator from "Someone's Got A Hold Of My Heart" has just returned from *a city of flaming red skies*, the little boy and the little girl live "under the red sky", *the clouds are turnin' crimson* in "Moonlight", the protagonist from "Things Have Changed" is *looking up into the sapphire-tinted skies*, and idyllically meant as well is *'neath crimson skies* in "Beyond The Horizon". So, in itself not too remarkable, a red sky. But the choice of words is: *clouds of blood.*

Clouds of blood has an inescapable, lugubrious connotation that seems rather out of place in this song. The overall tenor evokes the image of a washed-out, faded-out man who, like a grey old tusker, is heavily and lonely making his last journey to the elephant graveyard. *The fields have turned brown, beginning to hear voices, heart torn away, the fat's in the fire, torn to shreds...* the song lyrics offer an accumulation of images that are ambiguous enough to associate with a farewell to life. None, however, with the fatal, violent implication of *clouds of blood*, an image that seems to have imposed itself via William Blake.

In interviews during the nineties, Dylan often mentions his renewed fascination with William Blake, even unsolicited. "My latest thing of just reading was back into reading the William Blake poems again," he says in a telephone interview with Stuart Coupe. "In the last couple of lines, it might just open a door for another song. William Blake could have written that," he tells Gary Hill in San Diego in October '93 (on "Love Henry"). Often enough, in any case, to guess that three years later, Dylan, sitting with his draft inspired next to the drumming David Kemper, is incorporating echoes of Blake lecture; *The Divine Vision dimly appear'd in clouds of blood weeping*, for instance (from "Jerusalem", in which the bloody clouds drift by every few pages anyway). Or *The sound of a trumpet the heavens / Awoke & vast clouds of blood roll'd*, from "The Book of Urizen"(1794) - William Blake did like grand, apocalyptic settings. And iron. Iron whips, iron thorns, iron rocks, iron tears, iron arms of love, you name it. And iron chains, obviously. Lots of them. Like on the Little Boy Lost;

> *The weeping child could not be heard,*
> *The weeping parents wept in vain:*
> *They stripped him to his little shirt,*
> *And bound him in an iron chain*

... bound him in a *cold* iron chain, no doubt. Far from his friends with their laughter and their songs.

V   A very ornate, beautiful box

> *Oh, the winds in Chicago have torn me to shreds*
> *Reality has always had too many heads*
> *Some things last longer than you think they will*
> *There are some kind of things you can never kill*
>
> *It's you and you only I been thinking about*
> *But you can't see in and it's hard lookin' out*
> *I'm twenty miles out of town in cold irons bound*

It is a beautiful, revealing glimpse behind the scenes that scriptwriter Larry Charles (*Masked And Anonymous*, 2003) gives us, when he describes one of Dylan's working methods. It turns out that Dylan keeps hundreds of scraps of paper, in a "very ornate, beautiful box", and on those scraps are hundreds of one-liners, ideas, short rhymes and aphorisms. He turns the box upside down onto the table, and starts shuffling back and forth - rather like William Burroughs is drawing from his *Word Hoard*, his collection of paragraphs, sentences and fragments of sentences from the pile of paper (about a thousand sheets) that Brother Bill, with the help of among others Allen Ginsberg and Jack Kerouac typed away in Tangier, spring 1957. Burroughs writes his *Nova Trilogy* in this way, and ever since "Gates Of Eden", or "Tombstone Blues" at any rate, Dylan has occasionally used this cut-up technique for some of his songs.

The witness to the making of "Cold Irons Bound", drummer David Kemper, does not mention a box, but this fourth verse seems to demonstrate that Dylan can also topple that ornate, beautiful box in his head, sitting with his notepad next to the drum kit. The four stanza lines seem to be sorted together like a painter sorts his crayons; the blues to the shades of blues, the greys to the shades of grey. In terms of content, these lines have no clearly recognisable relationship, no epic quality; only the lyricism, the colour, the grey-blue mood of the protagonist, matches.

They are beautiful opening lines, lines from a Nobel Prize-winning poet. *Oh, the winds in Chicago have torn me to shreds* is a skilful anapaestic tetrameter, the four-footed anapaest (da da DUM, da da DUM, da da DUM, da da DUM) we know mainly from Dr Seuss, Lord Byron and T.S. Eliot, and for which Dylan also seems to have a soft spot ("Where Are You Tonight?", for example). And in terms of content, it is a stunningly rich verse that evokes a world in just ten words; it connects the cliché *Windy City Chicago* with urbane loneliness and despair with an admittedly somewhat showy yet heart-breaking metaphor. With as a bonus the cross-pollination of

blues and bluegrass, of a blues cliché like in Bo Diddley's "Diddley
Daddy" (1955), one of the many songs in which a protagonist loses
his sweetheart to the temptations of the Windy City;

> I got a baby that's oh-so pretty
> Diddley-diddley-dum, dum, dum-diddley
> I found her right here in the windy city
> Diddley-diddley-dum, dum, dum-diddley
> Somebody kissed my baby last night
> Diddley-diddley-dum, dum, dum-diddley

... with a popular bluegrass metaphor, as in the classic "Maybe You
Will Change Your Mind" (1959) by banjo legend Don Reno (*The tie
that binds our love, sweetheart / Was torn to shreds by you*).

The continuation, *Reality has always had too many heads*,
has at best a lyrical resemblance to the state of mind of the man
being torn to shreds in Chicago, and may even have fallen out of
the inner *ornate, beautiful box* just for the rhyme word. But the
emotion fits, regardless, and it is again a wonderful, loaded image
to express the dazed lostness of the protagonist. The choice of
words itself is perhaps initially reminiscent of the comic scene from
the beginning of *Moby-Dick*, when Ishmael asks the innkeeper
where his as yet unknown roommate is, the stranger with whom
he has to share his bed tonight. The innkeeper does not know;

> "May be, he can't sell his head."
> "Can't sell his head?—What sort of a bamboozingly story is this
> you are telling me?" getting into a towering rage. "Do you
> pretend to say, landlord, that this harpooneer is actually
> engaged this blessed Saturday night, or rather Sunday morning,
> in peddling his head around this town?"
> "That's precisely it," said the landlord, "and I told him he
> couldn't sell it here, the market's overstocked."
> "With what?" shouted I.
> "With heads to be sure; ain't there too many heads in the
> world?"
> "I tell you what it is, landlord," said I quite calmly, "you'd better
> stop spinning that yarn to me—I'm not green."

178

... the *comedy-of-errors*-like scene in which the innkeeper fails to reveal that Ishmael's prospective roommate is a tattooed cannibal who sells his *balmed New Zealand heads*, "and he's sold all on 'em but one, and that one he's trying to sell tonight."

Of its comic content - obviously - nothing remains in Dylan's lament, but for the alienating word combination *too many heads* the poet finds a splendid function in a oneliner that, in just seven words, contains as much richness as the preceding Chicago line. *Reality has always had too many heads* has an aphoristic depth that suggests that the narrator has had to learn, at the expense of his happiness, that there is never one truth, that truth lies in the eyes of the beholder. In addition, the personification of Reality has the antique elegance of a medieval allegory, and *many heads* echoes mythological many-headed horrors such as Hydra, Cerberus and Medusa. A richness, in short, which may not add anything to the plot of "Cold Irons Bound", but does add to its couleur, to its universal, timeless power.

After these two hits, the poet slows down a little. The following distich still is elegant as well, but

> *Some things last longer than you think they will*
> *There are some kind of things you can never kill*

... hardly has the Nobel Prize-worthy depth of the preceding verses. It seems to be a not too elaborate, Dylanesque improvisation on *Kill Your Darlings*, as shown by the weakness of settling for *some things* - twice even. If we are to believe Kemper, the song was recorded immediately after its conception - presumably Dylan would have sharpened these two lines a bit more, if he had let the song mature another day.

The same goes for the following lines of the verse. *It's you and you only I been thinking about* elaborates nicely on *the things you can never tell* and on *the things that last longer than you will*, but is otherwise rather lazy poetry. Just like the following *But you can't see in and it's hard lookin' out*; a dime-a-dozen antithesis from the same drawer as, but without the brilliance of poetic antitheses like *in through the outdoor* or the playfulness of *come all without, come all within* or the layered quality of *I've been in and out of happiness* and *drifting in and out of dreamless sleep*.

But then again: who cares. Surrounding those lesser, throwaway lines are those two shining jewels before them and the brilliance of the indestructible chorus line *I'm twenty miles out of town in cold irons bound* thereafter.

VI   The cat's in the stew

Well the fat's in the fire and the water's in the tank
The whiskey's in the jar and the money's in the bank
I tried to love and protect you because I cared
I'm gonna remember forever the joy that we shared

But here I am in prison, here I am with a ball and chain...it doesn't end well, for Captain Farrell's killer. The money he had stolen from the Captain has not been deposited in the bank, but purloined by that treacherous Molly. In cold irons bound he sits in the cell now, dreaming of Molly's bedroom, and he sings his refrain once more;

Musha rain dum a doo, dum a da, heh, heh
Whack for my daddy, oh
Whack for my daddy, oh
There's whiskey in the jar, oh

The indestructible Irish classic "Whiskey In The Jar" is an ancient, irresistible folk monument with dozens of versions in circulation. The rock version by Thin Lizzy (1972) is probably the best known and inspired Metallica to do a Grammy-winning heavy metal cover in 1998. And in between, it sneaks into a Dylan song, into the final verse of "Cold Irons Bound".

The in itself meaningless phrase steers the narrative of "Cold Irons Bound" down a side path. Down the wrong path, to be more precise, on the path to evil. Suddenly, through that highwayman connotation from the old folksong about a criminal who actually ends up in ball and chains, the poet highlights the possibility that *in cold irons bound* is meant literally, that the narrator has just murdered the woman he so pitifully longs for, and that he is now being carried off - jogging along in chains, already twenty miles on the way to the penal camp.

It is - of course - not unequivocal. The opening, "the fat's in the fire", fits in a bit - it does, after all, mean something like *trouble ahead, imminent crisis*. Squeezing in, however, is not possible with the other two expressions, "water's in the tank" and "money's in the bank". In themselves, again, without much relation to each other or to the text at all. But strangely enough, the accumulation of the four (quasi-)proverbial expressions does actually suggest, without any substantive basis, something like *the die is cast, I crossed the Rubicon*.

The accumulation, however, seems mainly the product of an improvising, unleashed poet in the zone. Stylistically, but coincidentally also in terms of content, it resembles the enigmatic word processions that Jethro Tull's Ian Anderson is so fond of producing for the crypto-analytical faction of his fan base. Like in the outtake "Living In These Hard Times", from a somewhat forgotten, beautiful folky highlight of Jethro Tull's discography, from 1978's *Heavy Horses*:

> *The bomb's in the china. the fat's in the fire.*
> *There's no turkey left on the table*
> *(,,,) Well the fly's in the milk and the cat's in the stew.*
> *Another bun in the oven --- oh, what to do?*

... a beautiful song by the way, that is rightly added as a bonus track on the 2003 reissue (and again on the 2018 *40th Anniversary New Shoes Deluxe Edition* of course). Demonstrating the same playful enjoyment of language: the alienating mixing of existing expressions (*fat's in the fire, bun in the oven*) with catachreses, with non-existent word compounds that nevertheless sound familiar (*cat's in the stew, fly's in the milk*). Triggered, no doubt, by a love of antique nursery rhymes, again similar to Dylan's – for example, Ian Anderson's fourth verse begins with:

> *The cow jumped over yesterday's moon*
> *And the lock ran away with the key.*

... a not too veiled paraphrase of the age-old "Hey Diddle Diddle" (*The Cow jump'd over the Moon / And the Fork ran away with the Spoon*). And, to complete the circle, equally inspired by nonsensical refrains like in "Whiskey In The Jar".

It's all possible, the nonsensical expressions and the empty metaphors like *fly in the milk* and *water in the tank* and *whack for my daddy*, thanks to the context. "Whiskey in the jar" becomes something like *those were the days*. Ian Anderson embeds his invented sayings in a portrait of a life full of misfortune, making something like *cat's in the stew* suddenly meaningful. And Dylan offers a fitting meaning for his linguistic finds in the lines that follow:

> *I tried to love and protect you because I cared*
> *I'm gonna remember forever the joy that we shared*

So: "our good times are over now and out of reach", something like that. Like water in a tank, like money in a bank, like whiskey in a jar and like fat in a fire. Maybe not entirely watertight, but what the heck - Dylan shakes the lyrics out of his sleeve in a few minutes, doesn't feel like polishing them, records it straight away, and above all: *it sounds good. And you want your songs to sound good* (Nobel Lecture, 2017).

VII   Cosmic waste and space debris

> *Looking at you and I'm on my bended knee*
> *You have no idea what you do to me*
> *I'm twenty miles out of town in cold irons bound*

The sketchy, improvised impression of the last verse is confirmed by the last refrain. *I'm gonna remember forever the joy that we shared* is a farewell - it fits badly with the subsequent present tense of the chorus lines. But in terms of content, it once again gives food for the thought that "Cold Irons Bound" subcutaneously is a murder ballad: the scene described is a copy of the repentant murderess Frankie from "Frankie And Johnny";

> She said, "Oh, Mrs. Johnson
> Oh, forgive me please
> Well I killed your lovin' son, Johnny
> But I'm down on my bended knees
> I shot my man, but he was doin' me wrong, so wrong."

Dylan uses the image in his adaptation of the song ("Frankie & Albert", on *Good As I Been To You*, 1992), but shifts it to an even more dramatic scene:

> Frankie got down upon her knees, took Albert into her lap.
> Started to hug and kiss him, but there was no bringin' him back.
> He was her man but he done her wrong

... the death scene. After which Frankie is taken away - bound in cold irons, no doubt.

Not too far-fetched. "Frankie & Johnny" and its many adaptations (Leadbelly, Mississippi John Hurt, Elvis) is somewhere at the front of Dylan's inner jukebox, and echoes thereof easily seep in, when the songwriter is in a creative daze and has a murder ballad up his sleeve. But who knows - Dylan's meandering mind may also have led him past Muddy Waters, triggered by the preceding *money in the bank* (from Muddy's "You Can't Lose What You Ain't Never Had": *I had money in the bank / I got busted, boys, ain't that sad?*), which then might lead Dylan to Muddy's ode to his wife, to "Little Geneva" from 1949:

> I want to see Geneva so bad, so bad
> Right now I'm on my bended knee

Less fitting in a possible murder-context of "Cold Irons Bound", but on the other hand: almost all *bended knees* in Dylan's repertoire and in Dylan's record collection are of desperate men begging their (living!) wives to stay. George Jones's "There Ain't No

Grave Deep Enough", John Lee Hooker's "Wednesday Evening Blues", Blind Willie McTell's "Broke Down Engine" (which Dylan records for *World Gone Wrong* in 1993), Little Richard's "Can't Believe You Wanna Leave"... no, that record cabinet is filled to the brim with pitiful men on bended knees, but none of them is a murderer - they are all suckers humiliating themselves in front of an apparently dominant, but most of all *living* woman.

A remorseful murderer or a pathetic sucker - it seems Dylan doesn't know either at the time of conception. "It's one of those where you write it on instinct. Kind of in a trance state. Most of my recent songs are like that," as Dylan says about "I Contain Multitudes" in 2020, and: "They just fall down from space."

Okay, the latter is perhaps a bit too woolly. It does seem quite likely, after all, that large parts of Dylan's songs do not so much come from outer space, but rather from his own record collection. Which is a good thing, by the way; falling-out from Dylan's record cabinet undoubtedly sounds much better than incoming space junk.

And you do want your songs to sound good.

9   Make You Feel My Love

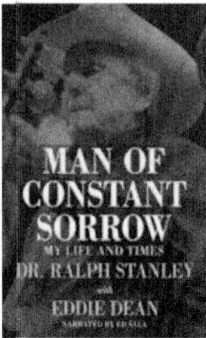

Man Of Constant Sorrow, the autobiography of Ralph Stanley (co-written with Eddie Dean, 2007), is a somewhat two-faced affair. The legendary bluegrass pioneer is a humble, down-to-earth and simple man, but emphasizes that so often that it is getting immodest. It's the fans, a grateful elderly Stanley says, who keep him sharp and lively. Fans like Bob Dylan he can not resist adding, a bit boastful. Quoting, among other self-congratulatory anecdotes, the telegram (the one with the *Fields Have Turned Brown* reference) he got from Dylan on the occasion of the celebration in Nashville of his fiftieth anniversary in the music business, in 1996. (The first radio show of The Stanley Brother And The Clinch Mountain Boys was December 26, 1946, WCYB in Bristol, Tennessee).

And with the same childish pride he tells us about that time "not too long ago" that an anonymous stranger with sunglasses and a hoodie visits the memorial at his birthplace, takes photos and at the local grocery store asks for directions to Ralph Stanley's home. "Don't you know who that was," the shelf stacker asks the cashier, "that was Bob Dylan."

Boastful or not, Ralph Stanley has, of course, every right to be proud of his career and Bob Dylan's admiration. That admiration is deep and sincere. In *Theme Time Radio Hour* radio host Dylan plays five times a song by The Stanley Brothers, the last time (episode 72, More Birds) introduced by a rousing recommendation:

> "We played The Stanley Brothers many many times. You can't go around when you see a Stanley Brothers record. If you're at a flea market or a yard sale, and you see a record with their name on it, it's gotta be good."

In 1997, Dylan plays three songs from the brothers on stage ("I'll Not Be A Stranger", "Stone Walls And Steel Bars" and "White Dove"), the cover of "Man Of Constant Sorrow" on his very first album is due to his love for the Stanleys and in the *Newsweek* interview (1997) he calls songs like "Let Me Rest On A Peaceful Mountain" his 'religion'. "The songs are my lexicon. I believe the songs."

A 'lexicon', a dictionary rather, is "Highway Of Regret", the Stanley Brothers song from which he uses the opening and the third line for "Ain't Talkin'" (*Ain't talkin', just walkin'* and *Heart's burning, still yearning*), and borrows the second line (*Down that highway or regret*) for one of his biggest hits, for "Make You Feel My Love".

The metaphor immediately stands out, among the little original, tear-jerker poetry and worn-out images. Ironically, the lovingly stolen *highway of regret* is still the most dylanesque, is a metaphor like Desolation Row, Heartbreak Hill, river of tears and Rue Morgue Avenue, which in turn are all probably located in the vicinity of Presley's Lonely Street.

The sweet character of the rest of the lyrics is also noticed by the most successful ambassador of the song, Adele. Her reservations initially concern her unwillingness to include a cover on her debut album (*19*, 2008). But her manager is a huge Dylan fan and keeps on bugging her, until she finally listens to that song.

> "And then I heard it in New York when he played it for me, and it just really touched me. It's cheesy, but I think it's just a stunning song, and it really just summed up everything that I'd been trying to write in my songs."

Because of that kitschiness the song is usually not very popular with the seasoned fans. The most disappointed do not shun the big words, on fan forums like *expectingrain*: "horrible", "indefensibly mediocre", "disgusting sentimentality". The slightly more loyal fans sputter that the song is or can be "quite nice" (and refer to illegal live recordings on which things are not *that* bad), a few hide behind the dubious compliment that the song is a guilty pleasure and a faction pleads that "Make You Feel My Love" truly is a very good song.

The professionals are equally unimpressed. Clinton Heylin dismisses the song briefly and concisely; with disdain he states that it indeed belongs "on a Billy Joel album" (Billy Joel is in fact the first who releases the song, earlier than Dylan, on *Greatest Hits Volume III*, 1997) and that Dylan's live performances do not reveal any hidden depths either. Greil Marcus is full of praise for *Time Out Of Mind*, but ignores this song completely, Greg Kot in *Rolling Stone* thinks that the album's spell is broken by this "spare ballad, undermined by greetingcard lyrics" and an acid Ian Bell snaps that the song "should have been shipped off instantly, gratis, to Billy Joel, Garth Brooks, and the rest of the balladeers who would take the vapid things to their sentimental hearts."

That seems a bit all too bold and short-sighted. The song is really not that trivial. The music, for example, manages to push enough buttons to let "Make You Feel My Love" slowly but surely enter the canon. Among the up to hundreds of artists who now have the song on the repertoire are certainly not the least; In addition to the aforementioned megastars such as Adele, Billy Joel and Garth Brooks, it has also been picked up by colleagues like Neil Diamond, Bryan Ferry, Joan Osborne, Timothy B. Schmit and Ed Sheeran. Artists about whom one may have an opinion, but in any case musicians who have an understanding of pop music, catchy melodies and appealing compositions.

The indestructible melody Dylan seems to have borrowed largely from a song that apparently buzzes through his head: "You Belong To Me".

"You Belong To Me" is a beautiful song from 1952, which Dylan probably admires in the performance of Dean Martin - or else the hit version of Jo Stafford, or Gene Vincent's rock 'n roll rendition, or the one of The Duprees, or Bing Crosby, or Patsy Cline … it is a song that is often recorded and is often a hit in the years that Dylan's music taste is formed, so under his skin it is anyhow. He himself records it in 1992 for *Good As I Been To You*, but ultimately does not select it. Dylan's recording eventually surfaces in '94, on the soundtrack of Oliver Stone's film hit *Natural Born Killers*.

Likewise, arguments can be cited against the supposed sweetness of the text. Admittedly, on hearing the song for the first time it does come across as the work of a lazy lyricist who dashes off a bunch of clichés. But at a second listening, and especially when dry re-reading the lyrics, something starts to gnaw. The narrator is quite pushy, is he not? And is it not strange that he makes no mention whatsoever of his beloved, not a single word, apart from the intriguing fact that she apparently has some serious doubts (*you haven't made your mind up yet*). Furthermore, the narrator merely sums up what he would do to make her "feel his love". And for that matter: that "I will make you feel my love" does not sound very tender either - certainly not after such a dubious vow like "I could hold you for a million years".

By then, one also starts to notice that it is nothing but abysmal misery. The rain hits her face, the whole world is nagging at her, tears, hunger, black and blue, storm and a "highway of regret"... and yet this girl still has her reservations about his "warm embrace", his consolation and any of his offers at all. Smothering, to say the least, if not: stalker alert. No, perhaps it's a good thing that this lady refuses to commit.

The majority of the covers is pretty much identical. Almost everyone chooses the same pace and similar arrangements, and sugar prevails.

Of all those uniform operations, Adele is indeed one of the finest; the English talent really is a great singer and she seems to have an innate, superior music feeling.

Behind that big leading group of superstars marches a huge platoon of artists of the second category. Ane Brun from Norway (who by the way performs one of the most beautiful versions of "She Belongs To Me") does it beautifully, fragile and lonely at the Nobel banquet in 2016, much more poignant than the posed kitsch parade of another Girl From The North Country, Sissel Kyrkjebø in 2014. A second absolute hit also comes from

Scandinavia: the Swedish Pernilla Andersson manufactures a heart-breaking, sparsely arranged "Make You Feel My Love", driven by a muted guitar, in 2004 on her album *Cradlehouse*.

The crown is for a man, this time. Josh Kelley from Georgia is a reasonably successful singer-songwriter who wins with his contribution to the soundtrack of the film *A Cinderella Story* (2004). With some good will one might hear how Jakob Dylan would address this song from his father; Josh' voice sounds like him and Josh opts for a Wallflowers approach: prominent drums (great drumming arrangement, by the way), sound effects, organ and electric guitars - and no swooning with violins and sensitive piano tinkling or stuff.

Boy, what a most beautiful song of constant sorrow it turns out to be.

10   Can't Wait

I   That dog song

In the connection between Bob Dylan and Pink Floyd, there seems to be a well working diode; the current only goes in one direction. From Dylan to Pink Floyd, that is. And the current already flows even before Pink Floyd exists: somewhere at the end of '64, beginning of '65 the founder of the band, crazy diamond Syd Barrett, writes his "Bob Dylan Blues". We know the background to this almost lost song thanks to then girlfriend Libby Gausden. On the fansite *sydbarrett.com*, Libby is kind enough to release parts of Syd's letters:

> "I have written a song about Bob Dylan. Yeh! Yeh! Soul, God, etc. It starts off *I got the Bob Dylan blues and the Bob Dylan shoes and my hair an' my clothes in a mess but you know I just couldn't care less*. In fact a bit satirical and humorous. Ho! Ha! Hee! Tee! for Syd."

And Libby also tells about the background; how Syd took her to a Dylan concert in London in May '64; how fond they both were of *The Freewheelin'*, *The Times* and *Another Side*; how Syd's eyes began to sparkle when she had her hair bubbled ("done in that image of Dylan on the cover of 'Blonde on Blonde', which we had endlessly listened to, and identified with") and how glad she was that David Gilmour still had the song on tape somewhere.

The song was recorded in 1970, on the second day of recording for *Barrett*, Syd's second and last solo album. After that, the song was lost for years, and was eventually found in the garage of producer and guitarist Gilmour. "I probably took it away to have a listen and simply forgot to take it back. It wasn't intended to be a final mix. Syd knocked it off, I took a tape home." When he finds it back, some thirty years later, it is a welcome enhancement to the 2001 compilation *The Best of Syd Barrett: Wouldn't You Miss Me?* With Gilmour's comment: "*Bob Dylan Blues* is a bit of fun. He was quite a Dylan fan, though there was a bit of jealousy there, too."

"A bit of fun" is a good description, indeed. Loosely based on the melody and chords of "Chimes Of Freedom", references to "Blowin' In The Wind", "Masters Of War", "I Shall Be Free #10", and in the title, obviously, and the song is mainly what the title promises: a tribute.

Gilmour was also hooked on Dylan at the time of Syd's song conception. Way before Syd even, if we should choose to believe him in the BBC documentary *Wider Horizons*, March 2016 (and we may, up to a certain point). His parents have moved to New York for work, he tells us, to Greenwich Village ("They could see the end of Bleecker Street out of their window") and also support their son's musical dreams from a distance: "I got Bob Dylan's first record for my sixteenth birthday, which they sent me from Greenwich Village." Which seems odd... Gilmour turned sixteen on 6 March 1962, thirteen days before Dylan's first album was released. He must mean a seventeenth or an eighteenth birthday then.

The Dylan love, however, is real and lasting. When he is the castaway in BBC 4's *Desert Island Discs* in 2003, Gilmour calls Dylan "fabulous" and "wonderful", and his second Desert Island choice is a Dylan song, though a surprising one: "Ballad In Plain D". "I've lived through a lot of his heavy protest stuff. This was another side I'm very keen on, this sort of love song approach."

In the trailer for the unreleased Italian documentary *Who's Ever Met Bob* (2012), people like Bernardo Bertolucci, Pretty Thing Phil May and Joe Boyd talk about their encounters with Bob Dylan. Dream Academy frontman Nick Laird-Clowes tells how he and David Gilmour were admitted to the dressing room just before a gig in London, presumably sometime in the 1990s.

> "There's Bob. Seeing David – he doesn't know who I am – seeing David coming towards him, he's trying to get his silver lame trousers over his motorcycle boots, and you could see it's a thankless task, they are much too... ah! And then he sees us and he launches himself towards us, trips as he comes and it's like *my God he's gonna break his arm!* [...] And then we stand, and he suddenly says: *Hey Dave, I love that dog song.* And David says: *Dog song, Bob? What dog song?* I say: *Dogs Of War, your song!* And he goes: *Ah, thanks Bob.* And Bob says: *We should really write together sometime.* "Yeah". And then Bob goes: *I better get ready for the show but it's great you guys stopped by.* And we say: *Sure!* We shake him by the hand. He squints up at us, and we leave."

David Gilmour also speaks in the same documentary, and the interviewer comes back to that story of Nick Laird-Clowes. Gilmour remembers, and remains, as usual, modest:

> *And he liked Dogs Of War very much?*
> So he said, yeah.
> *So it's like mutual fans. You're fan of his, and he's fan of yours*
> Well, I don't know if he is. But he certainly... he seems remarkably well-informed.

It's a bit hard to imagine. "Dogs Of War" (1988) is a fairly archetypal Pink Floyd song, not particularly loved by fans, and in many ways a kind of "Money" rip-off. But then again, content-wise the lyrics are a clone of Dylan's "Masters Of War", and the basis of the music is a pretty successful variation on the structure of a twelve-bar blues in minor (Gilmour goes from C minor to *E* flat minor rather than F minor) - both pillars could appeal to Dylan indeed. In addition, Dylan often expresses dissenting, highly unorthodox preferences, such as in the 2020 *New York Times* interview, in which he qualifies The Eagles' "Pretty Maids All In A Row" as "that could be one of the best songs ever".

Still, other candidates do seem more obvious. Dylan compliments *"that dog song"* and Laird-Clowes hastily fills in for Gilmour: "He means Dogs Of War!" That is quite questionable. For one, it's pretty unlikely that the "remarkably well-informed" Dylan, with his uncanny memory for songs, would recall the striking title of a recent song like "Dogs Of War" as *that dog song*. A better candidate is already "Dogs" (from *Animals*, 1977), but Pink Floyd's only real *dog song* is the most obvious: "Seamus", the funny little throwaway that closes side 1 of *Meddle* (1971).

Just as reviled by the fans, but for the non-Pink Floyd fan a charming country blues, and for the dog lover (as Dylan is) a witty leading role for the howling of Steve Marriott's border collie Seamus – by all standards a ditty that Dylan *would* remember a quarter of a century later, and which he would quite possibly remember as *that dog song*.

Too generic, though, to be qualifiable for an upgrade to *influential song*. That, Pink Floyd influence on a Dylan song, is really only indisputable one single time: on the rejected "Can't Wait", alternate version No. 2, which can be found on CD3 of the DeLuxe Edition of *The Bootleg Series Vol. 8: Tell Tale Signs: Rare and*

Unreleased 1989-2006, illustrating the one single time when the diode falters and the current flows in the other direction:

> By the way, the *Live at Pompeii* version of "Seamus" is re-titled "Mademoiselle Nobs" because the howling is now done by the beautiful, white Russian wolfhound Nobs. In a drastically changed arrangement, with David Gilmour on harmonica. "He'd introduced the harmonica," says Gilmour in that same trailer, "not, obviously, as a new instrument, but a new way of using the harmonica." In this particular song, Gilmour's approach is quite traditional, though.

II   Has he got a passenger service vehicle license?

Dylan does not only get under the skin of David Gilmour and Syd Barrett. Drummer Nick Mason counts Dylan, just like Gilmour does in *Desert Island Discs*, among his all-time favourites, when Jools Holland asks him in 2020 to compile a Top 5 for a radio broadcast of *Later... With Jools Holland*. Mason calls Dylan "still the greatest songwriter in rock music history" and chooses *The Freewheelin'* as number 1 in his Classic Albums Top 5. "There's an abstraction to some of them," Nick explains, "that means that you can interpret them in the way it means the most to you. I think that's one of the great skills of great songwriting." But equally remarkable he considers the fact that Dylan often gets behind the wheel of the tour bus himself.

Mason: He does like touring and actually driving the bus.
Holland: So why does he do that, then?
Mason: Well, I never actually had the opportunity to ask him,
but it's not something that ever appealed to me.
Holland: Has he got a passenger service vehicle license?
Mason: I haven't checked his credentials, I'm afraid. But it's
obviously something we should do, straight after the show.

More explicit and, as always, unambiguous about Dylan's influence is Roger Waters. When he is the castaway in *Desert Island Discs* in May 2011, he still pays his respects in the well-known clichés ("Leonard Cohen and Bob Dylan were the two men who allowed us to believe that there was an open door between poetry and song lyrics"), but eight months later, in January 2012 in the radio studio of Howard Stern, he does not shy away from the Big Words, bordering on melodrama:

> "Sad-Eyed Lady Of The Lowlands sort of changed my life. When I heard that, I thought, if Bob can do it, I can do it. It's twenty minutes long. It's a whole album. And in no way gets dull or boring, or anything. You just get more and more engrossed, it just gets more and more hypnotic, the longer it goes on."

With which Waters quite specifically defines Dylan's influence on Pink Floyd: the courage to deviate from three-minute songs, to let songs expand into whole album sides (okay, *Sad-Eyed* lasts a little over 11 minutes, not "twenty minutes", but still a whole album side), and the encouragement to allow poetry into song lyrics.

Opinions differ as to the poetic qualities of Waters' lyrics, but we can at least agree that the Pink Floyd catalogue contains a considerable number of exceptionally successful one-liners. *There's someone in my head but it's not me* ("Brain Damage"), "Careful with That Axe, Eugene", "Set the Controls for the Heart of the Sun", sometimes even with a Dylanesque quality: "So you think you can tell Heaven from Hell?" for instance ("Wish You Were Here") or

> You pick the place and I'll choose the time
> And I'll climb
> That hill in my own way.
> Just wait a while for the right day.
> And as I rise above the tree lines and the clouds
> I look down, hearing the sound of the things you've said today

... from "Fearless" (1971). Although the most Dylanesque verse was not written by Roger Waters, but by Rick Wright, for that bloodcurdlingly beautiful opening to "Summer of '68":

> Would you like to say something before you leave
> Perhaps you'd care to state exactly how you feel
> We said goodbye before we said hello
> I hardly even like you, I shouldn't care at all
> We met just six hours ago, the music was too loud
> From your bed I gained a day and lost a bloody year

The one time we hear Pink Floyd in a Dylan song, it is - of course - not due to some Floydian poetry in the song lyrics. "Can't Wait" is a beautiful song, and the lyrics are larded with shiny, Dylan-worthy one-liners, but in essence the lyrics are not that spectacular; a classic blues lament of a rather desperate man tangled up in a one-way love - the lady apparently finds him much less desirable than he does her. Large parts of the text are interchangeable. Literally; in the three officially released versions (on *Time Out Of Mind* and on *Tell Tale Signs*) and in the live versions, it's a coming and going of verse lines, some moving to other songs (*Well, my back is to the sun because the light is too intense* moves eventually to "Sugar Baby", for instance) and really only the opening (*I can't wait / Wait for you to change your mind*) is fixed in all versions.

The tone does shift, though; in the final album version it is desperate and sombre, as illustrated by the closing words:

> Well I'm strollin' through the lonely graveyard of my mind
> I left my life with you somewhere back there along the line
> I thought somehow that I would be spared this fate
> I don't know how much longer I can wait

...in other versions the tone is reproachful, such as:

> Loneliness around me diggin' at me like a ray
> What a piece of work she is to cause my heart to pray
> I thought somehow that I'd be spared this fate
> And I don't know how much longer I can wait.

That's what Dylan sings in "Alternate version #2", the second version that can be found on *Tell Tale Signs*. Which is also the version that for the sake of convenience is called the "psychedelic version", but even better is the nickname "the Pink Floyd version" - on account of the arrangement, obviously. And there we have it: the one time Floyd shines through in a Dylan song.

From the first bar, it is unmistakable: "Us And Them". Same organ sound, half a tone higher, identical, mesmerizing larghissimo tempo. Drums and hypnotic bass as subdued and tasteful as in "Shine On You Crazy Diamond" and "Breathe". And the guitar parts adapt almost automatically to the Floyd mode; sharp, guiding accents like in "Echoes" and "Money", and as a bonus a slide guitar with the unsurpassed elegance as Gilmour plays in classics like "Breathe", "Us And Them" and especially "The Great Gig In The Sky". Incomparable, at any rate, with the mosaic parts Lanois puzzles together on the album version and the Dr. John/New Orleans voodoo vibe he puts underneath. Or with the Chicago/Albert King's "Stormy Monday" colouring of "Alternate version #1" on *Tell Tale Signs*.

The same goes for the many, many arrangements Dylan chooses in the many, many live performances of "Can't Wait". *I'm looking for anything that will bring a happy glow*, as Dylan sings. Colours and sounds from every corner of the canon, but never again does Dylan switch back to the *engrossing, hypnotic* (in Roger Waters' words) cadence and colouring of that one time Pink Floyd penetrated a Dylan song.

A pity, perhaps. But comparing the restless shuffling with accents, verse fragments and arrangements is a fascinating consolation. What Tony Attwood demonstrates in his article exploring the arrangements of the live versions on his website *Untold Dylan*. Tony does have the credentials to do so, by the way. A song arrangement exploration license, so to speak.

11   Highlands

I   Wild rose in the heather

A boy saw a wild rose
growing in the heather;
it was so young, and as lovely as the morning.
He ran swiftly to look more closely,
looked on it with great joy.
Wild rose, wild rose, wild rose red,
wild rose in the heather.

("*Heidenröslein*, Wild Rose", poem by Goethe, set to music
by Schubert, transl. Richard Wigmore)

In the liner notes to the various records of Schubert songs, it is often and gladly repeated. Schubert, who was a great fan of Goethe's lyricism, sent him his set of Lieder in 1816 and again in 1825 three songs that he had dedicated to Goethe. On the one occasion, Goethe sent back the consignment, which contained such small masterpieces as "Erlkönig" and "Heidenröslein" without comment; on the other, he did not reply at all.

The undertone in these liner notes when quoting this anecdote is usually: how is it possible that the *Dichterfürst,* the poet laureate did not recognise Schubert's genius, and how strange is it that the civilised, broad-minded Goethe bluntly ignored Schubert's outstretched hand? And for two hundred years now, musicologists and literary scholars have been thinking they have an answer to this. "Schubert's music was too strong a competitor for the musicality of his lyricism," for instance, and "Schubert's songs did in fact not set Goethe's poems to music - at best, he was inspired by them."

That "explanation" is a somewhat romantic notion, which assumes that Goethe actually studied Schubert's arrangements of his lyricism and felt threatened by them. Which is rather speculative. Indeed, it is rather unlikely. Goethe himself, a meticulous chronicler of his own life, makes no mention of Schubert and his dispatches either in his diaries, letters or autobiography. Yes, a small marginal note in one of his diaries, 16 June 1825, a day summed up in 95 words. The last 33 of which are:

> "Dispatch of Count Sternberg. News of his intended journey. Consignment of Felix from Berlin, quartets. Consignment of Schubert from Vienna, compositions of my songs. In Dodwell and Stanhope Morea and the Greek affairs."

And that throws some light on Goethe's alleged disinterest. An identical picture emerges from the other, thousands of diary entries: Goethe's house at *Frauenplan* in Weimar is inundated week in week out, for years on end, with letters, parcels and shipments from all over Europe. Goethe made the conscious decision to be very selective fairly early on in his life. "If I could not tell someone something special and appropriate, as the particular issue demanded, I preferred not to write at all," he tells his secretary Eckermann in the last years of his life (*Conversations with Goethe*, 1836). And:

> "Thus it came to be that I could not answer many an honest man whom I would have liked to have written. You can see for yourself what is going on at my place and what kind of shipments arrive every day from every corner of the world. And you must admit that it would need more than one human lifetime, if one wanted to respond to everything just briefly."

It is much more likely, in short, that Schubert's correspondence simply went down in the tsunami of mail. Well, it did not, thank God, discourage Schubert.

The custom of setting literary poems to music took off in the nineteenth century. Schubert, Schumann, Wolf, Richard Strauss - in fact, all the great composers - loved to be inspired by the works of Schiller, Goethe, Eichendorff, Heine and all the others. And some poets owe their eternal fame to the musical setting of their actually mediocre poetry. Wilhelm Müller's work, for example, we know mainly because Schubert composed his immortal *Winterreise* on it.

In the twentieth century, when poets place less and less value on the musicality of their poems, and thus make it more difficult for musicians to write music to their non-rhyming, arrhythmic and unstructured poems, the nineteenth-century duality of poets and song composers fades. The most successful examples generally fall back on solid, classical poetry. The Waterboys set poems by Yeats to music (*An Appointment With Mr. Yeats*, 2011), Leonard Cohen adapts Federico García Lorca's poem "Pequeño vals vienés" ("Take This Waltz", 1988), Edgar Allan Poe is picked up by Alan Parsons and Lou Reed, among others, and William Blake does reasonably well too (in The Verve's "History" from 1995, for instance).

Dylan has his own approach. He does not set other people's poems to music, but he likes to borrow a line here and a word combination there. Even to this day, as is well known; "I Contain Multitudes" from 2020 is a line from Walt Whitman, for instance. William Blake echoes have been in Dylan's oeuvre for half a century. In "Roll On, John" and in "Every Grain Of Sand", to name just two, and here on *Time Out Of Mind* in "Cold Irons Bound" and in the outtake "Marchin' To The City". We hear T.S. Eliot in "Visions Of Johanna", and dozens of verses and word combinations from -

especially - Civil War era poems that can be found in the songs on Dylan's aptly titled album *"Love And Theft"* (2001) and in the monumental song "'Cross The Green Mountain".

"Highlands" is another variation on this practice. The core of Robert Burns' chorus is set to music, and then largely, as in the "normal" folk tradition, reworked;

Robert Burns (1789)
My heart's in the Highlands, my heart is not here,
My heart's in the Highlands, a-chasing the deer;
Chasing the wild-deer, and following the roe,
My heart's in the Highlands, wherever I go.

Bob Dylan (1997)
Well my heart's in the Highlands gentle and fair
Honeysuckle blooming in the wildwood air
Bluebells blazing where the Aberdeen waters flow
Well my heart's in the Highland
I'm gonna go there when I feel good enough to go

Dylan sings five variants of this refrain in his song, all of which in substance boil down to the same thing as Burns' refrain; nature's idyll and longing. And routinely picks the botanical additions thereto from songs that are somewhere at the front of the canon; "Wildwood Flower", "Honeysuckle Rose", "The Twelfth Of Never" (*I'll love you till the bluebells forget to bloom*), and in the chorus variants comparable bluegrass clichés like "over the hills and far away", and comparable rural scenery like "horses and hounds" in the fourth, and "buckeyed trees" in the second chorus.

The local botanist would object, by the way; it is *buckeye* trees. A detail, but it does grate a bit nevertheless, because apparently a spelling correction already has been made. The misspelling *bluebelles* on the official site and in *Lyrics 1962-2001* has been corrected to *bluebells* in *Lyrics 1961-2012*, and *buckeyed* has also been considered: it has been changed to *buck-eyed* - with a hyphen, but still wrong.

It would not have happened to Goethe. The *uomo universalis* from Weimar was not only a statesman, poet, scientist and philosopher, but also a naturalist; his botanical studies, (like *Geschichte meines botanischen Studiums,* 1817), are considered to be a precursor for Darwin, also according to Darwin himself. In the historical introduction that he includes in the third edition of *On the Origin of Species*, Darwin acknowledges Johann Wolfgang von Goethe as "an extreme partisan" of the transmutation view. Goethe was, in short, botanically as well as linguistically versed enough to know how to spell *buckeye* and *bluebells*.

But he could not write beautiful songs.

II   You can hear the air around it

"Probably the last time I bought a record that was just brilliant all the way through was Nick Cave," Henry Rollins tells in an interview with *DVD Talk,* in 2004. "I wrote him a letter after I played it and said 'you and Dylan are like the only guys writing songs right now.' I think the last two Dylan records have just been incredible - *Time out of Mind* and *Love and Theft.* Those were just amazing." And further on in the same interview he explains what touches him, apart from the songs, even more: the sound. Henry Rollins is a man of knowledge and moreover blessed with the gift of words, so he can perfectly articulate what touches him so, in terms of sound: "I miss the space, I miss the sound of a guitar in a room where you can hear the air around it. Who makes records like that still? Tom Waits does, Bob Dylan does."

Rollins demonstrates a kinship with Dylan, as evidenced by the words of session musician Jim Dickinson, the keyboardist on "Highlands":

> "One thing that really struck me during those sessions, Dylan, he was standing singing four feet from the microphone, with no earphones on. He was listening to the sound in the room."

... almost the same words Rollins uses to describe his preferred sound, the sound he hears on *Time Out Of Mind*. Which is also confirmed by engineer Chris Shaw:

> "And I'd say about 85 per cent of the sound of that record is the band spilling into Bob's microphone, because he'd sing live in the room with the band. Most of the time without headphones. That's why the record has this big, I think, almost kind of swampy sound to it, and he loves it, he really goes for that sound."

... the sound that Dylan hears on those famous "reference records". In an interview with Robert Hilburn, September 2001, Dylan leads the Dylanologists to Charley Patton:

> "I had the guitar run off an old Charley Patton record for years and always wanted to do something with that. I was sitting around, maybe in the dark Delta or maybe in some unthinkable trench somewhere, with that sound in my mind and the dichotomy of the Highlands with that seemed to be a path worth pursuing."

But that seems to be a misdirection; a Patton recording with a similar riff cannot be found. It can be found in Slim Harpo, though. Who is also mentioned elsewhere by Dylan as an example of the "reference records" with which he tried to put producer Lanois on the right track. Similar riffs as in "Highlands", which is a quite generic riff in itself, can be heard more than once on Slim Harpo's records. "That's Why I Love You" comes close, for instance, but "Tip On In" even more so, as well as in sound - in fact, all those old Excello recordings have the "air", the "space" that Dylan and Rollins love so much. Reduce the tempo of "Tip On In" to 75%, and you're pretty close to "Highlands".

It is not unlikely that Dylan is simply mistaken, with his Patton hint. Fans and followers often think that Dylan is putting up smokescreens on purpose or having fun sending journalists into the wind, but we have seen for 60 years now that Dylan is not familiar with details of his own discography, mixes up facts about recordings, such as the names of session musicians, and only superficially remembers circumstances surrounding recording sessions. Facts and details just don't interest him enough. He rarely if ever listens back to his own records, as he has said repeatedly for the past sixty years. During interviews, he often makes mistakes in dates and tracklists, and this happens again when he is asked about *Time Out Of Mind* and "Highlands" in 2001, more than four years later. Even nine months after the recordings, in September 1997, he does not remember exactly anymore:

> "I don't think we had a full ensemble playing on that, as I remember. There can't be more than four people playing. I can't say that the musicians didn't know the song or the lyrics. I don't know,"

... he says to Edna Gundersen. And in 2001, with Mikal Gilmore for *Rolling Stone*, he is half wrong when he says about "Highlands":

"That particular song, we worked with a track that I had done at a sound check once in some hall. The assembled group of musicians we had down at the studio just couldn't get it, so I said, "Just use that original track, and I'll sing over it." It was just some old blues song I always wanted to use, and I felt that once I was able to control it, I could've written about anything with it. But you're right – I forgot that was on that record."

That peculiarity, that exceptional technical fact, "a track that I had done at a sound check once in some hall" concerns the recording of "Dirt Road Blues", as we know thanks to both Daniel Lanois and drummer Winston Watson. For "Highlands", a pre-recorded loop is indeed also used, but it was fabricated by Lanois and Tony Mangurian, while playing along with a reference record, and further edited by Lanois and Dylan at the Teatro in Oxnard sometime in late 2016.

In short, it is not too daring to question Dylan's memories and statements about the recording process and song inspiration. Nor is it deliberate deception - recordings are simply not that important to Dylan. His head was in the Highlands, probably.

III   That long rambling talking thing

It is, of course, not that surprising, Henry Rollins being so moved by *Time Out Of Mind* and by *"Love And Theft"*; after all, he is hearing himself. Or rather: his own words. Some of Rollins' verses seem to inspire whole songs ("Million Miles"); in the masterpiece "Mississippi", at least four fragments seem to have been borrowed from him, both in the outtakes and in eight of the eleven *Time Out Of Mind* songs Scott Warmuth finds Rollins quotations, and "Highlands" is one of them too. The lines *All the young men with their young women looking so good / Well, I'd trade places with any of them / In a minute, if I could* as well as *"I think what I need might be a full-length leather coat / Somebody just asked me / If I registered to vote"* are lovingly stolen. And diluted, more fragments qualify for the *Rollins* label. A terrifying line like *Insanity is smashing up against my soul*, for instance, does smell an awful lot like the work in the poetry collection *See A Grown Man Cry*, like a ferocious six-liner as

> *Alone looking for the quickest way to get to pain*
> *I am my soul smasher love call death trip*
> *I slashed the wrists of Destiny and took total control*
> *I watch the night strangle the sun*
> *Hail night*
> *Darkness, my brother*

... "a few bad turns" Dylan also reads in *Now Watch Him Die*, as well as "I have new eyes" ("*I got new eyes*" in the last verse), and there are more whole and half borrowings like that.

"Highlands" is particularly peculiarly structured. Twenty quatrains, which for some reason on paper are all represented as quintains;

> *I'm listening to Neil Young, I gotta turn up the sound*
> *Someone's always yelling turn it down*
> *Feel like I'm drifting*
> *Drifting from scene to scene*
> *I'm wondering what in the devil could it all possibly mean?*

... for example, which is of course just a simple four-liner, both in recitation and in rhyme;

> *I'm listening to Neil Young, I gotta turn up the sound*
> *Someone's always yelling turn it down*
> *Feel like I'm drifting, drifting from scene to scene*
> *I'm wondering what in the devil could it all possibly mean?*

A "restructuring" that can be done for all twenty verses plus choruses. After all, the twenty stanzas are modelled on the template, on Robert Burns' "My Heart's in the Highlands": four-liners in the simplest rhyme scheme *AABB*.

Which is not the peculiar thing. Concealing the "real" form is something Dylan, or his editor, does with prodigious tenacity in every decade and every edition of *Lyrics*, God knows why. No, the peculiar thing is the function structuring, the chaotic formal tripartite structure:

- choruses: 1, 4, 7, 15, 20
- lyrical couplets: 2, 3, 5, 6, 16-19
- "Boston one-act play": 8-14

So, during seven stanzas, the song seems to have a traditional *verse-verse-refrain* structure, then this framework is interrupted by an epic intermezzo of seven stanzas, not to return to the original structure afterwards. This seems to be mainly due to inattention, by the way: it seems that Dylan simply forgets a refrain - if he had added a refrain after stanza 17, at least the part of the traditional *verse-verse-refrain* structure would have been maintained. *And* we would have had a balanced unit of three times seven stanzas.

The eight lyrical couplets are interchangeable. They are, in any case, not connected by a plot, but they are eight separate tableaux, connected only by the voice of the narrator: by an elderly first-person narrator who eight times expresses uneasiness, fatigue and unfulfillable longing. Most tableaux seem to be triggered by a Rollins fragment, which is then developed into a quatrain by an associating, improvising Dylan. Rollins' "shake the bars in front of my windows" (from *Now Watch Him Die*), for example, seems to trigger Dylan's opening line *"Windows were shakin' all night in my dreams"*, *"feel like a prisoner"* from the second verse can literally be found in *See A Grown Man Cry*, and like this, Rollins traces can be found in each of the eight lyrical stanzas. Dylan confirms the improvised character of the song by his explanations during a press conference in London, 1997:

> Q: *On your album, the song Highlands seems very improvised. How well prepared are you when you go into the studio?*
> BD: "Well, I think that long rambling talking thing... I think I've recorded things like that before, real early on. In that type of form, a person can say whatever they want because the form is simple. I wouldn't say it was improvised, but a lot of different thoughts were connected in a lot of different ways that might necessarily not be what they seem to be on the paper when they were written. This is like thoughts, you know, that could be connected over a two-month period of time."

Beautiful tableaux, visually strong and moving enough, but in itself not that special; "just dylanesque" as it were, comparable to language, tone and content of, say, "Cold Irons Bound" or "Standing In The Doorway". No, the real attention grabber, the distinctive strength of the song is, obviously, that bizarre "Boston interlude".

IV   She studied the lines on my face

> I'm in Boston town, in some restaurant
> I got no idea what I want
> Well, maybe I do but I'm just really not sure
> Waitress comes over
> Nobody in the place but me and her

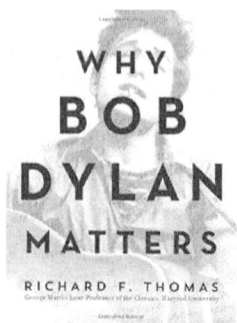

We owe to the unsurpassed Harvard professor Richard F. Thomas a special, fascinating plot interpretation of that alienating intermezzo halfway through the song, those seven stanzas forming a kind of one-act play for two in an empty restaurant in Boston. In his wonderful Dylan study *Why Dylan Matters* (2017), Professor Thomas points to the return of the image of the waitress. A return from that other monumental song in Dylan's catalogue, from "Tangled Up In Blue" (*Blood On The Tracks*, 1975).

Now we also recognise the male protagonist from "Tangled Up In Blue". Now, in "Highlands", he is in the "wrong time", *you picked the wrong time to come*, says the waitress, who by her looks and her behaviour has thrown him back in time, back to 1974. Just like her predecessor, she observes the restaurant guest intently (*She studied the lines on my face* vs. *She studied me closely*), we are again in an otherwise empty catering facility, and when she insists on drawing her portrait, he has to draw it, strangely, *from memory*, although she is standing right in front of him. It doesn't *look a thing like me*, she says a little later, a bit indignantly. On the contrary, the satisfied artist contradicts her, *it most certainly does* - after all, he has fabricated a fine portrait of the memory of that waitress in *the topless place* at the time. The last stanza definitively illustrates that the narrator is in a different time zone: when the waitress asks which female authors he has read. "Erica Jong," he replies triumphantly. Erica Jong's controversial *Fear Of Flying* is from 1973.

The return of the waitress is not the only striking thing that seems to hint at Dylan doing some retrospection in "Highlands". Reminiscence is a sub-motive, at the very least, or so it seems. *Time Out Of Mind* is a double album released thirty-one years after Dylan's first double album *Blonde On Blonde*, and again the last record side, Side 4, is reserved for one single song. Back then, "Sad-Eyed Lady Of The Lowlands", in which a young, lovesick narrator sings a lady from the *Lowlands*, now "Highlands", in which an old, disillusioned narrator longs for the loneliness of the *Highlands*. Unreachable they both are, by the way; *"Sad-eyed lady of the lowlands, where the sad-eyed prophet says that no man comes"* as the narrator sang thirty years ago, willing to wait, though. Worn out, but nevertheless more optimistic, the narrator is thirty years later:

> *Well, my heart's in the Highlands at the break of day*
> *Over the hills and far away*
> *There's a way to get there and I'll figure it out somehow*
> *But I'm already there in my mind*
> *And that's good enough for now*

... a beautiful, peaceful, thoroughly melancholic ending to a wonderful song. And if Dylan keeps up this rhythm, we will hear what happened to this protagonist on Side 4 of the next double album, sometime around 2028.

Weird scenes inside the gold mine

Strictly speaking, "Mississippi" is a *Time Out Of Mind* outtake. Dylan made three attempts, in January 1997 at Criteria Studios in Miami, to capture one of his most celebrated songs of late on tape, but in the end "Mississippi" was discarded. For inimitable reasons, as is often the case with Dylan. Becoming quite apparent in 2008 when both the first (*"Unreleased, Time Out Of Mind"*) and second (*"Unreleased version #2, Time Out Of Mind"*) and third takes (*"Alternate version #3, Time Out of Mind"*) are released on the gold mine *The Bootleg Series Vol. 8: Tell-Tale Signs*. One take is even better than the other, as drummer David Kemper agrees, when he hears those recordings four years later ("So they put it up on the big speakers, and I said, 'Damn - release it'!").

But Dylan is, for some reason, not satisfied with those Lanois recordings. Eventually, in 2001, he re-records the song, this time for *"Love And Theft"*.

Thus: from then on, the song is no longer a *Time Out Of Mind* outtake, but a *"Love And Theft"* track. And anyway: the song is so rich, majestic and outer category, that she deserves her own book - she really should not end up as a chapter somewhere in the back of a *Time Out Of Mind* book.

Tell-Tale Signs still offers three more "real" outtakes:

- the monumental "Red River Shore", which is even more ruthlessly discarded than "Mississippi" (the song is never re-recorded, never performed, nor, as far as we know, offered to a colleague);

- two versions of "Marchin' To The City", the song that will eventually be picked bare for "'Til I Fell In Love With You";

- "Dreamin' Of You", a beautiful song that, like "Marchin' To The City", also falls victim to scavenging. Nine verses move to "Standing In The Doorway", and Dylan re-uses some others for "Cold Irons Bound" and for "Things Have Changed". Still, the fate of "Dreamin' Of You" is a tad less sad: to promote *Tell-Tale Signs*, the song is released as a teaser, as a pre-release single, gets its own video clip with Harry Dean Stanton, and thus has its own fifteen minutes of fame.

A special case is the Oscar-winning "Things Have Changed". Definitely not an outtake, of course; the song was recorded two years later, in a different studio, in a different city, with different musicians and has nothing to do whatsoever with *Time Out Of Mind*. However - in the official editions of Dylan's collected song lyrics, *Lyrics 1962-2001* and *Lyrics 1961-2012*, the song is in the *Time Out Of Mind* segment, under the heading "additional lyrics".

Weird. Chronologically, "Things Have Changed" is closer to *"Love And Theft"*, and factually it's a stand-alone recording, but who cares. Apparently Dylan Inc. & Partners think it's a *Time Out Of Mind* song. And the music company Dylan Inc. & Partners outranks, obviously, any Dylanologist.

12   Red River Shore (1997)

I   She wrote me a letter

The Kingston Trio's track record is staggering. Five number-one albums, four of them consecutive (in 1959 and 1960, the successive records *At Large, Here We Go Again, Sold Out* and *String Along* all reached the top position); fourteen Top 10 albums; three Grammy's; in 22 of the 52 weeks of 1960, a Kingston Trio album was number one, and so on. As a result, the trio is considered mainstream and not appreciated in hardcore folk circles, among snobby college kids and other self-proclaimed purists, but Dylan has always remained a fan. In almost every interview in which he is asked about his musical idols, he mentions the men from San Francisco, among Odetta, Harry Belafonte and Woody Guthrie, and in his autobiography *Chronicles* he is unequivocal, with one small reservation, as well:

> "I liked The Kingston Trio. Even though their style was polished and collegiate, I liked most of their stuff anyway. Songs like "Getaway John," "Remember the Alamo," "Long Black Rifle."

... and further on Dylan is even rather exuberant in his admiration:

> "Folk music, if nothing else, makes a believer out of you. I believed Dave Guard in The Kingston Trio, too. I believed that he would kill or already did kill poor Laura Foster. I believed that he'd kill someone else, too. I didn't think he was playing around."

Dylan names three song titles that can be found on Side 2 of the millionseller *At Large* (1959, fifteen weeks at #1), and *poor Laura Foster* is of course referring to the landslide 1958 "Tom Dooley", the hit that pundits like Joan Baez, John Fogerty and Joni Mitchell say ignited the folk boom, the single that sold more than six million copies, and inspired envious peers The Four Preps to write the witty parody "More Money For You And Me";

> *Hang down the Kingston Trio,*
> *Hang 'em from a tall oak tree;*
> *Eliminate the Kingston Trio;*
> *More money for you and me.*

Dylan remains loyal to the Kingston Trio even after they are finally eliminated. From 1965 onwards, the commercial success is over. *Stay Awhile* does not get any further than a 125th place in the summer, *Somethin' Else* from November '65 doesn't even make it to the Billboard Top 150 LPs. But it reaches Dylan's turntable anyhow, apparently. The Dylan cover "She Belongs To Me" is dismissed for the final tracklist, remaining an outtake, which is a shame - although it is, like more of the tracks, a rather frenetic attempt by the men to fit in with the times, and a particularly atypical recording for the Kingston Trio, it still has most definitely an antiquarian charm. And the song is still way better than the slightly bizarre Dylan parody that does pass selection, the wacky "Verandah Of Millium August", a sort of psychedelic mutilation of "Tombstone Blues", with presumably satirically intended, bad Dylan imitations in the lyrics such as

> *The yellow window's hanging on the bed across the wall*
> *Well, always in the morning the yellowest of all*
> *And the faces of the people in the window look so small*
> *And the faces in the morning were the peoplest of all*
> *Standing on the verandah of Millium August.*

... and Dylanesque rhymes like *Victrola/crayola* and *someone else's odour/secret decoder*, Dyanesque meant images like *a prisoner on a cemetery lane* and Dylanesque meant idioms like *kaleidoscope* and *renaissance wallpaper*.

Dylan most likely has noted it with some bewilderment, but has in any case already been touched by the song that precedes that weird "Verandah Of Millium August", by the opening track of Side 2, by "Red River Shore".

The Kingston Trio's "Red River Shore" is, apart from the martial drum rolls in the background, a real, old-fashioned Kingston Trio song; the charm of a nineteenth-century folk song, banjo, nice harmony vocals and no new-fangled antics like elsewhere on the LP. No tomfoolery like the funky organ, electric guitar and intrusive percussion in Mose Allison's "Parchman Farm" (the opening and unlikely single choice), which by the way is spelled rather disrespectfully both on the single and the LP as Parch*ment*; no hooliganism like the all-electric pop rocker "Runaway Song" or the shameless Byrds rip-off "Long Time Blues" - songs the overenthusiastic writer of the liner notes probably is thinking of when he writes: "In places it has a beat born in that jailhouse and baptized in the waters of the Mersey."

But fortunately, "Red River Shore" is still old-school.

...a narrative ballad with an ancient melody, in a classical arrangement, with a Civil War colour and archaic language;

> At the foot of yon mountain, where the big river flows,
> there's a fond creation and a soft wind that blows.
> There lives a fair maiden, she's the one I adore.
> She's the one I will marry on the Red River shore.

... is the opening couplet, which right away explains the nineteenth-century colour; the Kingstons adapt the "Red River Shore" version as collected by the music historian John Lomax and recorded by The New Christy Minstrels (*Cowboys And Indians*, 1964), an adaptation of the time-honoured "New River Shore", of which the oldest version was indeed written down in 1864, during the Civil War. In all versions we find the text fragment Dylan eagerly saves for reuse:

> *She wrote me a letter, she wrote it so kind*
> *and in that letter these words you will find:*
> *Come back to me, darling, you're the one I adore,*
> *You're the one I will marry on the Red River shore.*

... the words Dylan will transfer during these very same recording sessions in Miami, January 1997, to that other Great Masterpiece, to "Not Dark Yet", also to the second verse:

> *She wrote me a letter and she wrote it so kind*
> *She put down in writing what was in her mind*

"All these songs are connected. Don't be fooled. I just opened up a different door in a different kind of way. It's just different, saying the same thing," as Dylan says in his brilliant MusiCares speech, February 2015.

For his own "Red River Shore", Dylan radically changes the plot. The Kingston Trio tells of the woman who so badly wants to marry the protagonist, but her father forbids it. The narrator wants to elope with his fair maiden, but Dad sees through it and awaits him with a private army of 24. With his six-shooter, the hero tries to fight his way through ("*six men were wounded and seven were down*"), but then he has to give up: "I can't fight an army of twenty and four / when I'm bound for my true love on the Red River shore."

Which may seem a bit excessive, twenty-four enemies, but compared to his predecessor in the original 1864 version of "New River Shore", he is still a pathetic sissy:

He raised for him an army   *He drew out his sword*   *And the rest of the number*
Of sixty and four   *And he waved it around*   *Lay bleeding in gore,*
To fight her old father   *Till twenty and four*   *And gained his own true love*
On the New River shore.   *Lay dead on the ground*   *On the New River shore.*

Somethin' else, indeed.

II   The importance of capturing spontaneity

"The great thing about the really great songwriters, is that the great songs, the really magic ones, they play themselves. There's very little question about what you're supposed to do. I love that when it happens. And Bob has done that over the years to a great extent, with a great variety of musicians."

That's what Jim Keltner says when, in Uncut's *Tell Tale Signs Special* (2008), he reminisces for the umpteenth time about one of his earliest recording sessions with Dylan, about "Knockin' On Heaven's Door" in 1973 ("I actually cried while we were recording it"). He tells it as an introduction to his story about recording "Red River Shore": "And that particular song, it was one of those really beautiful Bob moments: a great song, and he sang it really beautifully."

He is not the only session musician who is a fan, and who is disappointed that the song is not selected for *Time Out Of Mind*. Veteran keyboardist Jim Dickinson thinks it's "the best thing we recorded", and guitarist Duke Robillard is equally unequivocal: "I was mesmerised by it, completely blown away."

Dickinson is the only one who seeks some kind of explanation as for why Dylan passes over the song for the album. He is familiar with the bard's reputation ("Dylan is notorious for leaving off what appears to be the best one") and through a casual remark from Dylan he understands that "Red River Shore" has been tried many times before (engineer Chris Shaw reveals that there are four versions):

> "One of the things you really don't want to hear on a record is boredom. And, while, certainly, no one was bored by playing with Bob Dylan, once they did fall into playing repetitious parts, I think that had that same effect on him."

He does recognise it. Dickinson has worked with Alex Chilton, as a producer both for his solo album *Like Flies on Sherbert* (1979) and for the last record of the legendary Big Star, *Third* (1974): "After you did a song with Alex three or four times, he was past it."

And Keith Richards (Dickinson plays piano on "Wild Horses") has the same short span, has the real fire only in the moment of creation; "Keith Richards said, that's where the song comes alive, the first performance." More detailed, and infectiously, he recounts his three-day recording experience with *Sticky Fingers* in an interview for *ArtistHouseMusic*, shortly before his death in 2009;

"But the thing that I learned... what we did was the same thing every day. Insert the artist. Hamburger production. Assembly line. Lines, patterns, forms... insert the artist. Play it till it's right. I been on cut 132 with Aretha Franklin, I mean: play it till it's right. That was the way I thought you made a record. And here's The Rolling Stones. As they take literally the first cut they get through without a major mistake. Nobody says the words "should we do that again, can we do that better, why don't you do this, why you don't that..." those words were not spoken in three days. When they got to do a cut without a major mistake, Charlie Watts got up from the drums and, by God, it was over. And I'm sitting there and I'm thinking, well, this is certainly not the way we make records – who do you suppose is right here? I think maybe it's them. So I learned spontaneity, the importance of capturing spontaneity."

Dickinson asks Richards about it and Keef confirms that they really do it like this all the time. "We take the first performance, as we write the song. You know, you capture the moment of spontaneity and creation. The only problem is, when we go on the road I gotta learn all this stuff over."

It might be an explanation. And Jim Dickinson is no nitwit, of course. He is the man Dylan describes in his *Theme Time Radio Hour* as that *magical musical maestro from Memphis*, "the kind of guy you could call to play piano, fix a tractor, or make red cole slaw from scratch." And this magical musical maestro thinks "Red River Shore" is *the best thing we recorded*, calling the recording *amazing* and the song *remarkable*. Still, Jim's guess as to why Dylan rejects "Red River Shore", *bored by playing repetitious parts*, doesn't seem entirely conclusive. Apart from those four versions of "Red River Shore", Dylan also records a very long version of "Highlands", three versions of "Can't Wait" and three versions of "Mississippi"... Dylan's patience and stamina don't seem to be too bad these days.

Surely the music cannot be a problem either. The musical accompaniment of both versions we know (of *Tell Tale Signs*) is, as Dickinson also implies, beyond criticism. Well, obviously; Augie Meyers, Duke Robillard, Jim Keltner, Bob Dylan, Jim Dickinson, Bucky Baxter... in the studio there's an A-team of musicians with a grand total of about 200 years of experience at Premier League level - these guys could have made a good song out of "Driftin' Too Far From Shore" even on a bad day. The sound then, perhaps? Yes, the #2 on Disc 3 of *Tell Tale Signs*, the version with the even stronger Tex-Mex colour and Dylan's voice "drier" and mixed a bit further back, does have a different sound, but the first version, on Disc 1, is not at all that far away from the sound of *Time Out Of Mind*.

The lyrics then. Maybe the master is still dissatisfied with the lyrics – kind of how he explained the rejection of "Blind Willie McTell" at the time; because the song was "not finished". Possible. True, the lyrics do seem somewhat aimless. But on the other hand, it has more than enough gems to overcome something as debatable as "lack of direction". The opening, for starters, has a classic, cast-iron poetic power;

> *Some of us turn off the lights and we live*
> *In the moonlight shooting by*
> *Some of us scare ourselves to death in the dark*
> *To be where the angels fly*
> *Pretty maids all in a row lined up*
> *Outside my cabin door*
> *I've never wanted any of 'em wanting me*
> *'Cept the girl from the Red River shore*

Already looks like one of the great songs, the really magic ones, the ones that play themselves.

III   Pretty angels all flying in a row

The song does indeed start a bit undylanesque, a bit pre-war. An opening with such an aphoristic, moralistic reflection is not uncommon with Heine or Brecht, from parables and Christian lyricism, and from antique ballads altogether, but so far Dylan deemed it too old-fashioned. True, the archaic, slightly edifying-sounding introduction "some of us..." has been used twice in his catalogue, but both times at the end of the song, in the classical way, to express an overarching, concluding moral in the final couplet. Both times also quite similar in content, by the way. Both in "Walls Of Red Wing" (*Some of us'll end up in St. Cloud Prison, and some of us'll wind up to be lawyers and things*) and in "George Jackson (*Some of us are prisoners, the rest of us are guards*) to proclaim the cynical message that all of us are either victims of the system or enforcers of the system.

For "Red River Shore", Dylan moves the *some of us-*formula to the opening lines, but (fortunately) without a socio-critical undertone. It does foretell, though, a preachy, ethical morality; if the forthcoming lyrics turn out to be a ballad with a tragic life or love story, then we may expect some wise lesson – or so this aphoristic opening seems to promise. And then one as might be distilled from Oscar Wilde's famous aphorism, from "We are all in the gutter, but some of us are looking at the stars."

Semantically it is only a small step to Dylan's "Some of us turn off the lights and we live in the moonlight shooting by", and in terms of content it does seem to want to express approximately the same thing: we all are in the darkness, in the gutter, miserable, but comfort is to be found in beauty, something like that.

Wilde's aphorism, by the way, has completely detached itself from its original meaning. The quote comes from his first big hit, from his first comedy of society, from *Lady Windermere's Fan* (1892), is spoken by Lord Darlington and in the context of the dialogue means something like "all men are immoral bastards, but some can hide that very well behind charm". But freed from its context, the quote gains tremendously in poetic brilliance and depth, to be overshadowed perhaps only by that other perfect quote from *Lady Windermere*, "I can resist everything except temptation."

A first problem, and perhaps a first explanation of Dylan's apparent dissatisfaction with the song, is offered by these opening lines. *Some of us turn off the lights and we live in the moonlight shooting by*, as he seems to be singing, or *Some of us turn off the lights and we lay up in the moonlight shooting by*, as it says in the official *Lyrics* and on the website, is both semantically and poetically a bit weird - not to say just weak. "Moonlight shooting by"? All of us have the childhood memory of the night journey back home in the car, pleasantly warm and safe in the backseat, while the light of the street lamps shoots by. But the poet probably does not want to evoke this association. Nor, we may assume, anything like the Star Wars Stormtroopers shooting with light and missing all the time.

Comparably problematic is the next, equally aphoristic, metaphor: "Some of us scare ourselves to death in the dark / To be where the angels fly." This time not only semantically and poetically, but now syntactically a confusing mess as well. "We frighten ourselves, and very much so, in order to dwell in a place where celestial beings flutter around"? – it is hard to understand this particular sequence of words in any other way. Well alright, through laborious detours and with acceptance of cheap symbolism, something like "we live a cramped life in ignorance, for fear of not being admitted to Heaven's Kingdom," or something like that could be extracted - but that would be a very pathetic moral to accompany the coming, sad lost-love lament about the Red River Girl.

No, it actually seems as if Dylan is seeking his 1965 form, his *sound-over-meaning* mode, as if Dylan tries to do "consciously what I used to do unconsciously," as he says in 1978 Matt Damsker interview. And as he, in a variation, a few years after "Red River Shore" will repeat in the *CBS "60 Minutes" special* interview with Ed Bradley (2004):

> BD: I don't know how I got to write those songs.
> EB: What do you mean you don't know how?
> BD: All those early songs were almost magically written. Ah...
> "Darkness at the break of noon, shadows even the silver spoon,
> a handmade blade, the child's balloon..." Well, try to sit down
> and write something like that.

So, stylistically at most, this somewhat strange opening to "Red River Shore" is still Dylanesque in a way. We see a familiar stylistic feature, the surprising metaphor, the stylistic device that Dylan seems to use more consciously as the years go by. The poetic brilliance of a metaphor like *to be where the angels fly* may be debatable - and rigid Christian interpreters probably deny that it is meant metaphorically at all. And maybe a playful Dylan is only incorporating a playful nod to the Meat Puppets song played so smashingly by Nirvana in 1994 during the *MTV Unplugged session*, "Lakes Of Fire";

> *Where do bad folks go when they die?*
> *They don't go to heaven where the angels fly*
> *They go to the lake of fire and fry*
> *Won't see them again 'till the fourth of July*
> *I knew a lady who came from Duluth*
> *Bit by a dog with a rabid tooth*
> *She went to her grave just a little too soon*
> *And flew away howling on the yellow moon*

... but the *flying angels* metaphor is surprising anyway. With the same surprising power as *the whole world got me pinned up against the fence* in "'Til I Fell In Love With You", for example, or *my soul has turned into steel* in "Not Dark Yet". Or, for that matter, *shadowing a silver spoon*. But without the relevance that the metaphors in these other *Time Out Of Mind* songs have. At least, a bridge to the following *Pretty maids all in a row lined up outside my cabin door* is completely opaque.

In June 2020, when Douglas Brinkley interviews Dylan for the New York Times and asks about the Eagles reference in "Murder Most Foul", the *pretty maids*-verse retroactively takes on a different connotation;

> *Your mention of Don Henley and Glenn Frey on "Murder Most Foul" came off as a bit of a surprise to me. What Eagles songs do you enjoy the most?*
>
> *"New Kid in Town," "Life in the Fast Lane," "Pretty Maids All in a Row." That could be one of the best songs ever.*

Until that remarkable outpouring in 2020, the verse seemed an unspectacular derivation - from the eighteenth-century nursery rhyme "Mary" perhaps;

> *Mary, Mary, quite contrary,*
> *How does your garden grow?*
> *With silver bells and cockle shells,*
> *And pretty maids all in a row.*

... but a connection with Joe Walsh's atypical contribution to *Hotel California* seemed a bit absurd. And still isn't too obvious, really. *Melancholy* is a common denominator, but the line to "Red River Shore" is not much thicker than that. Which doesn't matter to Walsh, of course. Two months after that New York Times interview, fellow composer Joe Vitale tells *Rolling Stone* what an impression Dylan's words make:

> "Coming from Bob Dylan, it doesn't get any better than that. I called Joe immediately. And he goes, 'I know what you're calling about.' I said, 'This is so cool, Joe.' He was excited, too. He thought that was really cool. I printed out that article and framed it."

It was like, Joe means to say, to be where the angels fly.

IV I got a gal named Sue

> *Well, I sat by her side and for a while I tried*
> *To make that girl my wife*
> *She gave me her best advice when she said*
> *"Go home and lead a quiet life."*
> *Well, I've been to the east and I've been to the west*
> *And I've been out where the black winds roar*
> *Somehow, though, I never did get that far*
> *With the girl from the Red River shore*

In 2012, Rolling Stone publishes its list of the 500 Greatest Albums Of All Time and at no. 50 is *Here's Little Richard* from 1957. The eulogy ends with a stately certification: "*Tutti Frutti* still has the most inspired rock lyric on record: *A wop bop alu bop, a wop bam boom!*" Five years earlier, Mojo Magazine was even more enthusiastic. In June 2007, a panel of self-proclaimed experts compiles "Big Bangs: 100 Records That Changed the World" and "Tutti Frutti" is number 1 (*The Freewheelin' Bob Dylan* is 4, "Like A Rolling Stone" 17).

It is - naturally - a defensible choice. But if legendary producer Bumps Blackwell had been a little braver, or a little less commercial, he would have kept the original lyrics - which are truly a *most inspired rock lyric* and probably a few degrees more world-changing. In Charles White's *The Life and Times of Little Richard - The Authorised Biography by Little Richard* from 1984, the man himself tells the story:

> "I'd been singing *Tutti Frutti* for years, but it never struck me as a song you'd record. I didn't go to New Orleans to record no *Tutti Frutti*. Sure, it used to crack the crowds up when I sang it in the clubs, with those risqué lyrics: *Tutti Frutti, good booty/If it don't fit, don't force it/You can grease it, make it easy...* But I never thought it would be a hit, even with the lyrics cleaned up."

... and in the next verse the lyrics are no less "risqué", just as clearly the words of an excited homosexual man:

> *Tutti Frutti, good booty*
> *If it's tight, it's all right*
> *And if it's greasy, it makes it easy*

No, thinks Bumps Blackwell. First, he worries about Little Richard's appearance;

"He was so far out! His hair was processed a foot high over his
head. His shirt was so loud it looked as though he had drunk
raspberry juice, cherryade, malt, and greens and then thrown
up all over himself. Man, he was a freak"

... and then he let Dorothy LaBostrie clean up the text and partly
rewrite it to the less scabrous lyrics with which Little Richard would
change the world just as much. The Beatles, Chuck Berry, The
Stones, Elvis... all recognise the song's primal power. And up in the
High North, in Hibbing, "Tutti Frutti" hits the radio in November
1955 as well, crushing the young Bobby Zimmerman. On the so-
called *John Bucklen Tape* from 1958, the oldest tape recording of
Dylan making music, we hear a musical declaration of love, "Hey
Little Richard", in the first seconds, and further on how the
seventeen-year-old Bobby passionately puts his hero on a pedestal:
"Elvis copied all the Richard songs - *Rip It Up, Long Tall Sally, Ready
Teddy*, err – what's the other one..."

"The other one" is, of course, "Tutti Frutti" - it is clear that
the young Zimmerman by now has *Here's Little Richard* in his
record box. And that the songs have ingrained themselves in the
receptive brain of the adolescent. Echoes of *Long Tall Sally* can be
heard in "Subterranean Homesick" and in "Tombstone Blues",
Slippin' And Slidin' leaves traces in "Tom Thumb's Blues", and in the
Basement Little Richard's spirit hovers over enough fragments (*Rip
It Up* and *Ready Teddy* in "Tiny Montgomery", for instance).

And here, in 1997 we hear another slice of *Tutti Frutti*:

I got a gal, named Sue,
She knows just what to do.
I've been to the east, I've been to the west,
But she's the gal that I love the best.

"I've been to the east and I've been to the west" is deeply implanted in Dylan's memoria musica. The first incisions are done by Little Richard, and when Dylan immerses himself a few years later in Woody Guthrie, Pete Seeger, old folk songs and The Carter Family, the word order gets fixed. "John Hardy", for example, has also always been somewhere at the front of his inner jukebox;

> *I've been to the East and I've been to the West*
> *I've traveled this wide world around*
> *I've been to that river and I've been baptized*
> *So take me to my burying ground*

... as well as one of the founding fathers of American ballads and folk songs, "Reuben's Train";

> *I've been to the East, I've been to the West*
> *I'm going where the chilly winds don't blow*
> *Oh me, oh my I'm going where the chilly winds don't blow*

With which Dylan, by using that one classic line, comes pretty close to how he describes his early songs in 1984: "I crossed Sonny Terry with the Stanley Brothers with Roscoe Holcombe with Big Bill Broonzy with Guthrie... all the stuff that was dear to me."

The rest of the verse, the surrounding lines, suggest that with "Red River Shore", Dylan consciously, and perhaps somewhat forcefully, tries to return to precisely this method. *To make that girl my wife* is another formulaic line that has been around for centuries in broadside ballads, folk songs and variations of "Pretty Peggy-O", the song Dylan recorded back in '62. In the age-old "The Bonnie Woods o' Hatton" for instance;

> *Ye comrades and companions, and all ye females dear,*
> *To my sad lamentations, I pray you lend an ear;*
> *There was once I lo'ed a bonnie lass, I lo'ed her as my life,*
> *And it was my whole intention to make her my wedded wife.*

... and in almost every arrangement of "Buffalo Gals" (Louisiana Gals, Bowery Gals, Philadelphia Gals, Alabama Gals, Round Town Girls, Midnight Serenade... the nineteenth-century song exists in dozens of variations);

> *She was de prettiest gal in de room.*
> *I am bound to make dat gal my wife*

According to Alan Lomax's American Ballads And Folk Songs, her name is Sue, by the way; "*I met a girl named Sue*. So just like Little Richard's "Tutti Frutti": *I got a gal named Sue, she knows just what to do* – "all these songs are connected," as Professor Dylan said in his MusiCares speech.

Anyway, "Red River Shore". The most beautiful line of this second verse, *and I've been out where the black winds roar*, seems to be a Dylan original. True, with a clear echo from "A Hard Rain's A-Gonna Fall", but as an image it is unusual in the art of song. At most recognisable to viewers of the Finnish Netflix series *Sorjonen* (English title: *Bordertown*). Over the credits of Episode 3 of the for now final Season Three, on 15 December 2019, fans like Stephen King suddenly hear an appealingly dated-sounding folk rocker with garage sound:

> *Black winds, take this soul of mine*
> *Take me to the dark below*
> *Lord, I want to die*
> *In the night, I killed my love*
> *Black winds, take away my life*
> *Oh, Lord, let me die*

... "Black Winds", an obscure 1965 single by an obscure band from Oregon, Little John and The Monks. Obscure enough, in any case, to have a place in Dylan's mythical inner jukebox. Very unlikely, though. But still.

V   Mom says the pills must be working

Well I knew when I first laid eyes on her
I could never be free
One look at her and I knew right away
She should always be with me
Well the dream dried up a long time ago
Don't know where it is anymore
True to life, true to me
Was the girl from the red river shore

Calvin and Hobbes, the brilliant comic strip by Bill Waterson, is one of the best and most successful newspaper comics of the twentieth century. Graphically often small masterpieces (Waterson had to fight for a long time to be allowed to deviate from the standard, obligatory panel format), infectious humour - as often hilarious as it is sardonic and moving - great acting by all the characters both mimically and in terms of body language, and a wealth of highly quotable, intelligent one-liners ("A good artist's statement says more than his art ever does").

Calvin has his adventures with his great friend Hobbes, a stuffed tiger who is only in Calvin's imagination a real tiger - well, a real anthropomorphic tiger, anyway. Bill Waterson does view this plot-driving feature in a more nuanced way, though:

> "The so-called "gimmick" of my strip — the two versions of Hobbes — is sometimes misunderstood. I don't think of Hobbes as a doll that miraculously comes to life when Calvin's around. Neither do I think of Hobbes as the product of Calvin's imagination. Calvin sees Hobbes one way, and everyone else sees Hobbes another way. I show two versions of reality, and

> each makes complete sense to the participant who sees it. I
> think that's how life works. None of us sees the world exactly
> the same way, and I just draw that literally in the strip. Hobbes
> is more about the subjective nature of reality than about dolls
> coming to life."

... in which Waterson seems to get a bit caught up in his apparent, and understandable, desire to be *the* authority on *Calvin and Hobbes*; he argues rather cumbersomely that Calvin has his own version of reality, which is different from "everyone else's" reality. Which, of course, is a rather laborious way of saying "vivid imagination". Or, less innocently: "hallucinations". Waterson has, after all, already opened Schrödinger's box, and is past the point where he could claim that Hobbes can be simultaneously both alive and not-alive.

On 31 December 1995, ten years after the launch date, the very last *Calvin and Hobbes* appears, to the chagrin of millions of fans. It is an open ending. A melancholy, moody Sunday comic strip in colour, in which Calvin and Hobbes sled down the hill in the last panel, while Calvin exclaims: "Let's go exploring!"

"I believe I've done what I can do within the constraints of daily deadlines and small panels," Waterson writes in his farewell letter, and he never changes his mind.

The loss and the emptiness are still felt today and are countered by dozens of rip-offs, copies, unofficial continuations and loving fan-art. All build on the "gimmick" that Hobbes exists only in Calvin's imagination. The best, and usually most respectful rip-offs try to provide the series with a "real", closed ending. And the most successful of these is from an anonymous artist who uses a classic staging. Calvin is sitting at the kitchen table doing his homework. Hobbes is surprised. "You're working on your report already? It's not due til Tuesday!" "Yeah, I know," says Calvin, without looking up, "Mom says the pills must be working." It's snowing, says Hobbes, "and I thought, maybe... we could..." Now Calvin looks up for a moment. "Sorry, what? I wasn't listening. I really have to finish this." In the last picture, Hobbes is a stuffed tiger and Calvin is at work. In contrast to the three colourful ones before it, the panel is entirely in shades of grey.

But most artistic fans choose the "years later" variant, in which an adult Calvin holds his old stuffed tiger, wistfully realising that *the dream dried up a long time ago*.

The third stanza of "Red River Shore" seems to give away where the songwriter wanted to go with his song. "Dream", "True to me"... a narrator who, looking back, misses his imaginary lover, his hallucination perhaps. And it is fitting that the songwriter paves the way there with clichés, paraphrases and nods to old folksongs, those old songs *full of legend, myth, bible and ghosts*, as Dylan says in an interview - after all, he wants to express the melancholy of the man who longs for something he never had.

In previous stanzas we have heard echoes of "John Hardy" and "Buffalo Gals", the old "Red River Shore" and "Bonnie Woods" and "Mary" and whatnot, and here in this third stanza the songwriter persists; slalomming along fragments of mainly country classics, it seems. Hank Williams' "Be Careful of Stones That You Throw" and "Howlin' at the Moon", Charley Pride's "Please Help Me I'm Falling", Peggy Lee's "My Heart Stood Still", Marty Robbins... with a bit of cutting and pasting, the entire third verse, with its ingrained word combinations like "one look at you", "I could never be free" and "I knew right away", can be constructed from the country section in Dylan's jukebox. With a short turn to Warren Zevon, whom Dylan admired: *from the first time I laid eyes on her I knew that she'd be mine* from "Jeannie Needs A Shooter", another "New River Shore"-like song about a fatal crush on a girl whose trigger-happy father keeps the narrator away from his daughter;

The bard ignores a characterological problem along the way. The romantic, swooning *I knew when I first laid eyes on her I could never be free* is followed by the slightly threatening, stalkerish *One look at her and I knew right away she should always be with me*. In keeping with the tone and character of the narrator, of course it should have been: *I should always be with her*. But then, that doesn't rhyme. And you want your songs to sound good.

The suggestion that the narrator is wondering whether his memories of the Girl from the Red River Shore are *constructed memories*, memories of a fantasy with an imaginary pretty girl, is first suggested by the ambiguous *the dream dried up a long time ago*. The admission that he doesn't even know *where it is anymore* reinforces that suggestion, and the wistful *true to life, true to me* seems to seal it. "True to me" is clear enough, and "true to life" is a remarkable choice of words. "True to life", not "true to facts", that is. Dylan himself uses the phrase several times in interviews as well as in his autobiography *Chronicles*, and always to express the power of folk music. To explain the magic of "I Dreamed I Saw Joe Hill", for example, and less specific about folk music in general:

"It was so real, so more true to life than life itself. It was life magnified. Folk music was all I needed to exist."

... which, coincidentally probably, is also very similar to the words with which Odysseus praises the song of the blind bard Demodocus: "Surely the Muse has taught you, Zeus's daughter, or god Apollo himself. How true to life, all too true ..." (in the translation by Fagles, 1996).

Odysseus cannot hold back his tears when he hears Demodocus sing about the past. Dylan's hero is not far off either.

VI   Misery is but the shadow of happiness

Well I'm wearing the cloak of misery
And I've tasted jilted love
And the frozen smile upon my face
Fits me like a glove
But I can't escape from the memory
Of the one I'll always adore
All those nights when I lay in the arms
Of the girl from the red river shore

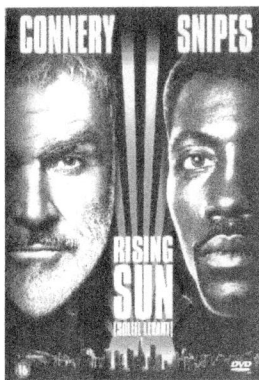

In *Overwatch*, Blizzard Entertainment's most successful multiplayer first-person shooter game, we hear it again, spoken by the Japanese fighting hero Hanzo: "If you sit by the river long enough, you will see the body of your enemy floating by." Presumably copied from the fairly successful crime thriller *Rising Sun* (1993), in which Sean Connery plays a former police captain, John Connor, expert on Japanese affairs. Throughout the film, "Connor-san" sprinkles ancient Japanese wisdom and proverbs, and towards the end of the film there is an appropriate moment to throw in the *floating corpse* aphorism. And the scriptwriter, in turn, presumably took it from James Clavell's bestseller *Shōgun* (1975), where it is also presented as a "Japanese wisdom".

Just as often it is attributed to - of course - Sun Tzu, to *The Art Of War*, and the Most Erudite Man of the Western World, Umberto Eco, muddies the already murky waters further in the Postscript to *The Name Of The Rose* (1980): "But there is an Indian proverb that goes, 'Sit on the bank of a river and wait: your enemy's corpse will soon float by'."

Enough confusion, all in all, to drive Western sinologists in particular to a mild state of frenzy. Especially since the original *Chinese* - not Japanese - wisdom is a completely unsuccessful translation of Confucius; "The time is passing like a river running day and night," is the best approximate translation - the Chinese characters for *passing time* can be understood as *passed away*, *deceased*, and from there a well-meaning, but slightly too creative translator went wrong. In any case, Confucius does not speak at all of *floating corpses*.

The beautiful metaphor *wearing a cloak of misery* has a similar life cycle. Throughout the centuries, it has been attributed to literary gifted journalists (New York Times reporter Paul Montgomery, 1968), to nineteenth-century Polish authorities warning against *dziady*, criminal beggars who swindle respectable citizens *"under the cloak of misery"*, to French composer Gabriel Fauré ("*Je ne me sense plus qu'un affreux manteau de misère et de découragement sur les épaules* - I feel that there is on my shoulders nothing more than a terrible cloak of misery and discouragement," from a letter dated August 1903, discussing his encroaching deafness), and whatnot. And to Dylan, of course.

However, the source is as old as that floating corpse: Confucius' colleague and contemporary Lao Tze. It may comfort the easily appalled sinologists that the quotation has survived more than twenty-five centuries undamaged:

> *Misery is but the shadow of happiness*
> *Happiness is but the cloak of misery*

... from the immortal *Tao Te Ching*, the most important writing of Taoism, *The Book Of The Simple Way*.

Still, it's not very likely that the songwriter Dylan, leafing through the *Tao Te Ching*, put a tick in the margin here. This whole fourth verse seems, after three verses full of country and folk clichés, a deliberate attempt to leave the Simple Way, and to take a turn to the narrow, thorny path. So: not *I'm feeling blue*, but *I'm wearing the cloak of misery*. Not: *my baby left me*, but *I've tasted jilted love*. And not: *I'll remember you*, but *I can't escape from the memory of the one I'll always adore*.

All right, that last line may have a vague echo of Hank Thompson's "I Cast A Lonely Shadow", which, not only because of its lyrics, but also because of its sound, could be a candidate for a place on Dylan's *Time Out Of Mind*;

> *I sit and watch the candle and the flicker of the flame*
> *My writhing shadow twists and turns as though it is in pain*
> *I'm trying to escape the memory my mind recalls*
> *And I cast a lonesome shadow on these lonely, lonely walls*

...and, of course, *"jilted love"* and variants with "jilted" can also be found in Dylan's jukebox. In Freddie King's "Woman Across The

River", for instance (1974, with a band, incidentally, consisting only of Dylan disciples: Jim Keltner, Leon Russel and Carl Radle). Or, to stay more in the Hank Thompson mood, Red Foley's "Jilted" (also a hit for Teresa Brewer in 1954). Even more attractive, though, is the idea that Dylan was inspired by his art brother Heinrich Heine, one of the greatest Jewish poets of the 19th century;

> *Wandere!*
> *Wenn dich ein Weib verraten hat,*
> *So liebe flink eine andre;*
> *Noch besser wär es, du ließest die Stadt*
> *Schnüre den Ranzen und wandre!*

> Away!
> If by one woman thou'rt jilted, love
> Another, and so forget her ;
> To pack up thy knapsack, and straight remove
> From the town will still be better

The same goes for the Cole Porter-like *the frozen smile upon my face fits me like a glove*. Poetic and *so visual*, as Dylan would say, and not too hackneyed. The formidable Etta James snarls a *frozen smile* (in the funky "Power Play"), and Dylan may have made a mental note when listening to the overly ambitious "The Modern Adventures of Plato, Diogenes and Freud" that his faithful organist Al Kooper wrote for the debut album of Blood, Sweat & Tears in 1968;

> *And the clock on the wall is a bore*
> *As you wander past the door*
> *And find him lying on the floor*
> *As he begs you for some more,*
> *you frozen smile*

... where the poet Dylan will at least notice the unusual AAAAB rhyme scheme, that he himself once used for "Love Is Just A Four-Letter Word". But the loudest association, and probably also a trigger for Dylan, is the evergreen "Behind A Painted Smile" (1968) by the indestructible Isley Brothers, who have now entered their eighth decade. With a protagonist who deals with adversity in a tougher way than Dylan's protagonist does: *"If I can't have your love, I don't need your sympathy."*

However, too thin all of it, to be worthy of the honourable label "paraphrase". And that *cloak of misery* is an absolutely unusual metaphor in the art of song. No, the song poet Dylan has now sat on the bank long enough, watching the river flow, has seen all kinds of wreckage float by, and now takes a turn to the narrow, thorny path.

VII   Please try to make it rhyme

Well we're living in the shadows of a fading past
Trapped in the fires of time
I've tried not to ever hurt anybody
And to stay out of the life of crime
And when it's all been said and done
I never did know the score
One more day is another day away
From the girl from the red river shore

Cosmologists will agree. Before the Big Bang there was an endless, timeless Nothing, then a brief flash of light, gravity, sulphur storms, atoms, C-beams glittering in the dark near the Tannhäuser Gate and event horizons, and after this brief flash, the flash in which we exist, the All shrinks back to a singularity and there will be an endless, eternal Nothing again. Nothingness without any Something, so also without matter, time or light. Nabokov puts it a little more simplified: "Life is just one small piece of light between two eternal darknesses," and Dylan a little more poetically: "We're trapped in the fires of time."

This fifth stanza of Dylan's "Red River Shore" illustrates (finally) that the song is a *Time Out Of Mind* song. After the *New Morning* rhetoric of the first verse, the *Freewheelin'* imagery of the second, the *Nashville Skyline* clichés of the third, and the *Street-Legal* poetry of the fourth, we're back to the world-weariness of "Standing In The Doorway", the melancholy of "Not Dark Yet", the despondency of "Cold Irons Bound". Just take the opening line.

"Living in the shadows of a fading past" is a great, classic line with which Dylan announces in eight words the overarching theme of his twenty-first-century oeuvre. It echoes *À la recherche du temps perdu* and Neil Young's Dylanesque gem "Time Fades Away", the old protest song "Which Side Are You On?" (*are we living in the shadow of slavery*) and Original Sin, it has the couleur of every film noir between *The Maltese Falcon* and *Touch Of Evil*, and it would have been an even nicer album title than *Time Out Of Mind*.

Classical, almost archaic beauty - though therefore not too original. All the stronger hits the subsequent image, *trapped in the fires of time*.

"Fires of Time" is a rather unusual image. Which is remarkable, really - after all, it's a not too far-fetched, extremely strong and very visual metaphor to express the destructive power of Time. It has the potential to trigger a plethora of related metaphors with *burning*, *heat*, *flames* and *smoke*, with the added bonus of the religious, autumnal connotation of *ashes to ashes*. But Dylan resists that temptation - this one, remarkable *trapped in the fires of time* remains unexplored, and colleagues don't pick it up either after this. Yes, a single exception like The Bellamy Brothers song makes an attempt. Little successful, unfortunately - their "The Fires Of Time" (on *The Anthology, Vol. 1*, 2009) is a somewhat overcooked throwaway with a tiresome enumeration of historical milestones á la Billy Joel's "We Didn't Start The Fire", but full of stylistic embarrassments ("*The Roman Empire fell, they found some dinosaur bones*"). And with a modest salute:

> *From Buddy Holly to Hendrix*
> *From Haggard to Jones*
> *From Elvis to Dylan*
> *From The Beatles to The Stones*
> *Well, the guitars twang*
> *And the poetry rhyme*
> *And they rocked our world*
> *Right through the Fires of Time*

... with some awkwardly mixed away, presumably Hendrixesque-meant guitar fury after "*Hendrix*", and ditto, presumably Dylanesque-meant harmonica honking after "*Dylan*".

The Bellamys are forgiven - they have given the world "Let Your Love Flow" and "If I Said You Had A Beautiful Body Would You Hold It Against Me", so they can do whatever they like. And in their defence: Dylan doesn't do any better with *fires of time* either.

The remainder of this fifth stanza, after that intriguing and potentially fruitful opening, is disappointingly flat - and stylistically rather weak, if we are honest. *I've tried not to ever hurt anybody and to stay out of the life of crime* is a bumpy verse line with clichés nonchalantly pasted together, and the following *And when it's all been said and done I never did know the score* is of the same ilk (though less bumpy). It even comes awfully close to *filler lyrics*; as if the song poet has already designed the beautiful closing line *One more day is another day away from the girl from the red river shore*, and for now just bridges the road thereto with rather haphazard grab finds from his inner jukebox.

I've tried not to ever hurt anybody has a somewhat alienating "John Wesley Harding" echo, for example (*he was never known to hurt an honest man*), although it is quite likely that Dylan has long since forgotten that song. Oh well, he knows the word combination from dozens of other songs too, of course. Charley Pride could, after borrowing *I could never be free* in the third verse, be a candidate supplier again (from "You're So Good When You're Bad", his no.2 hit from 1982). But another Nashville Cat probably appeals more to Dylan;

> *So let me say this, I never tried to hurt anybody*
> *Though I guess there's a few, that I still couldn't look in the eye*
> *If I've got one wish, I hope it rains at my funeral*
> *For once, I'd like to be the only one dry*

... the bittersweet, funny "I Hope It Rains At My Funeral" from 1971. By Tom T. Hall, who is so wittily dismissed by Dylan in his 2015 MusiCares Speech. He recalls reading an interview in which Tom was "bitching about" a James Taylor song. Coincidentally, Dylan tells, he was just listening to a song by Tom T. Hall on the radio; "I Love" - indeed a quite corny, über-sentimental drag of a song;

> "Now listen, I'm not ever going to disparage another songwriter. I'm not going to do that. I'm not saying it's a bad song. I'm just saying it might be a little overcooked. But, you know, it was in the top 10 anyway."

Still, he does quote effortlessly half the lyrics - and Tom T. Hall's name is of course also under "I Washed My Face In The Morning Dew" and especially the successful "Ode to Billie Joe" rip-off "Harper Valley P.T.A.", so *The Storyteller* probably does have some credit with Dylan.

Somewhere in that same corner of that inner jukebox, Dylan also finds the other clichés, or so it seems. *When it's all been said and done* we know from a hundred songs, and if Dylan's muse indeed does hang around in the country corner at the moment, then it may have been lifted from Charlie Rich's "Who Will The Next Fool Be" - or picked up via Jimmie Davis' evergreen "It Makes No Difference Now" (recorded by everyone from Gene Autry to Willie Nelson and from Fats Domino to Merle Haggard, but the ultimate version is Ray Charles's). Although Dylan himself will attribute this particular line to Buddy Holly's "I'm Gonna Love You Too";

> "Buddy Holly. You know, I don't really recall exactly what I said about Buddy Holly, but while we were recording [*Time Out Of Mind*], every place I turned there was Buddy Holly. You know what I mean? It was one of those things. Every place you turned. You walked down a hallway and you heard Buddy Holly records, like "That'll Be the Day." Then you'd get in the car to go over to the studio and "Rave On" would be playing. Then you'd walk into this studio and someone's playing a cassette of "It's so Easy". And this would happen day after day after day. Phrases of Buddy Holly songs would just come out of nowhere. It was spooky. But after we recorded and left, you know, it stayed in our minds. Well, Buddy Holly's spirit must have been someplace, hastening this record."
> (Murray Engleheart interview for *Guitar World*, 1998)

"Phrases of Buddy Holly songs would just come out of nowhere." And then Elvis probably does supply *I never knew the score* (from Lonnie Donegan's "I'll Never Fall in Love Again"). Or a dozen other songs, of course; the phrase is as generic as *the life of crime* in the verse line before. It is tempting, though, to think that Dylan subconsciously is revealing a secret love for the immortal Mose Allison there, and for his superior "Your Mind Is On Vacation";

> *You're quoting figures, you're dropping names*
> *You're telling stories about the dames*
> *You're always laughin' when things ain't funny*
> *You try to sound like you're big money*
> *If talk was criminal, you'd lead a life of crime*
> *Because your mind is on vacation and your mouth is*
> *Working overtime*

... not a very likely scenario, no. But *if* so, Dylan must have taken the last line to heart: "If you must keep talking please try to make it rhyme".

VIII   He is no one

> *Well I'm a stranger here in a strange land*
> *But I know this is where I belong*

According to legend, Sean Lennon, John and Yoko's son, triggered the song. In 1989, Sean visits Billy Joel in the studio, they got talking and Sean complains about the misery of our time, AIDS and wars and crises, and how hard it is to be 21 in this day and age. Ah yes, says Joel, we felt the same when we were 21. "Yeah, but at least when you were a kid," counters Sean, "you grew up in the fifties, when nothing happened." Do you really believe that, asks the Piano Man in surprise. Korean War, the Hungarian Uprising, the Little Rock Nine... a lot of stuff happened. I don't know anything about it, Sean answers. *I have to write about this*, Joel thinks, I have to explain to Sean's generation that this kind of *epic struggle* is of all times.

> "The chain of news events and personalities came easily—mostly they just spilled out of my memory as fast as I could scribble them down," says Billy. "I had a chord progression that originally belonged to a country song I was trying to write, and I sandwiched the words into those chords—'Harry Truman, Doris Day,' okay, so far so good—but then I didn't know what to call the song, and therefore what words to use in the chorus."

Something with "fire", anyway. *Rolling Stone* publisher Jann Wenner drops by the studio these same days and disapproves of both Dancing Through the Fire ("*that sucks*") and Waltzing Through The Fire. In the end, Jann thinks "We Didn't Start The Fire" is cool. The lyrics are a recapitulation of 118 events, loaded names, controversial films and influential books, interspersed with the now-familiar chorus, and it becomes a No. 1 hit. Not really one of Joel's great masterpieces, but at least more sincere and exciting than the bland "The Fires Of Time" by The Bellamy Brothers.

Looking back, Joel is not too proud of the song either;

> "Even I realized I hated the melody. It was horrendous, as I said at the time; it was like a droning mosquito. What does the song really mean? Is it an apologia for the baby boomers? No, it's not. It's just a song that says the world's a mess. It's always been a mess, it's always going to be a mess."
> (Fred Schruers - *Billy Joel. The Definitive Biography*, 2014)

Still, the song has a value. The *Scholastic Weekly* uses the lyrics as a teaching aid, and indeed, Sean's generation now does see the 1950s a bit more nuanced, with less rose-tinted glasses.

And just like in "The Fires Of Time", Dylan comes along in "We Didn't Start The Fire" as a historical landmark;

> *Hemingway, Eichmann, "Stranger in a Strange Land"*
> *Dylan, Berlin, Bay of Pigs invasion*
> *"Lawrence of Arabia", British Beatlemania*
> *Ole Miss, John Glenn, Liston beats Patterson*
> *Pope Paul, Malcolm X, British politician sex*
> *JFK – blown away, what else do I have to say?*

... when Joel, in his - almost chronological - enumeration, has arrived at the 1960s. Between Hemingway's suicide, the Eichmann trial, the construction of the Berlin Wall and the Bay of Pigs Invasion - so we are in 1961, the year Dylan scored his record deal. And the year in which the infamous "Stranger In A Strange Land" was published, the overwhelming socio-critical science fiction novel by Robert Heinlein.

Bowie didn't like it ("It was a staggeringly, awesomely trite book"), but the novel is on the bookshelf of the front fighters from the sixties scenes, as David McGowan shows in his wonderful book *Weird Scenes Inside The Canyon* (2020). Zappa is a fan, as are Gene Clark, Grace Slick, Charles Manson, Jim Morrison and David Crosby, to name but a few. Heinlein himself lives in Laurel Canyon (at 8775 Lookout Mountain Avenue) during those years, and not only his book, but he personally too lingers at the crossroads of revolution, hippie rock, avant garde and Hollywood.

It seems that Dylan is thinking of Heinlein's protagonist Valentine Michael Smith when he opens the sixth verse of his "Red River Shore" with the overused expression *stranger in a strange land*. The phrase itself, of course, has been around for 27 centuries or so (already spoken by Moses in Exodus 2:22, "And she bare him a son, and he called his name Gershom: for he said, I have been a stranger in a strange land", and Moses probably didn't get it from himself either), and is almost always used as Moses intended: to express displacement, literal non-home-ness and consequent discomfort. The feeling that even Bram Stoker's Count Dracula fears ("But a stranger in a strange land, he is no one"), the feeling that Mark Twain's Chinese alter ego Ah Song Hi incorporates into a letter home with words that we also hear in Dylan's "I Was Young When I Left Home": "I was to begin life a stranger in a strange land, without a friend, or a penny, or any clothes but those I had on my back" (*Not a shirt on my back, not a penny on my name*, sings *He-who-never-wrote-a-letter-to-his-home* in Dylan's song). Madonna ("Wash All Over Me"), Herman Melville, Pete Townshend, U2, journalists, Robbie Robertson (in the beautiful, atmospheric Lanois production "Somewhere Down The Crazy River"), Albert Camus and Sophocles... the expression is used gladly and often in all times in all corners of the cultural spectrum - and always to express that something or someone does not belong here.

But Heinlein's protagonist in *Stranger In A Strange Land*, Michael Smith, is a stranger who, as Dylan says, knows that *this is where he belongs*, here, on Earth. Michael is born aboard a spaceship on its way to Mars. The landing fails fatally and baby Michael is the only survivor. Raised by Martians, he is discovered twenty-five years later by a next, this time successful, Mars expedition and taken back to Earth. *He belongs here* - but remains an alien. About the situation Mowgli finds himself in when he goes to the village, how Tarzan feels like Lord Greystoke, the state of mind of the civilised savage John in *Brave New World* and of the surveyor K. in Kafka's *The Castle*: "But I know this is where I belong".

It is a beautiful, both poetic and Kafkaesque situation sketch, *stranger here in a strange land, but I know this is where I belong.* Uncanny and frustrating, meaningless and indeterminate; it is the existentialist version of an unrequited love - like the love for *a girl from the Red River shore.*

IX   A floating nothing

Well I'm a stranger here in a strange land
But I know this is where I belong
I'll ramble and gamble for the one I love
And the hills will give me a song
Though nothing looks familiar to me
I know I've stayed here before
Once a thousand nights ago
With the girl from the red river shore

It's a diesel, Dylan's lyrical engine. Today, anyway. It starts slowly and sputters, but is now almost at its optimum. After that wonderful opening full of alienation and melancholy, the engine sputters again, just for a second, and reluctantly produces one last filler. The unreal, dreamy atmosphere that the song poet evokes with the Kafkaesque *I'm a stranger here in a strange land but I know this is where I belong* evaporates at once with the introduction of a clichéd, earthy Rambling, Gambling Willie, the knave who indeed *rambled and gambled for the ones he loved* ("He supported all his children and all their mothers too"). A colourful protagonist, and a wonderful song - but a total miscast here.

Equally out of place is the meaningless, unrelated *And the hills will give me a song*. It's possible that the faltering engine seeks a shortcut via Bing Crosby ("The Singing Hills", 1940), or sputters past Rex Allen's "Song Of The Hills" from 1949. And if Dylan has a hidden drawer somewhere in which he keeps the ignored phenomenon of Kevin Coyne, we may owe the musical hills to one of his hidden treasures, to "Shangri-La" from 1976 (when the later Police star Andy Summers is still in Coyne's band, demonstrating his crushing talent);

> *Shangri-La is a million miles away*
> *You might see it on a clear blue day*
> *Over the hills and far away*
> *They're singing out:*
> *Duh-de-doo-doo, duh-de-doo-doo*

... who knows. After all, "Million Miles" also features in these same recording sessions for *Time Out Of Mind*, and our protagonist is also on a hopeless quest for unattainable happiness. Unlikely, though. *Singing hills* probably impose themselves on the poet Dylan the way the image will impose itself on almost every listener: via one of the corniest highs (or lows, depending on personal taste) of the twentieth century:

> *The hills are alive with the sound of music*
> *With songs they have sung for a thousand years*
> *The hills fill my heart with the sound of music*
> *My heart wants to sing every song it hears*

... the song with which Julie Andrews introduces the Unbearable Lightness of her Being in *The Sound Of Music*, an association that at the most a minority of Dylan's generation, and of the generation before that, and of the generation after that, will escape. And an association that, like Ramblin' Gamblin' Willie, quite seriously clashes with the mood and the setting that the songwriter in "Red River Shore" seems to want to evoke; the rather uncomfortable, Kafkaesque uncanniness. In Kafka's words:

> "To describe reality in a realistic way, but at the same time as a "floating nothing", as a clear, lucid dream, so as a realistically perceived irreality."
>
> *(Reflections From The Year 1920)*

... the mood that Dylan fortunately rediscovers after this little dip.

Though nothing looks familiar to me I know I've stayed here before is an oppressive outpouring from the protagonist. More sinister and less innocent, and even more unreal than a déjà vu - a *déjà venu*, as it were. It is a plot that is effectively used in mindfuck films such as *Total Recall* and *Before I Go to Sleep,* to evoke in the audience the same frightening feeling as in the protagonist, who usually has undergone something like a memory reset or implanted memories. Or, in the more criminal variety, the stories that suck us into the maddening frustration of victims of gaslighting; offices are dismantled, photos are swapped, walls are painted over, and when the protagonist returns with the police, the evidence is gone and everything is different. *Though nothing looks familiar to me I know I've stayed here before* - it's the paranoid version of the musical highlight from *The Muppets Movie* (1979), from Gonzo's heartbreaking "I'm Going To Go Back There Someday";

This looks familiar	*Close to my soul*
Vaguely familiar	*And yet so far away*
Almost unreal yet	*I'm going to go back there*
It's too soon to feel yet	*Someday*

It really does seem that the song poet Dylan has found the tone again now. The following *once a thousand nights ago* is not such a hollow cliché as, say, "ramblin' and gamblin'" or "when it's all been said and done", but has the same magical, poetic sheen as *cloak of misery* and *fires of time*; the paradoxical quality of being simultaneously fresh and old-fashioned. Its magical sheen can surely be traced back to Sheherazade, the Persian storyteller of the tales from *One Thousand and One Nights*, and is perhaps unintentionally reinforced by choosing not something like "once a long, long time ago" but rather "once a thousand nights ago".

The *poetic* power, then, is due to a kind of generally accepted metaphorical quality of "thousand"; although *thousand nights* covers a relatively manageable span of time (not much more than two and a half years, in fact), we all experience it as "endlessly long", "half a lifetime". Like Emmylou Harris uses it in her moving ode to Gram Parsons from 1985, "Sweetheart Of The Rodeo", in the beautiful opening line *A thousand nights a thousand towns I took the bows*, eventually leading to the equally beautiful final words

> *I stepped into the light you left behind*
> *I stood there where all the world could see me shine*
> *Oh I was on my way to you to make you mine*
> *But I took the longest road that I could find*

Or as it is used in "I've Made Love To You A Thousand Times" by Smokey Robinson, the man whose poetic value was once equated by Dylan with Rimbaud and Allen Ginsberg (jokingly, we may assume, in an interview with the *Chicago Daily News* in 1965). And like this, there are a few more songs in which *thousand nights*, usually in a romantic context, is used as a metaphor for "unbearably long time" - but except for Sinatra's "How Old Am I?" no songs from the canon - it's not too common. "Thousand nights" is a realistically perceived irreality, so to speak.

X   Send it to Lulu

Well I went back to see about her once
Went back to straighten it out
Everybody that I talked to had seen us there
Said they didn't know who I was talking about
Well the sun went down on me a long time ago
I've had to pull back from the door
I wish I could have spent every hour of my life
With the girl from the red river shore

Chancellor Merkel also plays along. In 2012, at a prize-giving ceremony, she happens to mention a recent visit to the town of Bielefeld, a city in North Rhine-Westphalia. She drops a dramatically perfect pause and then adds: "... *so es denn existiert* - if it exists at all." The audience laughs all the louder, as Frau Merkel very rarely allows herself to indulge in frivolities. When the laughter subsides, the Chancellor places, again perfectly timed: "*Ich hatte den Eindruck, ich war da* - I was under the impression that I was there."

Merkel is referring to a running gag that by then has been popular in Germany for nearly 30 years: the collective conspiracy to maintain that Bielefeld does not exist at all. Its existence is said to have been fabricated by, as befits a good conspiracy theory, an unnamed "THEY" ("*SIE*" - always written in capitals).

The city council deals with it somewhat ambiguously. For the first few years, until 1999, the increasingly popular joke is ignored, but then the council decides on a counter-offensive and launches the *Bielefeld gibt es doch!* campaign ("Bielefeld *does* exist!") with an official press release. Unfortunately, an inattentive official sends the official statement to the press on 1 April, so obviously, it backfires. In 2019, the next counter-offensive follows: the city council awards 1 million euros to the person who can prove conclusively that Bielefeld does not exist.

Usually it is less funny, such a collective conspiracy. Which seems to be Dylan's approach now; the less funny track. Apparently, the previous verse, the *I know I've stayed here before* verse, inspires him to the plot of an old-fashioned mystery thriller - the plot of a movie like *The Lady Vanishes*, to be more precise. Not too far-fetched; Hitchcock is on a pedestal with Dylan. In interviews, he does mention the director quite frequently, always admiringly, Hitchcock passes by once in *Tarantula* ("the world didn't stop for a second - it just blew up / alfred hitchcock made the whole thing into a mystery") and anyway: Dylan does have a fondness for old black and white crime thrillers in general.

In this old Hitchcock film (*The Lady Vanishes* is from 1938 and is considered one of Hitchcock's "early sound films"), the plot revolves around a young woman who seems to be the only one to notice the disappearance of a fellow passenger on the train, the elderly lady Miss Froy. The other passengers and the train staff all claim they never saw her. *Everybody that I talked to had seen us there said they didn't know who I was talking about*. A doctor present diagnoses hallucinations in poor, desperate Iris, and is not bothered by professional secrecy; he blabbers about it all over the train. An artifice that effectively contributes to the feeling of increasing suffocation for both the protagonist and the audience - in a more modern film (2005) with a similar plot, *Flightplan* with

Jodie Foster, poor Jodie is even tied to her plane seat by supposedly well-meaning airline staff, and a therapist present there diagnoses something like hallucinations due to an unresolved trauma. Which, of course, exponentially increases the helpless frustration of the audience and Jodie. Especially since the missing lady in this film is Jodie's six-year-old daughter - an extra traumatising dimension already added in Otto Preminger's *Bunny Lake Is Missing* (1965) and, in a variant, in Clint Eastwood's *Changeling* with Angelina Jolie.

There is a difference though, a psychological deepening in fact, with Dylan's protagonist - in all these films, the unhappy protagonist has at least one powerful ally: the audience. We have all witnessed that Miss Froy really exists, that Jodie Foster is not crazy and that little Bunny Lake is not a figment of a mentally ill lady's imagination either. In "Red River Shore", however, the screenwriter has already sown doubts about the protagonist; the audience has already heard him say that his time with that girl was "a dream", has heard him sigh that she was "true to me", and we even have some reason to suspect that the protagonist is a traumatised murderer - with all those whole and half references to a fatal event in *the shadows of the past*.

The build-up is good. "I went back to see about her once, went back to straighten it out" is an announcement that already makes the audience cringe: "Don't do it, man." The subsequent observation that everyone denies knowing her, all those people *that had seen us there* together back then, is then even a bit of a relief; thankfully, the whole village conspires to keep this dubious figure away from her. We, the audience, even become accomplices in a way; unlike in all those paranoia films, we are not on the side of the victim of the conspiracy, but we have sympathy for the conspirators.

It seems to break the I-person. "The sun went down on me a long time ago / I've had to pull back from the door" - Dylan's paraphrase of the poetic resignation from a recent pop song beyond categorization, from Elton John's 1974 "Don't Let The Sun Go Down On Me". The brilliant song, which superficially expresses a long jeremiad of a spurned lover, but with, as lyricist Bernie Taupin says, "a dark twist";

But you misread my meaning when I met you
Closed the door and left me blinded by the light
Don't let the sun go down on me
Although I search myself, it's always someone else I see
I'd just allow a fragment of your life to wander free
But losing everything is like the sun going down on me

An *hors catégorie* song that achieves a Holy Trinity: majestic lyrics with a dark twist, delightful melodies and a brilliant, just not over-the-top from babbling-mountain-brook-to-wilderness waterfall arrangement. Thanks to the chilling elegance of Davey Johnstone's guitar, Del Newman's superior horn arrangement and the heavenly backing vocals of the Beach Boys Carl Wilson and Bruce Johnston (and Toni Tennille of Captain & Tenille).

Elton, too, had an opinion, by the way:

"I'm not always the best judge of my own work – I am, after all, the man who loudly announced that 'Don't Let The Sun Go Down On Me' was such a terrible song that I would never countenance releasing it [...]. I hated the song so much we were going to stop recording it immediately and send it to Engelbert Humperdinck – 'and if he doesn't want it, tell him to send it to Lulu! She can put it on a B-side!' – I was coaxed back to the vocal booth and completed the take. Then I yelled at Gus Dudgeon that I hated it even more now it was finished and was going to kill him with my bare hands if he put it on the album."
(*Me* – Elton John, 2019)

Which, in retrospect, makes us regret that Gus Dudgeon was not the producer in Miami in January 1997. To coax Dylan back and complete the song.

XI   It's complicated

Now I heard of a guy who lived a long time ago
A man full of sorrow and strife
That if someone around him died and was dead
He knew how to bring 'em on back to life
Well I don't know what kind of language he used
Or if they do that kind of thing anymore
Sometimes I think nobody ever saw me here at all
Except the girl from the red river shore

Dylan also comes along for a moment. In "the Zone", the border area where the soul resides for a while when you are enraptured on earth - by music, for example. And that, "the Zone", is where Moonwind Stardancer's ship sails; to the sounds of "Subterranean Homesick Blues". Protagonist Joe roams around there, looking for Moonwind, because Moonwind knows how to bring him back to life. In *Soul*, the overpowering 2020 Pixar film, the soul of dying jazz pianist Joe Gardner can be brought back to life if he has a fully ticked off *Earth Pass* that grants him access to Earth, and thus back to his lifeless body. In *The Great Before*, the dimension where souls are prepared for Life, he must obtain one. A given used at about the same time by filmmaker Edson Oda for his thoroughly poetic film *Nine Days* (2020); in a lonely house on an unreal plain, the hermit selects, in nine-day interview sessions, the souls that are allowed to go to a body on Earth. The scenario is a Swiss cheese, but oh well; the images are pure poetry and the actors are sublimely cast.

Reanimation as a theme is of all times, but in most cases the plot leads to fright and horror, to sorrow and strife. The *Flatliners* who deliberately kill themselves and then reanimate each other do not exactly enjoy their regained, nightmarish lives (1990), and the life broker in the rip-off *The Lazarus Effect* (2017) also horribly regrets the monster he creates when he revives his own wrecked girl from the Red River shore, fiancée Zoë. She turns into an unstoppable killing machine with supernatural powers. And similar horror is provided by most reanimation stories and the dozens of Frankenstein films.

Only a handful of films have a positive twist like *Soul*. *The Crow*, although a gory revenge film, has a sort of happy ending for the revived Brandon Lee (whose actual death during the shooting is filmed, lugubriously, as a fake gun accidentally shoots a projectile into his stomach). And the cinematic monument *RoboCop* (Paul Verhoeven, 1987) is not quite a feel-good movie either, but the reanimated cop Alex Murphy is at least programmed to *serve the public trust, protect the innocent, and uphold the law*. And is inspired by the most famous reanimator of all time, the same one who also inspires Dylan;

> "The point of *RoboCop* is, of course, it is a Christ story. It is about a guy that gets crucified after 50 minutes, then is resurrected in the next 50 minutes and then is like the super-cop of the world, but is also a Jesus figure as he walks over water at the end."
>
> (director Paul Verhoeven in *MTV News,* 2010)

The final couplet of "Red River Shore" is, without a doubt, the most fascinating one of the song. Every line is striking and the whole, like Dylan's best final couplets, offers both a twist on the previous stanzas and a menu of possible scenarios.

The opening, *I heard of a guy who lived a long time ago*, masks through the choice of words ("a guy") the identity of Jesus, who therefore all the more surprisingly three lines later turns out to be "the guy". For the time being, the storyteller keeps the suspense going; the "guy" was *a man full of sorrow and strife*. Which pushes the associations, again through word choice, to medieval tragic heroes and ancient murder ballads. Identical word choice as in one of the many "Matty Groves" variants, for example. In the seventeenth century, troubadours sang about Matty (or rather: about *Little Musgrave*, as he was called in those days):

> *'To lodge wi thee a' night, fair lady,*
> *Wad breed baith sorrow and strife;*
> *For I see by the rings on your fingers*
> *You're good Lord Barnaby's wife.'*

... and to the nineteenth-century "Arthur McBride", the song Dylan interprets so lovingly, seven years before "Red River Shore", on *Good As I Been To You* ("And he pays all his debts without sorrow and strife").

But on the other hand, it already has an evangelical connotation; "Sorrow and strife" does indeed have a New Testament colour, is a word combination that is otherwise only to be found in gospel music. In "Wait For Me" by The Statesmen for example, Brenda Lee's "Some People", and in old hymns like "Jesus, I Come" and "Out Of My Darkness Into Thy Light" - all edifying songs in which a longing for liberation from earthly sorrow and strife and for union with Jesus is sung. With the single use of those two words *sorrow* and *strife*, in short, the poet builds a bridge from the old-fashioned folk atmosphere of the previous seven stanzas to the introduction of the gospel in this finale. A bridge that becomes all the more solid with the following *if someone around him died and was dead*; again that Biblical tone, the tautological of John ("he who is of the earth is earthly and speaks of the earth," 3:31), Esther ("and fast ye for me, and neither eat nor drink," 4:16), Proverbs 14:24 ("the foolishness of fools is folly"), to name but three examples - the Bible is rich in tautologies like *he died and was dead*.

The road is paved. So, in this chapter 8, verse 4 we get to know who *the guy* is: the most famous reanimator of all time, that is. But still described with the same pleasantly disrespectful, folksy tone: *He knew how to bring 'em on back to life*. Undertones: boy, he was quite something, this guy Jesus. The same tone Dylan uses in "Highway 61 Revisited" in the dialogue of Abraham and God; *man, you must be puttin' me on*.

Apart from that: the insinuation confirms the veiled hints from the previous verses; the narrator is looking for a guy who can bring the dead back to life - and thus insinuates that his girl from the Red River shore is dead. More than that, he reaffirms the vague suspicion that he himself is the murderer. After the cryptic opening in which he suggests that he has *scared her to death in the dark*, after which she has left for an area *where the angels fly*, and after the in this scenario rather lugubrious words *she should always be with me*, and all subsequent ambiguous outpourings, this is then relatively unambiguous - after "death" in the opening the narrator, neatly cyclic, returns in his closing words to the words *dead*, *died* and *back to life*. Words of a desperate, repentant sinner who needs a deus ex machina to undo auld lang syne, to dissolve the shadows of his past.

But: this is a Dylan song in the same category as "Desolation Row" and "Mississippi", in the category of monumental songs that meander between lyricism and epicism, that insinuate more than they tell, that don't show anything more than what the broken glass reflects. The poet has one final twist up his sleeve...

JOE
Does this mean I'm... dead?
COUNSELOR JERRY A
Not yet. Your body's in a holding pattern. It's complicated.

XII   I see dead people

Now I heard of a guy who lived a long time ago
A man full of sorrow and strife
That if someone around him died and was dead
He knew how to bring 'em on back to life
Well I don't know what kind of language he used
Or if they do that kind of thing anymore
Sometimes I think nobody ever saw me here at all
Except the girl from the red river shore

In *The Graham Norton Show*, former *Friends* actor Matthew Perry tells the amusing story of how, in a bar, he met M. Night Shyamalan, whom he knows a little because six months earlier he had presented an award to Bruce Willis for his impressive role in *The Sixth Sense*. And in the process, he got to say hello to the rest of the cast and the director. Perry spends an exceptionally enjoyable, alcohol-soaked evening with the world-famous director, they go to another joint together and Matthew is already dreaming of a major role in one of Shyamalan's next films. When the director goes to the toilet, Perry is approached by an acquaintance who happens to be passing by.

> "He said, how's your night going, and I said: what, are you kidding? I'm having the greatest night of my life. M. Night Shyamalan and I have been hanging out for the last two and a half hours. It's been great. And M. Night Shyamalan came back from the bathroom and my friend said: that's not M. Night Shyamalan.
> And it wasn't. It was just an Indian gentleman who looked a lot like M. Night Shyamalan."

Perry's eagerness is understandable. He is offered plenty of roles, but all in the romantic comedy corner, and M. Night Shyamalan is Hollywood's golden boy at the time, after the smashing, worldwide success of the occult thriller *The Sixth Sense*. (1999). That success is for 90% due to the script, also written by director Shyamalan. And especially because of its mindfuck quality, the bewildering twist at the end that the main character, psychologist Malcolm Crowe (Bruce Willis), is dead - we have unsuspectingly been sympathising and identifying with a ghost all this time, a ghost that, apart from the audience, is only seen by the other main character, nine-year-old Cole "I see dead people" Sear.

Cole also learns why these ghosts are wandering around: they have unfinished business, only see what they want to see and don't even know they're dead. And that all sounds awfully close to Dylan's protagonist, after hearing the last two lines;

> *Sometimes I think nobody ever saw me here at all*
> *Except the girl from the red river shore*

... lines spoken by the protagonist after he announces that he is looking for a guy who can bring the dead back to life.

There are enough lines to be drawn from Shyamalan to Dylan. He uses Dylan's music in his films, calls Dylan one of his great heroes in interviews and even confesses to feeling a kind of telepathic connection with the Bard (in Michael Bamberger's weirdly hagiographic, authorised study *The Man Who Heard Voices*, 2006). But the suggestion that these two Dylan lines inspired his one great masterpiece is way too far-fetched. It is highly unlikely that the script-writing director could have heard the unreleased song from January 1997 at the time he was writing the screenplay for *The Sixth Sense*. And then again, the concept of *the-one-who-can-see-ghosts* is not that unique. Meg Ryan sees the angel Nicolas Cage in *City Of Angels*, the Hollywoodised version of the brilliant Wim Wenders film *Der Himmel über Berlin* (1987). Whoopi Goldberg is the only one who can hear the murdered Patrick Swayze in *Ghost* (1990). Nicolas Roeg's classic *Don't Look Now*, in a way. And the witty Ricky Gervais as a blunt dentist in *Ghost Town* (2008) is also the only one who can see dead people - the idea was of course created for horror, but is surprisingly often used in romantic comedies and child-friendly family films as well.

But what sets Dylan's "Red River Shore" apart from all those stories, and what it shares with *The Sixth Sense*, is its surprising twist. *I think nobody ever saw me here at all* offers, in its final lines, a new scenario that overturns all that has gone before; the scenario in which the narrator dwells in the *shadows of a fading past*, wanders in the dimension *where the angels fly*, *living in the moonlight*, seeks his soul's rest there *where the black winds roar*, for whom *the sun doesn't shine anymore*... The closing lines offer the advanced insight that we have listened to a jeremiad of a wandering soul, of a spirit that has unfinished business and that probably does not even realise that he is dead. At least, he seems to be surprised that no one can see him. Except the girl from the Red River shore. And it turns the motivation to find the guy who can bring the dead back to life; this is not a repentant murderer trying to undo his misdeed with the reanimation of the Red River girl, but *he himself*, like the angel Nicolas Cage and the jazz pianist Joe Gardner, wants to be brought back to life.

Nice twist - though far from conclusive. Dylan's apparent dissatisfaction with "Red River Shore" (the song is discarded for *Time Out Of Mind* and never put on the setlist either - it belongs to the rather select club of songs completely ignored by the master) may have something to do with its imbalance. Comparably great works like "Blind Willie McTell" and "Series Of Dreams" are, after initial rejection, eventually rehabilitated. "Series Of Dreams" is admitted to the stage in Vienna, Virginia (8 September 1993) four years after its demotion to outtake, and performed nine more times thereafter. "Blind Willie McTell" takes longer to be rehabilitated, but then returns all the more glorious; to the dismay of producer Mark Knopfler, among others, it was rejected for *Infidels* in 1983, only to be released on *The Bootleg Series* in 1991, and after The Band records it and enjoys success with it, Dylan surrenders: since 1997, fourteen years after its conception, Dylan has performed the song 227 times.

A reluctant capitulation, still. Dylan seems only half convinced, judging by his statements in the interview with Jonathan Lethem for *Rolling Stone*, 2006 (when he has performed the song already about a hundred times):

> "It was never developed fully, I never got around to completing it. There wouldn't have been any other reason for leaving it off the record."

"It was never developed fully" also seems to be the key to explain the fate of "Red River Shore". Presumably, the poet only gradually, around the seventh verse, recognised the beautiful ambiguity of *traumatised killer or wandering soul*, made a mental note, but *never got around to completing it*. And now the song is dead.

It needn't be too late. Perhaps Dylan should consider a night on the town with the writer/director of *The Sixth Sense*. Storyteller M. Night Shyamalan is, after all, a guy who knows how to bring 'em on back to life.

XIII 'Twas in the merry month of June

"*Girl From The Red River Shore* I personally felt was the best thing we recorded. But as we walked in to hear the playback, Dylan was in front of me, and he said, 'Well, we've done everything on that one except call the symphony orchestra.' Which indicated to me they'd tried to cut it before. If it had been my session, I would have got on the phone at that point and called the fucking symphony orchestra. But the cut was amazing. You couldn't even identify what instruments were playing what parts."

Jim Dickenson (keyboards on *Red River Shore*) in *Uncut*

So, there should be four versions, according to engineer Chris Shaw, who together with manager Jeff Rosen is ploughing his way through the tapes to come to a selection for *Tell Tale Signs: The Bootleg Series Vol. 8* (2008). "Dreamin' Of You", the unreleased song they want to put on the website as a teaser, is easily found, Shaw says, but...

"... there were others that took forever to find, like "Red River Shore", there were four versions of that that we had to go looking for. It's an archival process, and it's fun digging through that stuff, especially all the banter you hear between tracks and stuff."

— Chris Shaw (engineer *Red River Shore*) in *Uncut*

Those closely involved, like Dickenson and Shaw, have no idea why the song was rejected. Neither do drummer Jim Keltner or producer Daniel Lanois. Guitarist Duke Robillard seems to have at least indirectly a clue, and is either remarkably well informed, or he can read the tell-tale signs remarkably well:

There was one song that I'm not sure will make the cut, that when I first heard Bob do it, right away I thought it was a Jimmie Rodgers thing circa 1929, it was that genuine. I was mesmerized by it, completely blown away . . . Lanois and Dylan talked about [how the album] was all designed to create a mood. The record is set in another time . . . it's steamboat, civil war, very Mark Twain.

Duke Robillard (electric guitar on Red River Shore) in *Isis #73*

Number 73 of the fanzine *Isis* is published in June 1997, so the interview with Robillard has taken place months before the release of *Time Out Of Mind* (30 September 1997). And at that time Robillard apparently already realises that "Red River Shore" will be dropped. Notable are the last words from the *Isis* quote, about the mood: "The record is set in another time . . . it's steamboat, civil war, very Mark Twain." Words that, apart from "Red River Shore", fit just as seamlessly on that other legendary dropout, on "Mississippi". Fitting with what Dylan himself says about "Mississippi", and his disagreement about it with producer Lanois: "I tried to explain that the song had more to do with the Declaration of Independence, the Constitution and the Bill of Rights than witch doctors." And especially fitting for the next record, the one on which "Mississippi" will eventually make its glorious debut, four years later, on «*Love And Theft*» (2001).

Now, *that* is an album where it does make sense to say: *steamboat, civil war, very Mark Twain*. "Mississippi", "Summer Days", "Bye And Bye", "Floater"... songs that all share the same nineteenth century mood as "Red River Shore" - a mood that, strangely enough, wouldn't characterise *Time Out Of Mind* that much. Despite the fact that Lanois and Dylan, if we are to believe Robillard, seem to seek it out so explicitly. But then: "Love Sick", *a highway of regret*, the Scottish Highlands, *a jukebox playing low*, *from London to gay Paree*... no, on large parts of *Time Out Of Mind* the poet definitely has discarded the steamboats and the Civil War. To pass it on to his next project.

"Mississippi" is then, thankfully, rescued from oblivion. Thanks to an outside intervention, too, as drummer David Kemper reveals:

> "I know of two versions of Mississippi. We thought we were done with "Love And Theft", and then a friend of Bob's passed him a note, and he said, oh, yeah, I forgot about this: Mississippi."

... manager Jeff Rosen would be an educated guess if we had to guess the identity of "a friend of Bob's". But no such luck for "Red River Shore"; the song really only surfaces more than ten years after its conception, on *Tell Tale Signs* from 2008. Again, on Jeff Rosen's instruction, praised be his name.

And further on, we find "The Girl from the Greenbriar Shore", one of several candidates that can be considered as a template for the song. Although both chord progression and melody are actually far too generic to attribute to one "mother song", of course. And we know the combination *girl + shore*, as well as the vague topographic location "Red River", from dozens of songs too. No, "Greenbriar Shore" seems to be an isolated burp that we owe to the rather prosaic fact that Dylan has the obvious association with "green shore" and the song that begins with the words "'Twas in the year of '92, in the merry month of June" when he is on the Côte d'Opale near Dunkerque in June 1992.

Two performances are given to *Greenbriar Shore* (both in the merry month of June '92). Two more than "Red River Shore", which otherwise does not make waves either. In fan circles, it is celebrated as a lost masterpiece of a similar category as "She's Your Lover Now" and "Blind Willie McTell", but neither the master himself nor his colleagues seem to agree.

In fact, only a few usual suspects, artists who have already made a name for themselves with Dylan interpretations, put the song on the repertoire. In the Netherlands, one of the most successful musicians of the 80s, Ernst Jansz of the million-selling band Doe Maar, has distinguished himself with translated Dylan songs, a successful Dylan tribute album (*Dromen Van Johanna* - "Dreaming Of Johanna", 2010) and a theatre tour. The album and the set list include "Het Meisje Van De Rode Rivier". And when he performs with his old pals from the folk group CCC Inc., he occasionally manages to coax them into an English "Red River Shore". Acoustic, with a lot of guitars, harmonica and accordion bag, as it should be. Just like the Austrian phenomenon Ernst Molden does, a shorter version in a smaller line-up, sung in unintelligible Viennese dialect, but with the same magic as Dylan.

And we understand, at least, that with Molden she is *a Madl aus der Lobau* - a girl from the Lobau, the Vienna floodplain on the northern side of the Danube, loved by nudists.

More international allure is given by the only celebrity to record the song in its original English: the late, great Jimmy LaFave, the Texan with the high pitched voice and unique phrasing. On the wonderful 2012 album *Depending On The Distance*, which features the equally successful Dylan interpretations "I'll Remember You" and "Tomorrow Is A Long Time".

Over nine and a half minutes, and every second is wonderful. It's steamboat, civil war, and very Mark Twain.

13   Dreamin' Of You

I   Dreamin' of Henry

Just like the equally compelling time document *The Bootleg Series 12 - The Cutting Edge 1965-66* (2015), on which we can voyeuristically follow the evolution from run-up to final studio recording (such as the twenty takes of "Like A Rolling Stone"), the brilliant *The Bootleg Series Vol. 8: Tell Tale Signs: Rare and Unreleased 1989-2006* from 2008 does give us a glimpse into the phase before as well, into the sketchbook, into the process of coming up with a lyric. We hear how lines and word combinations from the rejected "Marchin' To The City" are transferred to "Not Dark Yet" and "'Til I Fell In Love With You", and we get alternative recordings with textual differences ("Born In Time" and "Dignity", for example).

The rejected outtake "Dreamin' Of You" offers the same insight as "Marchin' To The City", and more: apart from the gems Dylan picks out to use for other songs, it seems to reveal what a very first seed for a Dylan lyric can be. At least, that's what the opening lines appear to give us, the opening which will eventually, after the rejection, be transferred to "Standing In The Doorway":

> *The light in this place is really bad*
> *Like being at the bottom of a stream*
> *Any minute now*
> *I'm expecting to wake up from a dream*

The opening line, as Dylan researcher Scott Warmuth found, is lifted in its entirety from Henry Rollins' poem "One Way Conversation" (in *See A Grown Man Cry*, 1992);

> *There's lots of things that I don't tell you*
> *Lots of things that don't have words to wear*
> *The light in this place is really bad*
> *I'm thinking about your eyes*
> *Hell, we're tied up in this shit you know*
> *Stuck behind walls, frozen in doorways*
> *I hope these bugs don't get into my food*

... and from the remaining eight lines, which are similar in content, it becomes clear that the narrator is talking to an answering machine and is in a slightly detached state; he does not know exactly where he is, for example. Somewhere halfway through, there is then the line that Dylan has underlined, "The light in this place is really bad", and which initially inspires him to the somewhat alienating, and in any case original metaphor, "Like being at the bottom of a stream". Alienating, because few listeners or readers will have an aha-experience with "the light at the bottom of a stream" – given that a metaphor is actually meant to make something clear by naming a resemblance to something familiar. But then, of course, this characteristic does not apply so much to poetry. And to an even lesser extent to Dylan's poetry.

"Being at the bottom of a stream" forces the associations to lugubrious distances, as a matter of fact. It is a location where we find victims of a witchcraft trial, where Ophelia ends up after her suicide, it is a classic dumping ground for murder weapons whose owner wants to get rid of, and more macabre connotations just like these - but there are really no positive links with a river bottom. The gloominess is triggered, presumably, by the morbid

Now Watch Him Die, the 1993 work in which Henry Rollins processes the horror of the gruesome, senseless murder of his friend Joe Cole (who is shot through the head point-blank right before Henry's eyes in a brutal robbery). Dylan incorporates more fragments from that chilling work into his *Time Out Of Mind* songs, like in this stanza; the fourth line, "I'm expecting to wake up from a dream", is also taken from *Now Watch Him Die*:

> "In semi darkness I think about my friend. In a few days it will be a year since his death. I remember when it was a week. I sat behind the desk of the office space I was living in and I was amazed at how unreal the entire week had been. I kept expecting to wake up from it like a dream."

… whereby Dylan will have poetically associated the setting, *in semi-darkness*, with that other Rollins quote *The light in this place is really bad* - and the morbid context might then trigger the sinister décor, *the bottom of the stream*. In any case, the continuation of this first stanza confirms that we should not understand the title *Dreamin' Of You* romantically, not as the title of a love song:

> *Means so much, the softest touch*
> *By the grave of some child, who neither wept or smiled*
> *I pondered my faith in the rain*
> *I've been dreamin' of you, that's all I do*
> *And it's driving me insane*

…the grave of "some child", a crisis of faith at a funeral in the rain, the longing for a comforting hand - this is the despair of a narrator left behind after the death of his loved one. With similar word choice and identical emotion as one of Bob Forrest's (well, officially The Bicycle Thief's) most beautiful, raw mourning songs "Everyone Asks" from 1999, in which he poignantly tries to come to terms with the death of a loved one almost a year ago:

Why do I always
Call your name
If it doesn't stop
I'll go insane
I just know

Wonderful song by the devout Dylan fan Forrest, in whose work we hear more Dylan echoes - although usually more raw, more unadorned than Dylan's of course. Dylan, meanwhile, is apparently also pleased with the word combinations in this first stanza: after the song's dismissal, the line "means so much, the softest touch" moves to "Standing in the Doorway" as well (as "Dreamin' Of You" will be the purveyor to that song anyway).

For the colour of his song the poet aims, or so it seems, at the nineteenth century, at *"steamboat, civil war, very Mark Twain,"* as guitarist Duke Robillard would say about that other discard, "Red River Shore". The *grave of a child* is already a Chekhovian background, the disturbing character description *who neither wept or smiled* seems to come from Henry James ("she only looked at him silently in return, neither weeping, nor smiling, nor putting out her hand," *Madame De Mauves*, 1874), and *pondering faith in the rain* is a rather Walt Whitman-like image.

It appears, all in all, as if Dylan has ticked those two Rollins lines, and then opened the floodgates. In the run-up to *Time Out Of Mind*, he has already dug a bed, the nineteenth-century steamboat, Mark Twain bed, and inspired the stream of consciousness leads him along Checkhov, Whitman and Henry James, along nineteenth-century word combinations and images. Far, far away from Henry Rollins, in any case.

II   The Lay of the Last Minstrel

The only official publication of the lyrics of "Dreamin' Of You" is on the official site, on *www.bobdylan.com*. In *Lyrics 1962-2001* from 2004 there are no lyrics of outtakes in the chapter *Time Out Of Mind*, only the lyrics of "Things Have Changed" under "additional lyrics". In the successor *The Lyrics 1961-2012* (2016) "Red River Shore" is added too, again with the indication "additional lyrics". The word "outtake" is never used anyway, and would of course be incorrect in the case of the Oscar-winning "Things Have Changed"; that song was recorded two and a half years after *Time Out Of Mind*, somewhere between May and July 1999. When compiling the book edition, the choice was apparently made to place the song with *Time Out Of Mind* for practical reasons only - although chronologically it is actually closer to *"Love And Theft"* (recorded May 2001).

On that only official publication then of "Dreamin' Of You", the lyrics are presented in ten stanzas. Each second verse ends with the recurring lines *I've been dreamin' of you, that's all I do / And it's driving me insane*, which we can call the refrain with some tolerance. Some irregularities do stand out, though:

- the ten stanzas alternate between four and six verses, except for the second stanza, which has five verses;
- the poet seems to have fixed a rhyme scheme in mind, but that scheme is not correct in a few places - or not yet, assuming that Dylan has recorded a work in progress;
- the line breaks in the published text seem rather arbitrary, hence

perhaps the "wrong" second stanza with the different number of five lines - in any case, presented like this, the lyrics ignore existing rhyme and a content-wise logical division into strophes.

All in all, it does seem that Dylan had a much tighter, more logical structure in mind: not stanzas of varying length, but five stanzas of ten lines, rhyme scheme AABBCC - DEED, where the last four lines have a chorus function. A rhyme scheme like Sir Walter Scott, for instance, uses in the nineteenth century (in *The Lay of the Last Minstrel*). The published text is fairly easy to rearrange into this structure, or rather: to restore. The first two stanzas, for example, are on the site shown as a six-line stanza plus a five-line stanza:

> *The light in this place is really bad*
> *Like being at the bottom of a stream*
> *Any minute now*
> *I'm expecting to wake up from a dream*
>
> *Means so much, the softest touch*
> *By the grave of some child, who neither wept or smiled*
> *I pondered my faith in the rain*
> *I've been dreamin' of you, that's all I do*
> *And it's driving me insane*

Illogical sentence breaks (verse 3 to 4, for example), only two end rhymes, an overdose of inner rhymes... a restructuring to a ten-line couplet seems much more obvious:

> *The light in this place is really bad, like being at the bottom of a stream*
> *Any minute now I'm expecting to wake up from a dream*
> *Means so much,*
> *The softest touch,*
> *By the grave of some child,*
> *who neither wept or smiled.*
> *I pondered my faith in the rain -*
> *I've been dreamin' of you,*
> *That's all I do*
> *And it's driving me insane*

The strongest indication for this option is the *AABBCC - DEED* rhyme scheme. The whole text can be reformed into this scheme (still having three "wrong" rhymes, though - again: work in progress, presumably). So, the next two stanzas are not stanza 3 and 4, but the second ten-line stanza:

> *Somewhere dawn is breaking / Light is streaking 'cross the floor*
> *Church bells are ringing / I wonder who they're ringing for*
> *Travel under any star*
> *You'll see me wherever you are*
> *The shadowy past*
> *is awake and so vast*
> *I'm sleeping in the palace of pain*
> *I've been dreamin' of you,*
> *that's all I do*
> *But it's driving me insane*

The same number of lines, a similar syllable distribution per stanza, an identical rhyme scheme... it seems very likely that this was the form the poet had in mind. Why Dylan, or the book editor, or the web editor, conceals this form is unclear. Maybe he thinks it looks corny, or uncool, or whatever. It does occur quite often, actually - that the layout of the official publication ignores or disguises the "true" form of a song text. The most extreme example is "No Time To Think", which is in fact a long, cleverly composed sonnet cycle of nine inverted sonnets, and there are plenty of other examples ("Where Are You Tonight", "Love Is Just A Four-Letter Word", "Just Like Tom Thumb's Blues", to name but three). The rearranging of the lyrics into their "real" form, as with this song, usually reveals cast-iron, classic poetry forms - and shows authentic, honest craftsmanship. Nothing to be ashamed of, in any case.

Anyway, "Dreamin'Of You". The content of this second ten-line stanza builds on the first. Again, it starts with a stage direction for the lighting technician, and there is again a reference to a grave, to a cemetery, to a death, at any rate. At least, variations of the expression *Church bells are ringing / I wonder who they're ringing for* in blues lyrics always refer to death bells (not to an ordinary church service, hardly ever to wedding bells). Dylan knows it from blues classics as Roosevelt Sykes' "Sad And Lonely Day" from 1933, from "Stop And Listen Blues" by The Mississippi Sheiks (1929) and Muddy Waters' "Buryin' Ground Blues"(1947). And Dylan himself sings it on his debut album, in "See That My Grave Is Kept Clean":

> *Did you ever hear them church bells tone*
> *Means another poor boy is dead and gone*

... as Dylan himself incorporates it in the *Blood On The Tracks* outtake "Call Letter Blues" (*Well, I walked all night long / Listenin' to them church bells tone*). And in the big sister of "Dreamin' Of You" of course, in "Can't Escape From You" on *Modern Times*:

> *The dead bells are ringing*
> *My train is overdue*
> *To your memory I'm clinging*
> *I can't escape from you*

Ringing church bells, in short, always mean *death*, both in the blues and with Dylan. Something similar applies to *shadowy* in the verse "The shadowy past is awake and so vast". In the canon, in American Songbook classics like "I Surrender, Dear", or "The Lamp Is Low", or the song of which "Dreamin' Of You" is a kind of negative image, in "I Thought About You", *shadowy* usually signals: idyll, romance, the place where lovers meet:

I took a trip on a train
And I thought about you
I passed a shadowy lane
And I thought about you

... but with Dylan it is always threatening, ominous. The *shadowy sun* from "Only A Pawn In Their Game", the *shadowy world* from "Jokerman", and the passage about Fred Neil in the first chapter of *Chronicles*:

> "I'd heard stuff about him, that he was an errant sailor, harbored a skiff in Florida, was an underground cop, had hooker friends and a shadowy past."

... and like *shadows* and *shadowy* is also used dozens of times by Henry Rollins - almost always metaphorically, and almost always with a sinister connotation;

Walk away from me as fast as you can
Never speak of me or to me again
It's too late
For all that
Death is the only shadow on my road

(from "Don't Come Close", *Now Watch Him Die,* 1993)

"Dreamin' Of You" is apparently, apart from being set up in a rigid, classical structure, also conceived as a sultry, uncomfortable cloak-and-dagger. "Confessions of an Assassin", perhaps. "Memoirs of a Strangler", or "Soon After Midnight", something like that...

III   I don't reckon I got no reason to kill nobody

*Maybe they'll get me, maybe they won't / But whatever it won't
be tonight*
*I wish your hand was in mine right now / We could go where the
moon is white*
For years they had me locked in a cage
Then they threw me onto the stage
Some things just last longer
than you thought they would
And they never, ever explain
I've been dreamin' of you,
that's all I do
And it's driving me insane

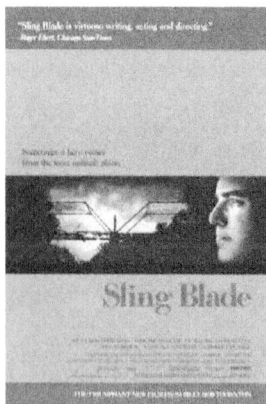

Allen Holdsworth was an inimitable British guitar magician for whom even men like Frank Zappa, Eddie Van Halen and Joe Satriani took their hats off. Contributions to projects by names like U.K., Stanley Clarke and Level 42 are, without exception, olympic, but Holdsworth (1946-2017) was never really a team player - perhaps a little too self-willed and uncompromising.

His true passion was his solo projects, filled with mainly instrumental exercises at the outer limits of guitar virtuosity and eccentric soundscapes. Perhaps not too accessible, but always fascinating. Like his eleventh and last studio album *Flat Tire: Music for a Non-Existent Movie* (2001). It is - as the title already reveals - a very atmospheric album with as one of the highlights the disturbing "Snow Moon" - just as disturbing and even more ominous than Dylan's *We could go where the moon is white*, by the way.

Holdsworth is not the first and not the last to try to capture a strong visual idea in music, or to think, after the creation of the music: my, this sounds like a movie soundtrack. Elton John calls his short instrumental interlude on his unjustly somewhat forgotten *Blue Moves* (1976) "Theme From A Non-Existent TV Series". Radiohead's pièce de résistance *OK Computer* contains the heartbreaking "Exit Music (For A Film)", which, incidentally, was indeed originally intended for the closing credits of the film *Romeo + Juliet* (1996). Complete albums by Eno (*Music for Films* from 1978, *Apollo: Atmospheres and Soundtracks*, and more), side 2 of Bowie's *Low*... non-existent films and fantasised scenes prove to be a fertile source of inspiration for many artists.

The suspicion that Dylan wanted to write a veiled murder ballad à la "Soon After Midnight" (*Tempest*, 2012) with "Dreamin' Of You", or at least leave the suggestion open, as in "Cold Irons Bound" and "Dirt Road Blues", gains more weight in this third decastich. "Maybe they'll get me", "locked in a cage', "thrown onto the stage"... this narrator chooses images and words that, at the very least, insinuate a conflict with law enforcers.

Fitting also with the chosen music, its arrangement and colour. The outtake we finally get in 2008, as a free download to promote the upcoming release of *The Bootleg Series Vol. 8: Tell Tale Signs* is, if anything, very, *very* Lanoisesque. This sound and atmosphere is familiar to us from Lanois' work for Robbie Robertson's first solo album, for instance, for a great song like "Somewhere Down The Crazy River", and equally from Lanois' more recent solo effort, the beautiful soundtrack for the film *Sling Blade* (1996). In musical highlights of that soundtrack like "Blue Waltz", "Asylum" and especially the brilliant "Jimmy Was", the colour of "Dreamin' Of You" is unmistakably already pre-cooked, probably also thanks to co-producer Mark Howard, who is the engineer for *Time Out Of Mind* a few months after recording *Sling Blade*. We hear the same space, the same reverb of Lanois' guitar notes swirling around in "Shenandoah", "Bettina" and "Secret Place", his very characteristic carpet of guitars are all over the soundtrack, and on "Jimmy Was" the drum part is even almost identical to "Dreamin' Of You";

Besides the sound of the soundtrack, Dylan's lyrics occasionally skim remarkably close along the film script - as this verse seems to express the introduction of Billy Bob Thornton's Karl Childers. Twenty-five years ago, as a twelve-year-old, the feeble-minded Karl murdered his mother and her lover, and has been put away in a mental hospital ever since. And now he is being released: *For years they had me locked in a cage / Then they threw me onto the stage*. He is cured, or at least: no longer considered a danger to society. Which Karl can relate to: "I don't reckon I got no reason to kill nobody." Incidentally, according to Dylan researcher Scott Warmuth the direct inspiration comes again from Henry Rollins; "For years they had me locked in a cage" is the opening line of one of the poems in his *Collected Work, 1988-1991*.

Likewise, the potentially romantic walk in the moonshine happens to be in keeping with a film scene;

> LINDA
> Karl, why don't you and Melinda go take a walk. It's nice out.
> KARL
> All right then.
> *He gets up and walks toward the front door. Melinda gets up and tries to catch up.*
> EXT. SIDEWALK - NIGHT
> *Karl and Melinda are walking in the moonlight. It seems a little hard for Melinda to keep up.*

... but that scene is above all touchingly awkward and funny, and has no relation whatsoever to the subcutaneous threat in Dylan's *I wish your hand was in mine right now / We could go where the moon is white*. The adjective "white" is particularly striking - in song and poetry, a colourless moon is actually always *"pale"*. "Copper Kettle", "Sleepy Time Down South", Hank Williams' "When God Comes And Gathers His Jewels", "East Of The Sun", the American Songbook monument "The Nearness Of You"... all songs from Dylan's jukebox with moonlight, and that light is always *pale*. "White" is a tad more ominous, maybe that's why. And a bit more nineteenth-century, perhaps - both Melville and Poe sometimes colour their moon white too. Melville in Dylan's beloved *Moby Dick* ("as the white moon shows her affrighted face from the steep gullies in the blackness overhead") and Poe in his early work *Tamarlane* (1827);

> What tho' the moon—the white moon
> Shed all the splendour of her noon,
> Her smile is chilly—and her beam,
> In that time of dreariness, will seem
> (So like you gather in your breath)
> A portrait taken after death.

... in both cases, evidently, to give a threatening, sinister touch to the narrative. And it is of course, for the third time already in this Dylan song, again a director's instruction for the lighting technician.

The repetitiveness of the endlessly repeated five-tone lick over the same four chords from start to finish strengthens the suspicion: the film fan Dylan sees a film scene in his mind's eye during the creation of the song – like one of those wordless interludes in which the camera follows the protagonist on his way to the next key scene. He walks along a dusty road at sunset, we get a backlit wide shot of a panoramic landscape and a lonely protagonist trudging along, a close-up of the man on a bridge staring at the water flowing underneath, usually interspersed with slow-motion flashbacks in sepia tones, of the man at the grave of a child, something like that. An interplay, in any case, where the director needs music, preferably with a repeating motif and minor chords.

It is beginning to look as if Henry Rollins has projected an unsettling character onto Dylan's inner white screen - and that the musician Dylan hears the soundtrack to it.

IV   If moonshine don't kill me

Well, I eat when I'm hungry, drink when I'm dry / Live my life on the square
Even if the flesh falls off my face / It won't matter, long as you're there
Feel like a ghost in love
Underneath the heavens above
Feel further away
than I ever did before
Feel further than I can take
Dreamin' of you
is all I do
But it's driving me insane

The Original Soundtrack to the 2007 Dylan biopic *I'm Not There* is a treasure trove. A double CD with 34 lovely Dylan covers, almost all of them surprising, original and quirky. Even such usual suspects as "All Along the Watchtower" (Eddie Vedder), "Knockin' on Heaven's Door" (Antony and the Johnsons) and "The Times They Are a-Changin'" (Mason Jennings), which are apparently unavoidable, qualitatively stand out from the thousands of covers that already exist of these songs. But the real magic of the collection comes from the dusted-off insider tips, from the covers of songs that suffer a languishing existence at the outer edges of Dylan's vast catalogue. "Can't Leave Her Behind", "I'm Not There", the brilliant "Goin' to Acapulco" cover by Jim James and Calexico, John Doe's unsurpassed "Pressing On", "Billy 1" by Los Lobos... both the selection and the performance show genuine, intrinsic Dylan love and knowledge.

Within that list of exotic birds, Bob Forrest's "The Moonshiner" is the odd duck out. Not because of Bob Forrest, obviously. The frontman of Thelonious Monster, who, after a devastating diversion through heroin hell in 1999, was helped back into the saddle by men from the Red Hot Chili Peppers and returned under the name The Bicycle Thief with the smashingly beautiful album *You Come And Go Like A Pop Song*, can still do no wrong in 2007. His contribution to *I'm Not There* is "just" another one of the heartwarming highlights. No, his song choice is remarkable, is the odd duck out: it is the only song on the 34-song track list that is *not* a Dylan song. "The Moonshiner" is a traditional, written probably half a century before Dylan was born.

However, it is defensible, up to a point, to call it a Dylan song. The song is still quite popular when Dylan records it during the *Times They Are A-Changin'* sessions in 1963, but it is not selected for the album at the time, nor is it ever on Dylan's set list. After 1963, "The Moonshiner" still does float around in hard-core folk circles for about thirty years (plus a peerless recording by Tim Hardin, 1971), until *The Bootleg Series Volumes 1-3 (Rare & Unreleased) 1961-1991* is released, featuring that forgotten Dylan recording. Which leads to a major reappraisal. In the years that follow, the song appears on the track and set lists of names such as Uncle Tupelo, Cat Power, David Bromberg and Rich Lerner - to name but a few; "The Moonshiner" is experiencing quite a revival, after the success of that bootleg box in 1991.

The origin is unclear, but the song is at least a hundred years old and there are - of course - dozens of text variants. After 1991, nearly all colleagues follow Dylan's lyrics. But Dylan himself seems, when he records "Dreamin' Of You" in 1997, to have the version in his head as he once learned it: the one by The Clancy Brothers from 1961. Not so much because of the lines that return word for word in "Dreamin' Of You", but because of the opening words with The Clancy Brothers:

> *I'm a rambler, I'm a gambler,*
> *I'm a long way from home*
> *And if you don't like me*
> *You can leave me alone*
> *I'll eat when I'm hungry*
> *And I'll drink when I'm dry*
> *And if moonshine don't kill me*
> *I'll live till I die*

... "I'm a rambler and I'm a gambler", which echoes almost literally in "Red River Shore", that other *Time Out Of Mind* outtake, is not sung in any version other than The Clancy Brothers. And "Moonshiner" playing in Dylan's head should be clear enough from the words that follow: *I'll eat when I'm hungry and I'll drink when I'm dry*, which is sung in virtually every version, including those by Dylan, Bob Forrest and The New Lost City Ramblers (Tim Hardin sings the "Kentucky Moonshiner" version; *Corn bread when i'm hungry, corn liquor when i'm dry*).

So, for some reason, perhaps the *white moonlight* from the previous stanza, the stream of consciousness in Dylan's creative mind meanders via Henry Rollins to an antique folksong that he had in his repertoire almost forty years ago. At least, the disturbing image from the next line, *Even if the flesh falls off my face*, is something Scott Warmuth has also found with Rollins, in one of the 61 dreams described in *Black Coffee Blues*:

> "One guy comes through the door and I unload an entire clip into him but he keeps coming at me. Flesh is falling off his face, his skull is made of metal. He smiles and falls."

In itself that is, of course, a bit too thin to draw an a-ha! line to Dylan. Flesh falling off bones or bodies or faces as an image of mortality and our corruptible lives is admittedly rather gruesome, and for that reason alone has never become mainstream, but it is hardly unique. We know the image from plenty of film horror scenes, Dylan himself has been singing along with "O Death" for years (*Leave the body and leave it cold / To draw up the flesh off of the frame*), Hieronymus Bosch was painting flesh-ripping scenes already five hundred years ago, and the opening line of Dylan's own "Foot Of Pride" uses a similar idiom: "Like the lion tears the flesh off from a man".

Still, these words are surrounded by literal quotes and unmistakable paraphrases from Rollins' work... it is quite likely that Warmuth is right, that Dylan got this gruesome image also from the ferocious poet from Washington DC. And he really likes them, these lines; they move almost unchanged to "Standing In The Doorway":

> I'll eat when I'm hungry, drink when I'm dry
> And live my life on the square
> And even if the flesh falls off of my face
> I know someone will be there to care

... where its beauty, arguably, indeed does shine even brighter. Well, less sinister anyway. In a soft, white moonshiner's light.

V   It's me, Cathy

Feel like a ghost in love
Underneath the heavens above
Feel further away
than I ever did before
Feel further than I can take
Dreamin' of you
is all I do
But it's driving me insane

It remains baffling, although it is actually not that extraordinary. Rimbaud is barely nineteen when *Un Saison En Enfer* is published, Hergé starts the *Tintin* series when he is twenty-two, Dylan is twenty-one when he records "A Hard Rain's A-Gonna Fall", Picasso and Mozart produce works of genius as teenagers, Stevie Wonder is twenty when he records his *thirteenth* album *Signed, Sealed & Delivered* (1970). And Kate Bush may also be placed in this line-up. Kate was nineteen when she released *The Kick Inside* (1977) - the oldest songs on it, such as the perfect "The Man With The Child In His Eyes", were written around the age of thirteen. And her biggest hit, the masterpiece "Wuthering Heights", was written when she was eighteen.

The song has more distinctive qualities, obviously, and one of them is its narrative perspective: the lyrics are narrated by Cathy, by a *ghost in love* - it is probably the only song ever where the protagonist is a love-struck apparition.

As an archetype, s/he has never really penetrated the upper world, the ghost in love. Only once in a while, in films like the witty *Ghost Town* (with Ricky Gervais, 2008), in *The Phantom Of The Opera,* in a way, and in the rather overpolished 1990 blockbuster *Ghost* with Patrick Swayze and Demi Moore, does a ghost in love play a leading role. A film, by the way, about which everyone may have their own opinion, but still: *Ghost* has firmly re-anchored "Unchained Melody" in the cultural baggage of yet another generation, so it has at least one big plus.

In songs however, apart from "Wuthering Heights", smitten ethereal beings do not appear at all. Radiohead's "Give Up The Ghost" from 2011 insinuates a spirit in love, as does Kristin Hersh's wonderful "Your Ghost" (1994) - but there, too, *ghost* is actually used as in most other songs: as a metaphor for "the memory of you". As Joan Baez introduces her former lover Bob Dylan in her remarkable Dylan ballad "Diamonds & Rust" (1975): "Well, I'll be damned, here comes your ghost again." No, not many *real* ghosts in love in songs.

Apparently, it does not have such potential, such dramatic power as - for example - the vengeful spirit or the wandering poltergeist; there are hundreds of stories around these archetypes. And Dylan, too, uses the image here only as a metaphor, of course. But then still in the spirit of those few stories in which a real *ghost in love* appears; not to represent a memory of a loved one, but to express something like "being ghosted", like *you can look but you cannot touch*, the frustration of being so-near-and-yet-so-far. Or, somewhat more literary, the frustration of Kafka's beetle in *Die Verwandlung* or the accursed judge from "Seven Curses": being able to hear and see everything, but at the same time invisible and unhearable to everyone.

The lines that follow seem to confirm that intention. *Feel further away than I ever did before* expresses a similar so-near-and-yet-so-far feeling, articulating the anguish of a narrator who feels an emotional distance from his beloved growing. And the lines reveal a fourth offshoot of the prolific "Dreamin' Of You"; apart from the text fragments and images that move to "Things Have Changed", "Cold Irons Bound" and especially "Standing In The Doorway", the cast-off is apparently also a supplier for "Million Miles". And especially for its motif ("tryin' to get closer but I'm still a million miles from you"), of which we had already seen that Dylan's inspiration for it came from Rollins, from *Black Coffee Blues*;

> "The next song I wrote was about the distance I felt when I thought about that girl. The song centered around the lines, "The closer I get, the farther away I feel." I was thinking that all the time I was with her, I worked hard to put that out of my mind. Romance passes the time."

Much more unlikely, and certainly more remarkable, is the source for the insubstantial middle line *Underneath the heavens above*: Glenn Frey. In themselves, of course, the words are far too mundane to attribute to any source of inspiration, but on the other hand, there *is* an all too coincidental match. In 2020, Dylan leads the attention of Dylanologists to the ex-Eagle through a name-check in "Murder Most Foul":

> *Play Don Henley, play Glenn Frey*
> *Take it to the limit and let it go by*

On his most successful solo album, 1984's *The Allnighter*, the piece of craftsmanship "I Got Love" stands out. Recorded in Muscle Shoals, in the same studio with the same men who assisted Dylan on *Slow Train Coming* and on *Saved*: Barry Beckett on keyboards and the studio's horn section. The lyrics of the second verse apparently made an impression on Dylan:

> *Jumped on the freeway with this song in my head*
> *I started thinkin' 'bout the things we said*
> *I said I'm sorry; she said I'm sorry too;*
> *You know I can't be happy 'less I'm happy with you*

… the distich "I started thinkin' 'bout the things we said / I said I'm sorry; she said I'm sorry too" moves almost literally to the monumental song Dylan writes and records during these very same days as the conception of "Dreamin' Of You" takes place: "Mississippi" (respectively *I was thinkin' 'bout the things that Rosie said* and *I know you're sorry, I'm sorry too*). Words that are far too specific to be attributed to coincidence or any other source, in any case. And with that, the chorus that follows in Glenn Frey's song suddenly gets more weight too:

> *I got love, it's my lucky day*
> *I got love, gonna keep it that way*
> *It's the sweetest gift from the heavens above*
> *I got you, babe, I got love.*

… so that Glenn Frey can suddenly call himself, with some right of speech, inspirator, or rather: contributor of at least *two* Dylan songs. Incidentally, at the end of the album's track list we find the horribly dated sounding "Living In Darkness" with its unmemorable chorus

You're living in darkness
You're living in the past
Living in darkness
Your dream is fading fast

... could just as well be about a ghost in love, come to think of it.

VI   The movement on your shoulder

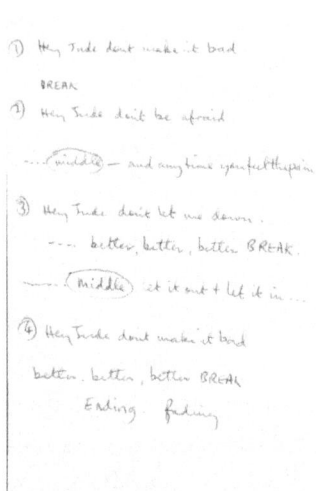

1) Hey Jude dont make it bad
   BREAK
2) Hey Jude don't be afraid
   ... (middle) — and anytime you feel the pain
3) Hey Jude don't let me down.
   --- better, better, better BREAK.
   --- (middle) let it out + let it in ...
4) Hey Jude dont make it bad
   better, better, better BREAK
   Ending. fading

From a formal point of view, the last ten-line stanza, or officially the last quatrain + sextet, is the most remarkable of the entire lyrics. And on the other two fronts, stylistically and in terms of content, it actually is too. Just as the entire text "in fact" seems to have another form than the one presented, namely ten-line stanzas in a fixed rhyme scheme, closed with a recurring refrain line, this ending also "in fact" seems to have a completely different form: in terms of stanza construction, a reversed sonnet. An inverted Petrarchan sonnet, to be precise; first the sextet, then the octave. Dylan chooses - for the time being, presumably - for a completely original mixture of classical rhyme schemes in the two quatrains of the octave (*AABB* and *CDDC*) and an open, modern rhyme scheme in the opening tercets (*AAB* and *CCD*).

So officially, on the site, this part of the lyrics is again formatted as ten lines, as a quatrain plus a sextet, but both content and rhyme scheme as well as Dylan's recitation leave little doubt:

Everything in the way
is so shiny today
A queer and unusual fall

Spirals of golden haze,
here and there in a blaze
Like beams of light in the storm

Maybe you were here and maybe you weren't
Maybe you touched somebody and got burnt
The silent sun
has got me on the run

Burning a hole in my brain
I'm dreamin' of you,
that's all I do
But it's driving me insane

... an inverted sonnet with even a neat classical chute between the sextet and the octave, as it should be. With the exposition in the opening sextet and the pointe in the concluding octave - Petrarch would have given his blessing. And probably would have tolerated the newfangled rhyme scheme of the sextet as youthful hubris. Maybe even appreciated it as a nod to McCartney's "Hey Jude";

So let it out and let it in,
hey Jude, begin,
You're waiting for someone to perform with.

And don't you know that it's just you,
hey Jude, you'll do,
The movement you need is on your shoulder.

... the second bridge, which McCartney actually only provided with filler lyrics for the time being, hence the "not right yet" rhyme scheme *AAB-CCD*. But he was overruled by Lennon, as Sir Paul tells us (in Paul Gambaccini's interview collection *Paul McCartney In His Own Words*, 1976):

Like "Hey Jude", I think I've got that tape somewhere, where I'm going on and on with all these funny words. I remember I played it to John and Yoko and I was saying, "These words won't be on the finished version." Some of the words were *the movement you need is on your shoulder*, and John was saying, "It's great! *The movement you need is on your shoulder*." I'm saying "It's crazy, it doesn't make any sense al all." He's saying "Sure it does, it's great."

Considering the fate of "Dreamin' Of You", it seems obvious that Dylan, like McCartney, fills this part of his song with the words that come up first, words that at least approximately cover the intended content, but for the time being without worrying about rhyme or reason. "These words won't be on the finished version," after all. A finished version that, as we know, never came.

Removed from the complete song lyrics, the last part of "Dreamin' Of You" seems to be an opening. Conceivable; ever since "All Along The Watchtower" (1967), or even earlier, Dylan has been resorting to a narrative technique he calls "the cycle of events working in a rather reverse order". Though not quite conclusive here; after all, "Dreamin' Of You" has a lyrical text, not an epic "cycle of events", but nevertheless this closing section definitely seems to have been set up as an opening:

> Everything in the way is so shiny today
> A queer and unusual fall
> Spirals of golden haze, here and there in a blaze
> Like beams of light in the storm

A traditional opening like for instance "Oh What A Beautiful Mornin'" (1943), the opening song of the hit musical *Oklahoma!*, incidentally the very first Rodgers/Hammerstein song that the world gets to know:

There's a bright golden haze on the meadow,
There's a bright golden haze on the meadow,
The corn is as high as an elephants eye,
An' it looks like it's climbing clear up in the sky.
Oh, what a beautiful mornin',
Oh, what a beautiful day.
I got a beautiful feelin'
Ev'erything's goin' my way

... an immortal song that sets the standard for all musicals to come. In addition to the same idiom, it has exactly the same cinematic, professional quality – starting with a wide shot of carefree idyll and sunshine, to warm up the audience: this cannot go on, this spells disaster. Underlined by Dylan in the very last word of the sextet, *storm*.

The idiom, the choice of words, also suggests that the poet started with this part of the text; "queer fall", "golden haze", "silent sun", "beams of light"... Dylan searches and finds archaic, elegant, nineteenth-century idiom and meanders among other things along shreds of Melville ("the golden haze that canopied this heaven," *Mardi*), which the associative mind of the walking music encyclopaedia Dylan no doubt leads to *Oklahoma!*, and William Blake. "Beams of light" is most likely anchored in the poetic part of Dylan's brain thanks to Blake's poem "Auguries of Innocence" (1803), the same poem whose opening line *To see a World in a Grain of Sand* already (partly) inspired him to write the masterpiece "Every Grain Of Sand" and whose closing lines he noticed too: *When the Soul Slept in Beams of Light*. Just like Dylan seems to have Blake's "Jerusalem", from which he also drew for "Every Grain Of Sand", on his bedside table again these days:

THEN the Divine Vision like a silent Sun appear'd above
Albion's dark rocks: setting behind the Gardens of Kensington
On Tyburn's River: in clouds of blood

... the *clouds of blood* are reserved for "Cold Irons Bound", and the *silent sun* is an equally beautiful, loaded and mysterious image for the threat that the poet Dylan wants to express in the next few lines. With the nineteenth century couleur of *steamboat, Mark Twain and Civil War* that Dylan still strives for in this phase of *Time Out Of Mind*'s genesis. Darker and more elegant than *the movement on your shoulder*, in any case.

VII   Perhaps soft-boiled egg shit

"Maybe I'm afraid of the way I love you," sings Sir Paul at the beginning of one of his many masterpieces, of "Maybe I'm Amazed" (1970). The first of many *maybes* in this particular song - seventeen more will follow. It has a poetic power and a wistful beauty that has been recognised in all ages by poets in all corners of art history: the single word "maybe". Dylan has already tapped into its power before in his songs, as in one of his most beautiful love songs, in "Mama, You Been On My Mind";

> Perhaps it's the color of the sun cut flat
> An' cov'rin' the crossroads I'm standing at
> Or maybe it's the weather or something like that
> But mama, you been on my mind

... in which the elusiveness of a strong emotion is, of course, reinforced by the equally helpless addition *or something like that*.

Part of the magic is due to the bonus value of "resignation" contained in *maybe*. A bonus like the one exploited by Cat Stevens in "Maybe You're Right" (1970);

Now maybe you're right
And maybe you're wrong
But I ain't gonna argue with you no more
I've done it for too long

... but which only becomes truly irresistible when combined with melancholy - like the heartbreaking melancholy of the sublime quatrain from one of Nick Drake's all-time great songs, from "River Man" (1969):

Betty said she prayed today
For the sky to blow away
Or maybe stay
She wasn't sure.

Mastery such as you would otherwise only find in French, the language that has an unfair advantage. After all, everything sounds more melodious and melancholy in French. We see it in the poets who have penetrated Dylan's work since the mid-1960s, in Verlaine, Rimbaud and Baudelaire, and we hear it in the chansonniers like Moustaki, Cabrel and Hardy, the artists who share an artistic affinity with Dylan in more ways than one. As demonstrated in a chanson like "L'arbre noir", the closing track of Nino Ferrer's *Blanat* from 1979 - a song that, in eight lines, captures Dylan's entire *Time Out Of Mind* plus the outtakes:

Rien n'est changé, tout est pareil
Tout est pourtant si différent
Il flotte comme un goût de sommeil

Nothing has changed, all is the same
Yet everything is so different
It floats like a hint of sleep

Ou de tristesse, je ne sais comment
Ce n'est peut-être que le temps
Qui passe et laisse une poussière
De rêves morts et d'illusions
Peut-être est-ce ton absence, mon cœur

Or sadness, I don't know
Maybe it's just time
That passes and leaves some dust
Of dead dreams and illusions
Maybe it's your absence, my love.

It is, therefore, arguably the most beautiful verse, or, depending on your point of view, the most beautiful octave of Dylan's "Dreamin' Of You": the closing lines. An ending that could stand on its own, a sestain like one by Byron, Schiller or Verlaine;

> *Maybe you were here and maybe you weren't*
> *Maybe you touched somebody and got burnt*
> *The silent sun has got me on the run*
> *Burning a hole in my brain*
> *I'm dreamin' of you, that's all I do*
> *But it's driving me insane*

... despite its technical imperfection. If Dylan had not discarded the lyrics so readily, he would undoubtedly have done some repair work on rhyme and rhythm. The weak repetition *burnt-burning* would not have survived, in all likelihood. And the *silent sun* line was probably sacrificed to achieve a troubadour-like AABCBC rhyme scheme, or something like that. But as it is, it is still a beautiful sestain - the lyrical power of the words is convincing even without a classical corset, the "minor" stylistic devices such as internal rhyme and alliteration provide the sextet with more than enough melody and euphony.

The opening *Maybe you were here and maybe you weren't* has its own almost magical power, which transcends its simple dialectic; with these few simple words, the poet colours all that has gone before a few shades more melancholic - and at the same time more resigned. In all its simplicity, a masterly line of text, with the same magical, elusive poetic power as Ferrer's "L'arbre noir" or Drake's "River Man". A magic that Dylan also seems to seek here, witness the following line *Maybe you touched somebody and got burnt*. The trigger is probably Dylan's love of rhyme; the rhyme *weren't-burnt* is yet another Dylanesque rhyme in the category of *sick-in-chicken* (from "Tombstone Blues") and *buy her-fire* ("Love Minus Zero"), of frenzied rhyme finds in short, for which Dylan has had a contagious weakness for over sixty years now. This rhyme *weren't-burnt* is probably only found in one place in all of Western culture. By the poet whose work in the 1960s was disqualified by Dylan as being "bullshit", "bad" and "soft-boiled egg shit" (in the *Los Angeles Free Press* interview with Paul J. Robbins, 1965), by Robert Frost, that is:

> *I name all the flowers I am sure they weren't;*
> *Not fireweed loving where woods have burnt-*

... from the beautiful poem "A Passing Glimpse" (1928), the poem with the brilliant, rather Proustian line *Heaven gives it glimpses only to those / Not in position to look too close*. A work of art, all in all, that the 55-year-old Dylan in 1997 will look at with considerably more respect and admiration than the 23-year-old angry young man Dylan in 1965. Frost as a direct source for the choice of words in this particular Dylan song is unlikely, but who knows: the following *silent sun* seems to have been borrowed from William Blake, but Dylan certainly did read Henry Rollins just before the creation of "Dreamin' Of You";

> *After life*
> *Miles away*
> *A life away*
> *Up a long river*
> *On a beach*
> *Silent sun will watch over me*

... from *Now Watch Him Die*, the poignant poetic mourning from which Dylan has drawn so much more for the *Time Out Of Mind* songs.

The closing *Burning a hole in my brain* seems to be another final product of the blender's work in Dylan's creative brain. "Holes in brain" abound in Rollins' oeuvre, who seems quite fond of metaphors describing destructive activities in the brain area ("I am left with hammer holes in my brain," for example, and "It drills a hole into your brain"), and perhaps Dylan's associations meander along songs in his inner jukebox like Connie Smith's "Burning A Hole In Mind". But a more obvious inspiration source, after those earlier borrowings, would seem to be lyrics by the unlikely purveyor Glenn Frey, the ex-Eagle who, apart from "Mississippi", also contributes several fragments of lyrics to "Dreamin' Of You". This time from the rather mediocre "Long Hot Summer" (*Strange Weather*, 1992):

> *You see the heat comin' up from the sidewalk*
> *You can feel the temperature rise*
> *All I see is a blazin' sun*
> *Burning a hole in the sky*

... in itself hardly specific enough to be considered a source for Dylan's *Burning a hole in my brain*, but then again: the verse before it also says "go insane", in the next verse Frey sings "It's too hot to sleep, we're in trouble so deep," which Dylan takes to "Not Dark Yet" and in two stanzas after that "There's a fire in the sky and the earth is so dry," which echoes again in "Mississippi". Too many similarities to be coincidental, anyway; for some reason Glenn Frey's "Long Hot Summer" also gets under Dylan's skin. Unbelievable and improbable, though still hardly surprising anymore: Henry Rollins, Junichi Saga, a Time Magazine from 1961, Proust's *À la recherche du temps perdu*.... Dylan has by now convincingly demonstrated that he can just as easily draw from improbable sources. Glenn Frey fits right in. Even though he writes, apart from a few okay lyrics, mostly soft-boiled egg shit.

VIII   Harry Dean

When "Dreamin' Of You" is released in the autumn of 2008, 21 years after its recording and subsequent discarding, the song gets the full glare of the spotlight. It is chosen to promote the upcoming release of the overwhelming *The Bootleg Series Vol. 8: Tell Tale Signs: Rare and Unreleased 1989-2006*. Fans can download the song for free, it is released as a single and a promotional music video is recorded.

The video is irresistible. Harry Dean Stanton is always a joy to watch, especially when he gets to play his own archetype: the old, worn-out, odd-jobber, preferably in a sweltering heat, driven by some private obsession. The Harry Dean Stanton from *Paris, Texas*, from his last movie *Lucky* (2017), the *lost yankee on gloomy Sunday-carnival-embassy-type*, as Dylan, in the 1985 *Biograph* booklet, typified the main characters in "Just Like Tom Thumb's Blues" and "Señor".

The Dylan-Stanton connection is documented, not least by the gentlemen themselves. In interviews, Stanton is often enough tempted to tell an anecdote about their friendship, which began in

1973 on the set of Peckinpah's *Pat Garrett & Billy The Kid*, in which both of them starred. And, a-typically, the friendship even moves Dylan to a rare on-stage revelation, in Blackbushe, 15 July 1978: "This song is inspired by a man named Harry Dean Stanton. Some of you may know him," at the announcement of "Señor". And three days earlier, in Gothenburg, Dylan lifted another tip regarding the same song:

"This is a new song written about six months ago on a trip through the southern part of the ... northern part of the States. Anyway it's entitled Tales Of Yankee Power"

... apparently referring to a road trip of which Harry Dean Stanton has given more details. The friends undertook sometime in 1977 a three-days holiday trip by car from Guadalajara to Kansas City to visit Leon Russell, so Dylan's apparent slip of the tongue "through the southern part of the ... northern part of the United States" is pretty much correct.

The anecdote, plus Stanton's film image, plus his unique charisma with the paradoxical quality of being simultaneously jaded and driven, make Harry Dean a perfect interpreter of the moving mini-portrait sketched in the video clip. Harry Dean, the slacker, who sells self-produced bootlegs and follows his hero Bob

Dylan across the United States. We see him sweating and slaving away with tapes and cassette tapes and covers, and we see the genuine love of a Dylan fan - occasionally Harry Dean picks up a guitar, a few times he mutters the words to "Dreamin' Of You". And we get a few snippets that suggest an underlying tragedy when we see Stanton looking at a photograph. A photograph that he always carries with him, in the car and in hotel rooms and in his workroom: an old black-and-white photograph of an attractive lady with an old-fashioned hairdo in old-fashioned clothes, about twenty-one years old. A love from the days gone by, apparently.

"I'm dreaming of you," Harry Dean mumbles wordlessly along with the lyrics.

14   Marchin' To The City

I   The last verses might be better

The two versions of "Marchin' To The City" that *Tell Tale Signs* bestowes upon us are a very kind gift from the compilers to the fans and Dylano-logists. The gift value is similar to "Dreamin' Of You" in terms of lyrics (revealing how fragments move to a different song), with as a bonus a glimpse into the musical evolution: we hear how #1 opens as a gospel ballad, evolving into a slow blues, the switch to midtempo in #2, and therein already tentatively the shouted exclamations on the guitar that will eventually be so distinctive for "'Til I Fell In Love With You".

The search for the definitive *Time Out Of Mind* sound, meanwhile, is just as voyeuristic to follow. The primal version, the slow blues, is crystal clear, crispy, and Dylan's voice hovers, with slight reverberation, over the music. In the second version, on Disc 3, Dylan's voice is brought down to the studio floor, standing warm and intimate between the band - over which, incidentally, a damp blanket has been placed. Somewhere after that, just before "'Til I Fell In Love With You", Lanois and Dylan seem to have decided to return to the sound of #1, and then square it, on almost every front: Dylan's voice has double the reverb, as do the drums, two of the three guitars and Augie Meyer's organ, but the bass, piano and third guitar retain the warm, humid #2 sound. The pace finally ends halfway between "Marchin' To The City" #1 and "Marchin' To The City" #2. All three songs have the same, generic blues scheme (only the key rises by half, from E♭ to the more guitar-friendly E).

Version 1 has seven stanzas, each ending with the same refrain:

> *Once I had a pretty girl*
> *She done me wrong*
> *Now I'm marching to the city*
> *And the road ain't long*

At least, almost the same. Now and then Dylan corrects the grammar (and sings *she did me wrong*), and the first time he sings the chorus, it's still plural: *once I had pretty girls*. Presumably a deliberate attempt to not copy too literally from Del Shannon's "Hats Off To Larry";

> *Once I had a pretty girl*
> *Her name it doesn't matter*
> *She went away with another guy*
> *Now he won't even look at her*

... Del Shannon's second single and second biggest hit after "Runaway". And in fact not much more than a rip-off of his own "Runaway". But apparently "Hats Off For Larry" is still at the front row of Dylan's inner jukebox; the chorus line *He told you lies now it's your turn to cry cry cry* is also borrowed by Dylan - we shall hear it a few years after the recording of "Marchin' To The City", in "Cry A While" on *"Love And Theft"* (2001).

Anyway, after that first chorus Dylan has already forgotten his semi-transparent cover-up - in the remaining six choruses plus all the choruses of #2 Dylan sings Del Shannon's line in the "right"singular: *Once I had a pretty girl*. The rest of Shannon's not-too-verbose schadenfreude song Dylan succinctly summarises with *she done me wrong* - a classic blues cliché we know from dozens of songs from the blues canon, from the country lexicon, to even symphonic rock (Genesis' "Robbery, Assault And Battery"). From Jimmie Rodgers' 1931 "Travelin' Blues", Joe McCoy's 1932 "You Know You Done Me Wrong", and from the great Elmore James ("Coming Home", 1957), but especially from "It's All Over Now", of course; the song that also cemented *her turn to cry*. A word combination Dylan, in variations, has sung often enough himself ("Man On The Street", for example, and "Frankie & Albert"). A line that entirely on its own will impose itself on Dylan.

The concluding lines of the verse did not cost any blood, sweat or tears either: also lovingly stolen. From the old spiritual "Wade In The Water", as recorded by Alan Lomax:

> *The enemy's great, but my Captain's strong*
> *I'm marching to the city and the road ain't long*

"Wade In The Water" is on Dylan's repertoire in the early 1960s, as we know from the bootleg *Minnesota Hotel Tape* (recorded 22 December 1961), but back then he does not yet sing these words.

It seems that Dylan had the chorus first, and then opened the floodgates. "So that's where the song was going all along," as he says in the 2020 *New York Times* interview with Douglas Brinkley about the creation of "I Contain Multitudes", adding "most of my recent songs are like that." We are now looking over the poet's shoulder into his draft. He is not yet concerned about cohesion, or even a motif. "Write twenty verses while you're in The Zone," is the writing advice Dylan gives to Mike Campbell. The polishing and scrapping will come later, the master teaches, just write uncritically first, and keep writing – "the last verses might be better than all the stuff you had."

The first verse is apparently already a demonstration of that method. Most of it will be deleted again;

> *Well I'm sitting in church in an old wooden chair*
> *I knew nobody would look for me there*
> *Sorrow and pity rule the earth and the skies*
> *Looking for nothing in anyone's eyes*

Initially a classic opening for a novella; in the first two lines the introduction by means of the traditional *who-where-what-why*, then an attention-grabbing, wisdom-suggesting aphorism, and finally the beautifully poetic, resigned despondency *Looking for nothing in anyone's eyes.*

Almost cinematic, this opening. *The Fugitive*, something like that. In a Catholic church, clearly, as the narrator seems mesmerised by an abundance of Stations of the Cross around him - *sorrow and pity rule the earth and the skies*. Which probably also brings in a first stagnation for the poet in The Zone; in the past decades, he has stated that *Mercury rules*, that the *masters make the rules*, that *whoever got the gold rules*, that *lawbreakers make the rules*, that *this world is ruled by violence*, and anyway: a protagonist who believes in the power of *sorrow and pity* is rather out of place on *Time Out Of Mind* - Dylan does, after all, create a world of despondency here, of abandonment and farewell, full of extinguished protagonists who at best strive for resignation.

So three lines that do not inspire the poet to a comprehensive narrative, but still lead him to the one line that will survive; *I ain't looking for nothing in anyone's eyes* will eventually be promoted to a verse line in one of the grandest black pearls of Dylan's late work: "Not Dark Yet".

Not a bad net result, all in all.

II   Loneliness is just a waste of time

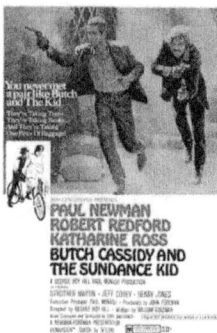

The freewheelin' poet finds no further inspiration in the church, lets his protagonist rise from his wooden chair and open the door to the outside world. We were not, as the gospel-like opening and languid blues accompaniment suggests, in a stuffy little church somewhere in Mississippi or Georgia on a sweltering summer's day;

Snowflakes are falling around my head
Lord have mercy, it feel heavy like lead
I been hit too hard, seen too much
Nothing can heal me now but your touch

But we are a lot farther north, and it's a bleak winter's day. Or perhaps a fairytale winter day, with snowflakes whirling picturesquely. The songwriter, meanwhile, seems to have made an inimitable associative leap to *Butch Cassidy And The Sundance Kid*.

The persistent story has been repeatedly denied by Burt Bacharach himself, but on 5 March 2021, B.J. Thomas is quite resolute, in conversation with Bart Herbison, in another great episode of *Tennessean*'s wonderful series "Story Behind The Song":

> "Burt had written the melody for Bob Dylan. I think he said he didn't do that but there was a time where he did pitch it to Bob Dylan. He was the first to turn it down. It seemed like a Dylan song, but maybe not."

... and B.J. Thomas is a well-informed source, of course. Ray Stevens also turns the song down, preferring to record "Sunday Morning Coming Down", so in the end B.J. is the lucky wilbury who gets to have "Raindrops Keep Fallin' On My Head".

This must have played out in the summer of 1969, shortly after Dylan recorded *Nashville Skyline* and "Lay Lady Lay"; Bacharach's idea of giving the song to Dylan would not have been that crazy - *and* it is an attractive fantasy, the fantasy of what Dylan would have done with "Raindrops Keep Fallin' On My Head" (aside from imagining how the confrontation with the notoriously perfectionist Bacharach would have gone down). It is, frankly, rather unlikely that Dylan could have done better than the untouchable monument built by Bacharach and B.J. Thomas. On the other hand: the cover by the Manic Street Preachers from Wales in 1995 demonstrates an unexpectedly tragic, gritty depth to the classic - a dimension that a *Time Out Of Mind* Dylan will surely enjoy.

Anyway, thirty years later, the song seems to be haunting Dylan's mind again and going through the Dylan-o-matic ("I'm listening to the song in my head. At a certain point, some of the words will change and I'll start writing a song," as Dylan explained in that Robert Hilburn interview, 2003).

But presumably Dylan also considers the word change from "raindrops" to "snowflakes" not radical enough. And he's right; *"snowflakes are falling 'round my head"* still keeps evoking Paul Newman and his antics on the bicycle. No, both this line and the subsequent filler *"Lord have mercy, it feels heavy like lead"* (Ray Charles' "Lonely Avenue" buzzes around as well, apparently) will not survive, and have already been scrapped in #2 of "Marchin' To The City".

Which does not apply to the second half: *"I been hit too hard, seen too much / Nothing can heal me now but your touch"* does seem to please. The words are even promoted unchanged to the opening verse of "'Til I Fell In Love With You". Conceivable; apart from the perfect *TOOM* colour and stylistical beauty, the words have an evangelical connotation that surely appeals to Dylan. Something like "Somebody Touched Me" by The Stanley Brothers, which will also be on Dylan's set list in the following years. Or Elvis' "He Touched Me" of course, which Dylan values at least as highly, and whose tenor is the same as these two lines from Dylan's song;

> Shackled by a heavy burden
> 'Neath a load of guilt and shame
> Then the hand of Jesus touched me
> And now I am no longer the same

...*first* the misery of the man "who has seen too much", *then* the healing power of a touch, as it should be.

The Dylan-o-matic, the inner engine of the songwriter who writes his verses one after the other while he is in The Zone, is now starting to come up to speed. The third verse of "Marchin' To The City" approaches the familiar poetic perfection;

Loneliness got a mind of its own
The more people around, the more you feel alone
I'm chained to the earth like a silent slave
Trying to break free out of death's dark cave

"Loneliness" is, evidently, a motif that perfectly lends itself to marble one-liners. Desolation is, after all, unambiguous, pitiful and universally recognisable. *"Loneliness is the cloak you wear,"* as the Walker Brothers unforgettably open their "The Sun Ain't Gonna Shine Anymore". Solomon Burke snarling that *"loneliness is just a waste of time"* ("Cry To Me"), Andy Williams looking for *"a place where there's just loneliness, where dim lights bring forgetfulness"* and finding it on "Lonely Street"... all brilliant, unforgettable one-liners that would be utterly insignificant if "loneliness" were replaced by, say, "happiness". After all, happy people are all alike; but every lonely man is lonely in his own way, to paraphrase Tolstoy.

And the Dylan of the late 90s, back at the top of his game, enriches this heartbreaking series of one-liners with the most beautiful of all: *"Loneliness got a mind of its own"* - the poet with frightening clarity expresses the irrational, destructive power of loneliness even with people around. And just as successful is the continuation; the suicidal despair of *"chained to the earth"*, the numbness of *"silent slave"* and the Odysseus-inspired suspense of *"trying to break free from death's dark cave"*... it has the gloomy shine of "Not Dark Yet" and the despondency of "Dirt Road Blues", the hopelessness of "Cold Irons Bound" and the sadness of "Standing In The Doorway" - with a stronger hint of metaphysics, though.

The ever-accelerating stream of inspiration seems to want to lead Dylan's imagery to a ghost story. A soul that cannot be released from the earth as long as a fateful love binds him, something like that. After all, he is in *death's dark cave*, is "chained" and seems unable to be seen by *people around* him. Which brings an evangelical connotation to the title and the chorus; the wandering soul is not on his way to, say, the Big Apple, not to just any city, but to a Heavenly Jerusalem, the city of gold, where the King, our Redeemer, the Lord whom we love, all the faithful with rapture behold.

A twist that Dylan will explore further in the following verses. But the beauty of this particular verse, the one that sets him on track, does not convince him. Too whiny, perhaps. The stanza still becomes the opening couplet of "Marchin' To The City #2", but after that, the self-directed loneliness, the silent slave and death's dark cave all disappear into the Waters Of Oblivion, never to be heard again. Well, who cares. Dylan is in The Zone – he'll write twenty more verses.

III   You'll be sorry when I'm dead

Most films and stories in which a ghost roams the earth have such a scene. Sometimes romcom-like, as in *Just Like Heaven* (2005) and *Ghost Town* (2008), sometimes even corny (*Topper*, with Cary Grant, 1937), but mostly melancholic to just plain sad: the spirit wanders unseen over the stopping places of his life, stares lonely at playing children, sadly observes smiling people at outdoor cafes and his shadowy presence is noticed at most by a passing dog. Who, to the incomprehension of his owner, starts growling at an emptiness.

His sojourn in The Zone brings Dylan's meandering creative mind a protagonist in *death's cave, chained to earth*, so that is the direction where "Marchin' To The City" now flows:

> Boys in the street beginning to play
> Girls like birds flying away
> I'm carrying the roses that were given to me
> And I'm thinking about paradise, wondering what it might be

... cinematic, indeed. First the wide-shot of a street scene where life goes on as usual, then the camera pans the protagonist with the loaded image of roses in his hand. Which reminds the Dylan fan of "Love Minus Zero", of course (*people carry roses, and make promises by the hour* - also illustrating something like "life goes on"), but here the ghostly narrator insinuates that he has just attended his own funeral and taken some flowers from it. All the while musing about the next stop, "paradise".

The latter does not survive. The image of the boys playing and the girls running has a lasting quality, is eventually taken to "'Til I Fell In Love With You". No such luck for the roses and paradise. Perhaps too sweet, too cute - both are discarded. The tenor is maintained, though; they are replaced by "When I'm gone you will remember my name" from verse 7.

In the end, the same net result as verse 5 will have, coincidentally;

> Go over to London, maybe gay Paree
> Follow the river, you get to the sea
> I was hoping we could drink from Life's clear streams
> I was hoping we could dream Life's pleasant dreams

The first two lines are so good that they are reserved for the highlight "Not Dark Yet", the lines after that survive up to and including "Marchin' To The City #2", and are discarded then. Beautiful lines, euphonious and beautifully poetically balanced with a not-too-bad imagery, lovingly stolen from William Blake's famous "You Don't Believe" from 1808;

> *You don't believe -- I won't attempt to make ye:*
> *You are asleep -- I won't attempt to wake ye.*
> *Sleep on! sleep on! while in your pleasant dreams*
> *Of reason you may drink of Life's clear streams*

... but ultimately rejected by Dylan. Perhaps for stylistic reasons; they are the only lines of the whole song with a "we" perspective - although confusingly fiddling with personal pronouns is exactly what the poet Dylan usually integrates (cultivates, even) without any problem. In terms of content, there seems nothing wrong with it, nor with the subtext, with Blake's conclusion *That is the very thing that Jesus meant, / When He said `Only believe! believe and try! / Try, try, and never mind the reason why!* - a message that must be close to Dylan's heart.

Anyway, Blake is deleted again, but still inspires Dylan to an aphoristic interlude, to a sixth verse that opens with:

> *Well the weak get weaker and the strong stay strong*
> *The train keeps rolling all night long*
> *She looked at me with an irresistible glance*
> *With a smile that could make all the planets dance*

Ironically, the weakest verse of the song under construction, and it is rejected immediately, even before the #2. Understandable; the "aphorism" is a rather gratuitous variant on a worn-out cliché, the *rolling train* is admittedly dylanesque, but not much more than filler in which, with some good will, one might see a link to "life goes on" or something like that, and the closing lines are just awkward. Undylanesque anyway ("dancing planets"?), but also *lousy poetry*, like Dylan once reportedly said about Joan Baez' writings.

The little slump does not derail the train. The last stanza, the seventh, is clearly only a sketch, but it does give the persistent poet in The Zone words and images that will make it to the gallery of honour, to *Time Out Of Mind*:

> *My house is on fire, burning to the skies*
> *I thought the rain clouds but the clouds passed by*
> *When I'm gone you'll remember my name*
> *I'm gonna win my way to wealth and fame*

Okay, that second line comes out a bit clumsy. Corrected in #2 to, of course, *I thought it would rain but the clouds passed by*, as it will eventually appear in "'Til I Fell In Love With You". And, although every word of this verse is deemed good enough for *Time Out Of Mind*, this combination of verse lines is not to the master's liking - nor its position in the lyrics; it really is not a final couplet. The first rudimentary steps to a ghost story in the third verse, the *death's dark cave* couplet, leads the flow to *When I'm gone*, but otherwise it's not very coherent. The mother of "Marchin' To The City", the gospel "Wade In The Water", pushes the associations with metaphors like *My house is on fire, burning to the skies* to religious connotations. "My soul is lost, I'm going to hell", something like that. But is still quite underdeveloped - the words will be better placed in "'Til I Fell In Love With You".

And: suddenly, the melancholy is gone. "Just wait, soon I'll be rich and famous and you'll be sorry"... this is beginning to sound more like the childish, vindictive bleating of the aggrieved protagonist of The Police's "Can't Stand Losing You":

I guess this is our last goodbye
And you don't care, so I won't cry
But you'll be sorry when I'm dead
And all this guilt will be on your head

No, this is going the wrong way. Dylan puts the last two sentences aside. They don't appear in #2. The burning house and the overhanging rain clouds are allowed to remain, but the wealth and fame are exchanged for the misery and regret from the first verse:

My house is burnin' up to the skies
I thought it would rain but the clouds passed by
Sorrow and pity through the earth and the skies
I'm not looking for nothing in anyone's eyes

... better, indeed. But still not good enough for "'Til I Fell In Love With You".

IV   I Just Don't Know What To Do With Myself

The second version, the up-tempo and smoother version of "Marchin' To The City", distinguishes itself, apart from the changed key (from E♭ to the guitar-friendlier E) and the different arrangement, mainly by the quite radical text intervention. The chorus is maintained, but the verses are cut back considerably. Of the seven, only four remain; two and a half old ones, supplemented by one and a half new ones. The only one to emerge unscathed from the battle is the most beautiful verse, the one that Dylan evidently finds hard to say goodbye to and which is even promoted to the opening verse:

> *Loneliness got a mind of its own*
> *The more people around, the more you feel alone*
> *I've been chained to the earth like a silent slave*
> *I'm trying to break free out of death's dark cave*

... which was originally the third verse. The first two are ruthlessly deleted, though this one will not survive either in the end. The theme of "'Til I Fell In Love With You" is "smaller", more intimate love despair - perhaps the poet finds the "larger", existential desolation of this *loneliness* couplet ultimately too dramatic.

From version #1, the *gay Paree/follow the river* lines are saved for "Not Dark Yet", the first line of that former fifth verse is allowed into this second verse:

> *I was hoping to my soul that we'd never part*
> *You took all the madness right out of my heart*
> *I was hoping we could drink from Life's clear streams*
> *I was hoping we could dream from Life's pleasant dreams*

So for the time being, William Blake's words from "You Don't Believe" may remain, now introduced by a much more intimate confession of love. Poetically not really an improvement, by the way. The rhyming of *we'd never part* with *broken heart*, or *with gave you my heart*, or with other variants, we've known for a hundred years from inspirational quotes, the back of matchboxes and sentimental lyrics like "Hello Mary-Lou" and "Wayward Wind" and "Hurt". Nothing wrong with that of course, but here, in this revised version of "Marchin' To The City", it is an impoverishment. At most, the "I Walk The Line"-like motif of *you took all the madness right out of my heart*, of the revelation that love has changed the personality of the protagonist, is a merit, opening the gate to the theme of the forthcoming "'Til I Fell In Love With You".

Which does not extend to the third verse, however. This third stanza seems to consist of rather haphazard cutting and pasting from #1;

> *My house is burnin' up to the skies*
> *I thought it would rain but the clouds passed by*
> *Sorrow and pity through the earth and the skies*
> *I'm not looking for nothing in anyone's eyes*

Which in turn is merrily cut up, and pasted into "'Til I Fell In Love With You" (lines 1 and 2), "Not Dark Yet" (line 4), and consigned to the wastebasket (line 3). This verse ultimately has little more than a bridging function, all in all; it fills a minute to the main verse of #2, the most important part, the closing couplet.

> *Wind is blowin' all troubles and dirt*
> *Time to get away 'fore someone gets hurt*
> *I just don't know what I'm a-gonna do*
> *I was all right 'til I fell in love with you*

Not so much important because of the rather generic opening lines, obviously. Skilful and provided with a pinch of appropriate melancholy, but the clichéd rhyme *dirt/hurt* is undoubtedly too easy in Dylan's ears as well. It's been used in thousands of songs, from Loretta Lynn to Marty Robbins, from Tom Waits to Mick Jagger and from Motörhead to Public Enemy... and Dylan himself has chosen this easy way out plenty of times too ("Do Right To Me Baby", "Don't Ever Take Yourself Away", "Last Thoughts On Woody Guthrie"). No, for this #2 Dylan does dash off these lines in a wink, including the trite rhyme, but after the recording they are discharged into the shredder just as easily.

The music-historical eternal value is, of course, in the closing lines. Again, presumably, a sample of the conclusion of

Dylan's songwriting class to Mike Campbell; the "twenty verses" you write while you're out there in The Zone, hoping that "the last ones might be better than all the stuff you had." Dylan, in this case, is not only merely content with these last lines; they even inspire a complete song – that's how much better than "all the stuff he had" these new lines are, apparently.

It is a change all right. Where the song initially seemed to be going in an almost metaphysical, transcending misery direction, these last two lines suddenly take a turn towards universally recognisable, "small" heartbreak, small heartbreak at which that new line in verse 2 already hinted (*"You took all the madness right out of my heart"*). And once again, after the "Raindrops Keep Falling On My Head" echo in #1, Burt Bacharach seems a signpost. At least, the opening of the change of direction, *"I just don't know what I'm a-gonna do"*, has the colour, tone and even word choice of the immortal "I Just Don't Know What To Do With Myself";

> *I just don't know what to do with myself*
> *Don't know just what to do with myself*
> *I'm so used to doing everything with you*
> *Planning everything for two*
> *And now that we're through*

... the song we all know and love in Dusty Springfield's unsurpassed 1964 version, but which, as we only discovered in the 1980s, was recorded much earlier by Chuck Jackson in 1962 (over the original track by Tommy Hunt) - with a similarly magical, thoroughly melancholic beauty as Dusty's masterpiece.

Although the magic, to be honest, actually shines through in each and every version. Marcia Hines, Isaac Hayes, White Stripes, Dionne Warwick... Elvis Costello has had the song in his repertoire since 1977, when he still was an angry young man and therefore initially misunderstood, as he explains:

> "It was a measure of how backwards things were in 1977 that some people actually thought I was making a joke when The Attractions and I began performing "I Just Don't Know What to Do with Myself". I was not being ironic. I was being extremely literal."
>
> (in his autobiography *Unfaithful Music & Disappearing Ink*, 2015).

Costello has performed the song at least 50 times during his career, was even allowed to perform it with Bacharach himself on piano in 1998, and still performs the evergreen in 2020, when he has already become a Grand Old Man himself.

Anyway, "Marchin' To The City". Bacharach or not, Dylan is in The Zone and, via *I just don't know what I'm a-gonna do*, eventually arrives at the key that will unlock an entire song; *I was all right 'til I fell in love with you* is the last line of the final version of the preliminary study of "'Til I Fell In Love With You".

15   Things Have Changed

Chronocentrism, it is called, the very human phenomenon that one believes to be living in an exceptional time. With politicians it is a chronic ailment; they refer to "these difficult times" in every discussion, or "these uncertain times", and variants. But intellectuals also fall for it. Respected Dutch philosopher Joke Hermsen meets broad agreement with her treatise *Quiet Down The Time* in which she notes how busy, busy, busy we are and that we have less and less time at our disposal - also an *idée fixe* that we have been telling ourselves for centuries. In *every* era, opinion formers and trendsetters sigh that we live in weird times, in troubled times, that time flies and that times are hard.

In 63 BC Cicero complains about the corruption and the badness of modern times with the famous exclamation *O tempora, o mores*, but in the centuries after him none of these *mores* seems to be time-bound. Goethe hits the nail on the head in *Faust* (1808). The great poet-thinker is annoyed by his valued colleague and former teacher Johann Gottfried Herder, who has just coined the term *Zeitgeist*, and replies through the old scholar Faust. Faust knocks some sense into his assistant Wagner when he starts twaddling about the *Zeitgeist*, the "Spirit Of Ages":

Was ihr den Geist der Zeiten heißt,
Das ist im Grund der Herren eigner Geist,
In dem die Zeiten sich bespiegeln.

(What you the Spirit of the Ages call
Is nothing but the spirit of you all
Wherein the Ages are reflected.)

Dylan follows Goethe and does not share the short-sighted view that we helplessly float along on the waves of an autonomous time. We ourselves will change times, he argues in '63, in "The Times They Are A-Changin'", the song that so calmly echoes in "Things Have Changed". In later songs, the narrator withholds commentary on chronocentric narrow-mindedness. The exhausted Ruby in "New Brownsvile Girl" may be sighing how hard the times are, the narrator does not participate. *We live in times where one commits crimes* from "Political World" is a despondent observation of a cynical narrator who sees that neither the times nor the people are essentially changing, and in "Floater" (2001) the poet has reached the maturity to conclude:

They say times are hard, if you do not believe it
You can just follow your nose
It does not bother me - times are hard everywhere.

It is a beautiful, resigned aphorism from a beautiful, enigmatic song, but it comes shortly after that one time Dylan blames the times for his detachment, a year earlier in his Oscar winning masterpiece "Things Have Changed". The wandering, lost protagonist has to give up, but that is not his fault: no, the *people are crazy and times are strange*.

It is a state of being in which Dylan's protagonists often find themselves, the lost, dream-like and passive state of detachment. We recognise it from *Tom Thumb*, from the young man who longs for *Johanna*, the *drifter* who escapes, the I-persons in "Watching The River Flow", "Going Going Gone" and "Simple Twist Of Fate", the interlocutor of *Señor* - and the list goes on through "Mississippi" and "Things Have Changed" until well into the twenty-first century. Just like "Just Like Tom Thumb's Blues" most of those songs have an epic quality, they tell (snippets of) a story. Here it hardly does. "Things Have Changed" is mainly lyrical, expresses in unrelenting, poetic images the discomfort of a displaced, numb narrator, through which the poet strings mysterious observations and half-known references.

The first verse starts as a classic novella, with the introduction of the protagonist, but it is confusing right away. He is worried, has nothing to gain, nor to lose. Admittedly, he only has to lift a finger for sensory pleasure, but apparently, he does not care anymore. For the description of his appearance the narrator confines himself to two characteristics: he is white and has the eyes of an assassin. That alone is already intriguing. This metaphor is usually reserved for sports heroes. According to his biographer, basketball legend Michael Jordan has "the gaze of an assassin" and in the summer of 2015 football coach Steve McLaren of Newcastle United introduces his new purchase Aleksandar Mitrovic to the press: "He's got assassin's eyes." With only eight goals from Mitrovic in thirty games, the club relegated in May 2016, so that turned out to be a bit disappointing.

Dylan's main character is probably not a sports hero, but he certainly is a man with a mysterious aura. He has not an open, honest gaze, at any rate, and resembles the man Angelina is looking for (*his eyes were two slits that would make a snake proud*) and also the Satan from "Man Of Peace" (*both eyes are looking like they're on a rabbit hunt, nobody can see through him*) or, on the opposite, the God from "Durango" (*with His serpent eyes of obsidian*). But perhaps Dylan just looked in the mirror.

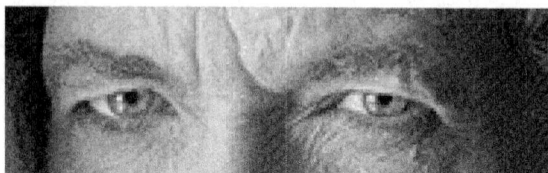

The film for which Dylan writes the song, *Wonder Boys* by director Curtis Hanson, appears incidentally, in the second verse, and then only indirectly. So indirectly that it could also be about another (film)character: Blanche DuBois from *A Streetcar Named Desire* (Elia Kazan, 1951) in particular. The closing words *do not get up gentlemen, I'm only passing through* are lifted from her closing monologue, when the men in the white coats drag the now completely empty Blanche into the institution.

With some effort, there are some similarities to the target film to be found in the lyrics, but the concerns of the drudging professor Grady Tripp (played by Michael Douglas) will not have been much more than a superficial source of inspiration. This is also evident from the words of gratitude that Dylan expresses at the Oscar presentation: "A song that doesn't pussyfoot around nor turn a blind eye to human nature." Dylanesque nebula, again. The lyrics are full of concealing language use ("some things", "so much", "things", "lot of other stuff" and so on) and dark imagery. "I've been walking forty miles of bad road" (Dylan writes in the fortieth year after his first record). He feels like he wants to put a beautiful lady in a wheelbarrow (?). The "next sixty seconds will last forever" (the singer sings exactly sixty seconds before the end of the song). And the ultimate enigmatic sentence of the last middle-eight, about one Mr. Jinx and Miss Lucy jumping into a lake. Mr. Jinks is the cat in the cartoon series *Pixie and Dixie*, the beagle that Dylan buys during the Rolling Thunder tour, he calls Miss Lucy. Those facts do not help. A jinx is a kind of curse that lays a constant stream of small accidents and bad luck on the accursed, or the name for a person who brings bad luck - that fits better. And Miss Lucy? Dylan knows Miss Lucy from the song "Miss Lucy Long", a song from the nineteenth century that is sung in the blackface minstrel shows and is analysed by Eric Lott in his "Love & Theft", in the work that is on Dylan's bedside table in this period. This Lucy does not jump in the lake, but still times do change for her. She has a big mouth and is therefore exchanged for a bag of corn.

Explicable or not, even the impenetrable verses contribute to that one image that rises from the song: the evening twilight of a extinguished human life that Dylan painted in a similarly large way in that other monument, in "Not Dark Yet". Imagery like *waiting on the last train* and *head already in the noose* is not necessarily overwhelming, but effective. Distinctive, however, are the philosophical one-liners. *All the truth in the world adds up to one big lie* has the same dark, sombre beauty as *my sense of humanity has gone down the drain* from "Not Dark Yet", like the masterly, melancholy phrase *I used to care, but things have changed* is an echo of *I just do not see why I should even care* from that same song.

The lament is accompanied by a driving, almost swinging music part with a high hum-along quality. The one who will most happily join in humming is Marty Stuart, who wrote the song from which Dylan stole the melody, the shuffle and the colour: "Observations Of A Crow" from his album *The Pilgrim*.(1999). It is not a sensitive matter, as evidenced by Marty's words in an interview with Jim Beviglia for *American Songwriter*, September 2014. Stuart tells how he spent an evening with Dylan in 1999, shortly before the recording of "Things Have Changed":

> "I took him to my warehouse to see all the country music treasures I have," Stuart said. "Bob said, Hey, I like that *Crow* song. I might borrow something out of that." I said, "Well, I probably borrowed it from you in the first place. Go ahead."

Unusual for Dylan are the many middle-eights; the master lets the bridge play no fewer than four times. It is not annoying, for it is indeed a beautiful bridge, as the whole song is captivating. "Things Have Changed" climbs quickly in Olof Bjorner's Top 20 of most performed songs - with over eight hundred performances, a proud Dylan has already played it more often than "The Times They Are A-Changin'".

There are not that many noteworthy covers, but among those few attempts some pearls shine. Most colleagues extrapolate the jazzy elements of the original, with walking bass and brushes, and opt for the wandering pace that Dylan already has abandoned in his live performances. Usually one enters J.J. Cale's territory. That applies in any case to the beautiful version by late bloomer Grant Peeples, on *Prior Convictions* from 2012. Pure swing jazz produces the hobby project *String Swing* from Swedish jazz singer Josefine Cronholm (*Waiting for the Good Times*, 2008, with a magisterial guitar solo á la Wes Montgomery), but Cronholm does not come close to her superior colleague Barb Jungr. Jungr continues to play tirelessly the Bob Dylan Songbook to this day and is still getting better every day. Her version of "Things Have Changed", which was recorded in 2002, is fascinating, and distinctive too: Jungr turns it into a tango.

However, the ladies competition is won by veteran Bettye LaVette. LaVette's soulful cover, opening the 2018 tribute album *Things Have Changed,* is rough, driving and swings like a pendulum.

The most beautiful cover so far is sung by another jazz celebrity, by Curtis Stigers. His *Don't Think Twice* from 2003 already is one of the most brilliant renditions of that evergreen, and with "Things Have Changed" (*Let's Go Out Tonight*, 2012) he reconfirms his class. Superb, supercooled production with dozens of small, loving surprises in the arrangement, and on top of that the declamatory art of Stigers; it is a version that earns a place next to the original. In every time.

I'm not the songs

"It is a spooky record," says Dylan in the David Gates interview, September 1997, "because I feel spooky. I don't feel in tune with anything." Which rather invites biographical interpretation. However, less than half a cup of coffee later in that same interview: "But I'm not the songs. It's like somebody expecting Shakespeare to be Hamlet, or Goethe to be Faust. If you're not prepared for fame, there's really no way you can imagine what a crippling thing it can be."

Time Out Of Mind is celebrated as a come-back immediately upon its release. Five-star reviews, top positions in hit parades all over the world, a rush on concert tickets, and prizes, lots of prizes.

Twenty-five years later, we have enough distance to qualify the record as what it turned out to be: the starting shot of Dylan's *Spätwerk*, as the Germans respectfully call it, the starting point of the final phase of Dylan's career - the phase when Dylan becomes an Old Master. In the twenty-first century, from 1997's *Time Out Of Mind* in fact, every new record effortlessly reaches the highest regions of the charts, no. 1 positions even, from now on the concerts are and stay sold out, Dylan is honoured with the highest possible prizes (Grammy Awards, an Oscar and even a Nobel Prize), and in 2020 he scores his first no. 1 hit with "Murder Most Foul". Even a bewildering Christmas album (*Christmas In The Heart*, 2009) is at worst called "ironic" by a non-comprehending journalist, but can otherwise count on polite applause and sympathetic reviews.

Dylan has transcended criticism.

Sources

Well, I investigated all the books in the library
Ninety percent of 'em gotta be burned away

Dylan:

- *Lyrics 1962 - 2001* (2004)
- www.bobdylan.com
- *Chronicles* (2004)
- *Time Out Of Mind* (1997)
- MusiCares speech (2015)
- Nobel Prize speech (2017)
- *Theme Time Radio Hour* (2006-08)

Interview fragments (in addition to the mentioned):

- *Every Mind Polluting Word* (collected interviews, 2006)

On Dylan (in addition to the titles mentioned):

- *Still On The Road* - Clinton Heylin, 2010
- *Liner notes Biograph* - Cameron Crowe, 1985
- *Dylan & de Beats* – Tom Willems, 2018
- Goon Talk (Scott Warmuth's blog; swarmuth.blogspot.com)
- About Bob (Olof Björner's blog, bjorner.com)
- de Bob Dylan aantekeningen (Tom Willems' blog,

  debobdylanaantekeningen.blogspot.com
- Untold Dylan (bob-dylan.org.uk/)
- Eyolf Østrem's *dylanchords.com*
- expectingrain.com

Notes

Between 2018 and 2022, most of these chapters were published as articles on the British site *Untold Dylan*. Some of them, such as *Love Sick* and *Tryin' To Get To Heaven*, have been reworked or expanded for this book.

Thanks

Tom Willems in the Netherlands, from *de Bob Dylan aantekeningen* - the mercury Dylan blog, author of *Dylan & The Beats,* 2018

Martin Bierens in Ireland- dear old Bobhead, from Utrecht to Amsterdam to Dornbirn to Stadskanaal to Tilburg to Bielefeld

Tony Attwood in England- webmaster of *Untold Dylan,* the place where it's always safe and warm

Larry Fyffe in Canada, the Knight with the Red Pencil

Scott Warmuth in the USA, the leading Dylan dissecting expert.from *Goon Talk,* his showcase on swarmuth.blogspot.com

Stephen Vallely in North Yorkshire, England – webmaster of *Bob Dylan: Street-Legal & Illegal* on Facebook, suggestions & hawk's eye

The author

Bob Dylan's songs continue to fascinate.

Jochen Markhorst (1964) grew up in Arnhem, The Netherlands and in Hanover, Germany, with *Highway 61 Revisited* and *Blonde On Blonde* as soundtrack, bought *Blood On The Tracks* and *Street Legal* from his pocket money, studied German language at Utrecht University, translated Russian at the Military Intelligence Service, teaches language training courses at companies and lessons in schools, translates German literature, Dutch websites and English subtitles and always plays the music of Dylan in the background.

Markhorst, however, is not one of the hardliners who honour the motto *Nobody Sings Dylan Like Dylan* – Jimi Hendrix is certainly not the only one who can brush up a Dylan song. He preaches this controversial opinion, among other things, in his fifteen books on Dylan songs, and continues to build on the Dylan library.

Jochen has been living in Utrecht for the past 40 years, is still married to the same great, attractive woman and has two sons who have left home by now, but fortunately still work and live in Utrecht.

In the same series:

Blonde on Blonde — Bob Dylan's mercurial masterpiece — Jochen Markhorst

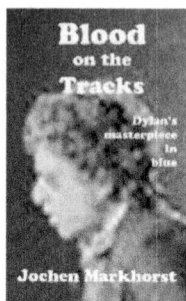
Blood on the Tracks — Dylan's masterpiece in blue — Jochen Markhorst

Bob Dylan's Greatest Hits — Jochen Markhorst

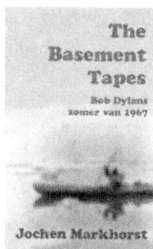
The Basement Tapes — Bob Dylan zomer van 1967 — Jochen Markhorst

John Wesley Harding — Bob Dylan meets Kafka in Nashville — Jochen Markhorst

Street-Legal — Bob Dylan's unpolished gem from 1978 — Jochen Markhorst

Bringing It All Back Home — Bob Dylan's 2nd Big Bang — Jochen Markhorst

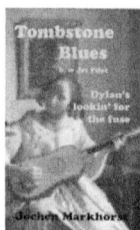
Tombstone Blues — Dylan's lookin' for the fuse — Jochen Markhorst

Desolation Row — Bob Dylans poëtische brief uit 1965 — Jochen Markhorst

Mississippi — Bob Dylans midlife meesterwerk — Jochen Markhorst

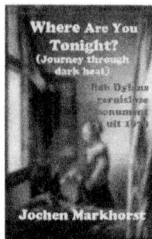
Where Are You Tonight? (Journey through dark heat) — Bob Dylans vruchteloze monument uit 1978 — Jochen Markhorst

Printed in Great Britain
by Amazon